INSTITUTE OF CZECH LITERATURE
KAROLINUM PRESS

CZECH LITERATURE STUDIES

EDITED BY TOMÁŠ GLANC

Samizdat
Past & Present

INSTITUTE OF CZECH LITERATURE
KAROLINUM PRESS

2018

INSTITUTE OF CZECH LITERATURE is part of the Czech Academy of Sciences
Na Florenci 3/1420, 110 00 Prague 1, Czech Republic
www.ucl.cas.cz

KAROLINUM PRESS is a publishing department of Charles University
Ovocný trh 560/5, 116 36 Prague 1, Czech Republic
www.karolinum.cz

This publication originated with the support of the long-term development
of the research institution 68378068.
This anthology was published as part of a Czech Literary Bibliography project
(LM2015059) supported by the Ministry of Education, Youth and Sports
of the Czech Republic.

MINISTRY OF EDUCATION,
YOUTH AND SPORTS

RESEARCH INFRASTRUCTURE
INSTITUTE OF CZECH LITERATURE, CAS

Editor Tomáš Glanc
Sub-Editor Gabriela Romanová
Translation Melvyn Clarke
Proofreading Gillian Purves
Cover and graphic design DesignIQ
Set and printed in the Czech Republic by Karolinum Press
First English edition

Cataloguing-in-Publication Data is available from the National Library
of the Czech Republic

ISBN 978-80-88069-76-8 (Institute of Czech Literature, CAS)
ISBN 978-80-246-4033-4 (Karolinum Press)
ISBN 978-80-246-4039-6 (pdf), 978-80-246-4065-5 (epub), 978-80-246-4064-8 (mobi)

Contents

Long Live Samizdat
Editorial note

Tomáš Glanc

Over the last few years, research into samizdat has undergone some significant development, the roots of which, as is commonly the case in such circumstances, can be found retrospectively in the fairly remote past. In simplified terms, this 'turn' can be described as the depoliticization of samizdat and in some cases the declining interest in its role in the history of literature, with a shift towards a more typological, medial and performative approach (samizdat as an act/activity in a particular place and community).[1] Also of importance is the attention being paid not only to samizdat as an object, but also to the consequences of samizdat culture, e.g. in the formation of subjectivity and the constitution of symbolic power as conceived by Pierre Bourdieu. His theory inspired Ann Komaromi, who is also actively engaged in preserving and providing access to samizdat.[2] This research field has also been created in the recent past, and is not just based on traditional archiving aspirations and (re-)editions of hard-to-find texts, but is much more to do with the issue of how to structure access to fragile, hand-made copies, how to digitize them and organize the 'architecture' of their publication, so that they serve not only as books available online, but also as a network of items that belong to a single unit, as well as to the set of all other published texts, periodicals and the like, while differing from them typologically. Ann Komaromi deals with this task in her Database project:

---

1   See e.g. CSEH-VARGA, Katalin. 'Innovative Forms of the Hungarian Samizdat. An Analysis of Oral Practices', *Zeitschrift für Ostmitteleuropa-Forschung*, No. 1, 2016, Vol. LXV, pp. 90–107.
2   KOMAROMI, Ann. *Uncensored: Samizdat Novels and the Quest for Autonomy in Soviet Dissidence.* Evanston (IL): Northwestern University Press, 2015.

'*Soviet Samizdat Periodicals*', which has been operating since 2011 at http://samizdat.library.utoronto.ca. The provision of access to samizdat as a 'museumization' issue and not just as a challenge for philological and cultural history research, but also as a curating challenge focusing on narration through objects and their arrangement, as well as through exhibitions, is highlighted by Daniela Šneppová in her contribution to knowledge of a broad range of samizdat activities.[3]

These more distanced approaches, which are less utilitarian in comparison with the political perspective of 'prohibited literature', bring about new ways of integrating samizdat into cultural history, not only from the standpoint of opposition to the state-controlled book market, but also as a particular publication strategy, generating increased sensitivity towards the media dimension of publication and special distribution. This is associated with particular acts (transcription, transport and circulation) in communities of users of samizdat as a communication framework, in which physical presence and the connection between individual participants plays a rather more obvious role than in the case of book culture in general. Moreover, in the most recent research, samizdat does not just mean printed matter, but also other media for information and works of art, both musical and audiovisual,[4] as well as performative (drama[5]). As for the spontaneous

---

3 ŠNEPPOVÁ, Daniela. 'Staging Samizdat: The Czech Art of Resistance, 1968–1989', *Zeitschrift für Ostmitteleuropa-Forschung*, No. 1, 2016, Vol. LXV, pp. 64–89.
4 For details of samizdat music see this dissertation: HAGEN, Trever. *Musicking in the Merry Ghetto. The Czech Underground from the 1960s to the 2000s*. Exeter: University of Exeter, 2012.
5 See LAZORČÁKOVÁ, Tatjana. 'Divadelní disent. K historii neoficiálních divadelních aktivit v sedmdesátých letech 20. století' [On the History of Unofficial Theatre Activities in the 1970s], in *Kontexty III. Acta Universitatis Palackianae Olomucensis*, M. SÝKORA (ed.). Olomouc: Univerzita Palackého, 2002, pp. 47–64. JUNGMANNOVÁ, Lenka. 'Neoficiální, nezávislá, paralelní, alternativní, nelegální, druhá, jiná, nelicencovaná, samizdatová, ineditní, undergroundová, podzemní..., ale naše. Pokus o vymezení problematiky neoficiální dramatiky v letech 1948 až 1989' [Unofficial, Independent, Parallel, Alternative, Illegal, Secondary, Other, Unauthorized, Samizdat, Unpublished, Underground, Subterranean..., But Ours.

distribution of various recordings, the term *magnetizdat* had long been established (at least in Russian).

One of the first programmatic manifestations of the post-political approach to samizdat can be considered to be the catalogue for the Präprintium exhibition in 1998,[6] published by the small Bremen publishers Temmen with a 'multimedia CD', which was something of a technical peculiarity in the late 1990s, matching the subject of the exhibition. The very name indicates that attention is focused on alternative duplication to (book) printing, thus developing an idea that had already been formulated: samizdat of a literary nature, and the 'production' of texts and books harked back to before the invention of typography.[7] The relatively narrow focus on the Moscow circle of primarily conceptual artists who in various ways developed samizdat practices in their work, raises the question of the extent to which this analogy can be pursued in other artistic communities at other times and in other countries.

Here samizdat is not a politically controversial topic, but an intimate cultural process, which forms and manages not only the works of art themselves, but also their distribution, documentation and even their reception and archiving/museumization.

Valentina Parisi, who includes poetic readings,[8] for example, in the category of samizdat, was also heading in the direction indicated by the Präprintium exhibition and the catalogue of the same name in her monograph on Soviet samizdat.

An Attempt to Define the Issues Surrounding Unofficial Drama between 1948 and 1989], *Divadelní revue* No. 3, 2003, Vol. XIV, pp. 3–11.

6   G. Hirt – S. Wonders (eds.). *Präprintium. Moskauer Bücher aus dem Samizdat (Ausstellungskatalog)* [Moscow Books in Samizdat (Exhibition Catalogue)]. *Dokumentationen zur Kultur und Gesellschaft im östlichen Europa, Forschungsstelle Osteuropa an der Universität Bremen*. Bremen: Edition Temmen, 1998.

7   See Skilling, H. Gordon. 'Samizdat: A Return to the Pre-Gutenberg Era?', in *Cross Currents. A Yearbook of Central European Culture*, L. Matějka – B. Stolz (eds.). Ann Arbor: Michigan Slavic Publications, 1982, pp. 64–80.

8   Parisi, Valentina. *Il lettore eccedente. Edizioni periodiche del «Samizdat» sovietico (1956–1990)* [Outreaching Reader. Soviet Periodical Samizdat]. Bologna: Il Mulino, 2013, p. 247 et seq.

Samizdat has naturally attracted attention in its most obvious form, i.e. as a publication strategy reacting to the unfree conditions in a closed society of an authoritarian or totalitarian nature. It would be a mistake to ignore the connection between samizdat and Communist censorship, the persecution of writers on political grounds and its connection with political dissent and rights to freedom of speech that had been trampled underfoot. However, nowadays, thanks to systematic study[9], we know that censorship is a phenomenon that appears in all periods of cultural development, and it would be limiting to see it exclusively as an instrument for the ideological persecution of writers.[10] Moreover, the attention of researchers is increasingly being drawn by phenomena which might indeed be associated genealogically with the conditions in which samizdat in Eastern Europe came about, but at the same time they go beyond the political framework or simply abandon it altogether and raise different types of questions that come under the current scope of the humanities in a way that casts new light on old subjects.

In Czech literary studies the subject of samizdat has continually been raised ever since the significant increase in the importance of this publishing activity in the 1970s during the period known as normalization after the Soviet-led military intervention in 1968, which

---

9   See e.g. PREČAN, Vilém. 'Unabhängige Literatur und Samizdat in der Tschechoslowakei der 70er und 80er Jahre', in *Der Zensur zum Trotz: Das gefesselte Wort und die Freiheit in Europa*, P. RAABE (ed.). Weinheim: VCH Verlagsgesellschaft, 1991, pp. 241–253. Ibid: 'Independent Literature and Samizdat in Czechoslovakia in the 1970s and 1980s', in *Literature and Politics in Central Europe: Studies in Honour of Markéta Goetz-Stankiewicz*. Columbia: Camden House, 1993, pp. 91–107.

10   The Institute of Czech Literature at the Czech Academy of Sciences first published a translation anthology on this subject: T. PAVLÍČEK – P. PÍŠA – M. WÖGERBAUER (eds.). *Nebezpečná literatura? Antologie z myšlení o literární cenzuře* [Dangerous Literature? An Anthology of Thought on Literary Censorship]. Brno: Host, 2013 – followed by an extensive two-volume collective monograph: WÖGERBAUER, Michael – PÍŠA, Petr – ŠÁMAL, Petr – JANÁČEK, Pavel et al. *V obecném zájmu. Cenzura a sociální regulace literatury v moderní české kultuře, 1749–2014.* [In the General Interest: Censorship and Social Regulation of Literature in Modern Czech Culture, 1749–2014]. Praha: Academia – Ústav pro českou literaturu, 2015.

radically changed the cultural policy of the ruling Czechoslovak Communist Party. Previous research into samizdat activities in the Czech lands, going back to the war period and the 1950s, but with their heyday in the 1970s, will culminate in the *'Encyclopedia of Czech Literary Samizdat 1948–1989'* and the *'Article Bibliography of Czech Literary Samizdat'* projects, which are under way from 2015 to 2019 at the CAS Institute of Czech Literature, Lexicography Department and the Centre for Information on Literary Studies at the same research institute with the assistance of the Czech Science Foundation and the Czech Ministry of Education research infrastructure.

Attempts to achieve an overview of samizdat that not only summarizes its sources, archives, libraries and even individual publications, but also offers an inspiring approach to the study of the phenomenon itself are made in parallel with many other countries, but unfortunately often with insufficient regard for the comparative aspect, which is increasingly attractive with the passage of time.[11] Studies are undertaken both in countries where samizdat has played an important cultural and historical role (e.g. Russia, Poland[12], East

---

11 The following publications, for example, have at least to some extent followed this route: W. EICHWEDE (ed.). *Samizdat. Alternative Kultur in Zentral- und Osteuropa. Die 60er bis 80er Jahre. Dokumentationen zur Kultur und Gesselschaft im östlichen Europa* [Samizdat. Alternative Culture in Central and Eastern Europe from the 1960s to the 1980s]. Bremen: Edition Temmen, 2000. A. CATALANO – S. GUAGNELLI (eds.). 'La luce dell'est: il samizdat come costruzione di una comunità parallela', *Il samizdat tra memoria e utopia*. eSamizdat 2010-2011, Vol. VIII, pp. 5-17. V. TODOROV (ed.). 'Publish & Perish: Samizdat & Underground Cultural Practices in the Soviet Bloc (I) and (II)', *Poetics Today: International Journal for Theory and Analysis of Literature and Communication*, 2008-2009, Vol. XXIX and XXX. V. PARISI, (ed.). *Samizdat. Between Practices and Representations. Lecture Series at Open Society Archives. Budapest, February – June 2013*. Budapest: Central European University, Institute for Advanced Study, 2015. FEINDT, Gregor. 'Opposition und Samizdat in Ostmitteleuropa. Strukturen und Mechanismen unabhängiger Periodika in vergleichender Perspektive' [Opposition and Samizdat in Eastern Europe. The Structures and Mechanisms of Independent Magazines in Comparison], *Zeitschrift für Ostmitteleuropa-Forschung*, No. 1, 2016, Vol. LXV, pp. 17-42.
12 BŁAŻEJOWSKA, Justyna. *Papierowa rewolucja. Z dziejów drugiego obiegu wydawiczego w Polsce 1976-1989/1990* [A Paper Revolution: From the History of the 'Second Circulation' in Poland]. Warszawa: Instytut Pamięci Narodowej,

Germany[13] and Hungary[14]) and at universities where attention is traditionally focused on Eastern Europe (in the USA, Italy, Germany[15] and elsewhere).

In this connection we have decided to publish English translations of several studies of samizdat that have been written in the Czech milieu or that involve Czech culture. We wanted to find out which relevant, inspirational studies are available that might also attract foreign researchers, as they contain many ideas that go far beyond the factographic and political framework, or that present the traditional aspects in a way that is inspiring to this day.

One of the characteristic features of independent culture in Communist countries during the latter half of the 20th century was its small-scale interconnections with counterpart communication circles in other Soviet bloc countries. Hence our publication is by no means just aimed at users whose native language is English, but also in equal measure at all those who might be interested in these subjects and who cannot read these texts in the original language.[16]

The selection of just a few articles out of dozens, if not hundreds of previously published studies of Czech samizdat was not an easy

2010. KANDZIORA, Jerzy – SZYMAŃSKA, Zyta. *Bez cenzury 1976-1989: literatura, ruch wydawniczy, teatr: bibliografia* [Censorship Free 1976-1989: Literature, Publishers, Theatre: Bibliography]. Warszawa: Instytut Badań Literackich, 1999.

13 KOWALCZUK, Ilko-Sascha. *Freiheit in Öffentlichkeit. Politischer Samisdat in der DDR 1985-1989* [Freedom in Public. Political Samizdat in Eastern Germany 1985-1989]. Berlin: Robert Havemann Gesellschaft, 2002.

14 HODOSÁN, Róza. *Szamizdat történetek* [Stories of Samizdat]. Budapest: Noran, 2004. DEMSZKY, Gábor – RAJK, László – SASVÁRI, Edit. *Földalatti vonalak* [Underground Lines]. Pécs: Jelenkor, 2000.

15 Particularly noteworthy is the connection between samizdat and the way the internet operates nowadays. This subject is dealt with competently by Henrike SCHMIDT in her monograph: *Russische Literatur im Internet. Zwischen digitaler Folklore und politischer Propaganda* [Russian Literature on the Internet. Between the Digital Folklore and the Political Propaganda]. Bielefeld: Transcript, 2011.

16 In the field of artistic practices and theories, this mediating role was played at the beginning of this century by Primary Documents: L. HOPTMAN – T. POSPISZYL (eds.). *Primary Documents: A Sourcebook for Eastern and Central European Art since the 1950s*. Cambridge (MA): The MIT Press, 2002. A fairly comprehensive publication of this kind is still missing in the field of samizdat.

task, and was not governed by any strict objective criteria. We have attempted to present views of samizdat that might be comprehensible and inspirational in the present-day situation, where, as already mentioned, the typological and theoretical standpoints go hand in hand with the historical viewpoint, or even take precedence over it. Chronologically, we have also taken into account both the era in which authors depicted samizdat, as it were, while it was still in operation, i.e. till the end of the 1980s, and research into the following period, when attempts were first made to systematize samizdat output and its reflections from the standpoint of the age in which samizdat had lost its previous urgency and had acquired new characteristics and fresh qualities in retrospect.

For the first group of texts (written during the samizdat era and distributed primarily through samizdat channels) an exceptionally significant role was played, from our point of view, by the texts of Miroslav Červenka (1932–2005), one of the most prominent Czech literary theorists of the latter half of the 20th century, a critical pupil and original successor to Roman Jakobson and Jan Mukařovský, who was not only an internationally famous versologist, but also a samizdat poet and samizdat theorist. He only wrote two studies on it, which actually overlapped to some extent, but both of them present a conceptual analysis relating samizdat to general textological and literary history and scholarship of the kind that displays sensitivity to the manuscript and its changeable semiotic nature during communication between the author, the publisher and the reader.

A study by prose writer and essayist Josef Jedlička (1927–1990), who emigrated from the working town of Litvínov to West Germany after 1968, describes the growing and increasingly genre-diverse samizdat output of the 1970s, which he compares to the cultural experience of the 1950s, documenting samizdat as a network not only of texts, but also of alternative institutions.

The controversial nature of the texts by literary critic, historian and writer František Kautman (1927–2016) and essayist, linguist and philologist Karel Palek (*1948) publishing under the pseudonym of

Petr Fidelius make them of special importance to our collection. Should it ever appear that samizdat culture before 1989 was exclusively in solidarity as it overcame its differences of opinion in its polemical relations with the official prosecuting and state authorities (as was the case to a large extent in political dissent between participants in the Charter 77 civic initiative), then Kautman and Fidelius's short articles indicate the opposite. There were harsh polemics even within samizdat over what samizdat actually meant and what terminology could be used to describe its ambitions and activities. Fidelius takes exception to the term *ineditní* (unpublished), which he believes contradicts the very essence of samizdat output, in which the term *edice* (publication, series) plays a key role. Moreover, in the Czech context these polemics refer to a specific terminological and ideological element that could not exist in the Soviet Union, the homeland and empire of samizdat. Some authors (including not only Fidelius, but also prose writer Ludvík Vaculík, one of the key samizdat participants) refer to a paradox which they seek a way out of (in vain), i.e. in an environment under pressure from linguistic Sovietization, how can we avoid the term samizdat, which might well express its subversive nature in the face of Soviet-style political power, but at the lexicological level it highlights the adoption of such irritating neologisms as *kolkhoz* and *khozrazchot*?

Texts by the brilliant stylist Jiří Gruša (1938–2011), poet, prose writer and later Czech Ambassador to Austria and Germany, never relinquish their personal tone in favour of scholarly propriety. His viewpoint is objective but in particular it is that of an author who was one of the prominent protagonists of his generation during the 1960s, the man behind the journals that were among the most important press platforms of their day (*Tvář* and *Sešity pro mladou literaturu*) and who was subsequently one of the first to personally experience the persecution and criminalization of literary activity. He was prosecuted for distributing pornography in his literary works, and during the 1970s he was involved in the establishment of Petlice, the largest Czech samizdat 'publishing house'.

Gruša's view of samizdat output includes historical intersections and comparisons relating not only to the Stalinist period in post-1948 Czechoslovak history, but also references to the Soviet regime and even Tsarist Russia. At the same time, however, his description includes the detailed testimony of a prominent participant in the events taking place in Czechoslovakia.

The articles by librarian and editor Jiří Gruntorád (*1952), translator, journalist and literary critic Tomáš Vrba (*1947) and Martin Machovec (*1956), literary historian, critic and editor of Czech underground literature, present an important stage that combines personal experience of samizdat with the opportunity to treat it historically with the hindsight of the ensuing period, in which samizdat ceased to fulfil its original function of publishing texts that could not be published, for various reasons, in the usual way.

The characteristic approach of the period starting in the early 1990s involved attempts to summarize, categorize and describe the material in an elementary way: the establishment of the Libri prohibiti samizdat library under the management of one of those most prominently involved in samizdat production, Jiří Gruntorád, the first collected bibliographical works, an anthology of texts examining the phenomenon of alternative, unofficial culture in the Czech lands,[17] the fifteen-part television serial *Samizdat* (2003), directed by Andrej Krob, one of those involved in samizdat activities, and Petr Slavík's television serial *Alternativní kultura* (1997–2005) inter alia. This flurry of typological arrangement and material registration activity also involved Tomáš Vrba, samizdat publication house and magazine editor, and in the 1990s the editor-in-chief of the *Lettre international* and *Přítomnost* magazines. An irreplaceable role combining that of eye-witness and protagonist with the competence of editor and textologist is played by the author Martin Machovec. We have not included his seminal

---

17 HANÁKOVÁ, Jitka. *Edice českého samizdatu 1972-1991* [Czech Samizdat Series 1972-1991]. Praha: Národní knihovna ČR, 1997 and J. ALAN (ed.). *Alternativní kultura. Příběh české společnosti 1945-1989* [Alternative Culture: The Story of Czech Society 1945-1989]. Praha: NLN, 2001.

study 'The Types and Functions of Samizdat Publications in Czech-oslovakia', 1948–1989 in this anthology, because it is easily available to all those interested in an English translation in *Poetics Today*.[18] Two of his contributions deal with some fundamental aspects of samizdat and research into it. The first one ('How Underground Authors and Publishers Financed Their Samizdats') looks at the economic dimension of independent publishing, which is often overlooked due to samizdat activists' voluntary participation in the preparation and distribution work, which might appear somehow exempt from economic mechanisms. For all that, however, samizdat is an attractive subject for research into its 'shadow economy' operations, even though it is only sporadically documented, as is the case with any black market. However, this lack does not mean that samizdat was not inter alia a material and inevitably an economic pursuit involving such categories as work and its value, material costs, time (working time), buying, selling, profit and the like. Machovec's study on the group of writers around the Půlnoc series (1949–1955) bore testimony to his erudition, with his detailed knowledge not only of individual texts, but also of their variants, transcriptions and the relations between biography and bibliography, as he reconstructed the emergence and activities of one of the first postwar samizdat communities, which came to be of decisive importance inter alia for the creation of the 'cultural underground', the most famous representatives of which were the poet and philosopher Egon Bondy, the theorist and poet Ivan Martin Jirous and the band Plastic People of the Universe.

The texts by literary historian and translator Alena Přibáňová (*1970), editor, writer and literary historian Michal Přibáň (*1966), Polish lecturer in Czech studies and cultural journalist Weronika Parfianowicz-Vertun (*1984), literary historian Petr Šámal (*1972), who is also editor of the classified journal *Česká literatura* published by the CAS Institute of Czech Literature, and Tomáš Glanc (*1969), doctor

---

18 *Poetics Today, Publish & Perish: Samizdat & Underground. Cultural Practices in the Soviet Bloc II*, No. 1, Spring 2009, Vol. XXX. Duke University Press.

in Russian studies and East European literature specialist, are remarkable for each individual author's unique perspective, since in contrast to the contributors referred to above they have at most only marginal personal experience of samizdat. Their relationship towards samizdat is primarily that of researchers, aided by the preserved material media and the methodological tools which they use in their efforts to find relevant approaches to the phenomena under investigation.

In the case of Alena Přibáňová, Michal Přibáň and their article on Sixty-Eight Publishers in contact with samizdat at home and the competition in exile, this is a specific example of the largest *tamizdat* (publishing in exile) producer and procedures involving movement of texts between the 'domestic' and 'foreign' environments.[19] Put in this way, the following question also problematizes and expands the category of samizdat: does it also include books published in the usual way at state-registered publishers that operated in other countries, whose output was distributed abroad (primarily within the 'émigré' environment, from which it was then smuggled into samizdat circulation in the 'domestic' environment?)

This topic is developed by Petr Šámal in his text on parallel circulation as a consequence of censorship, which was published as part of an extended study entitled 'In the Interest of the Working People' on literary censorship between 1949 and 1989.[20] It follows the effects of censorship on literary activity, resulting in the need to smuggle prohibited printed matter across totalitarian state borders and to publish it at publishers in an environment that placed demands on authors that were different to those they were used to in the domestic environment, and which many had difficulties accepting. This question also raises the possible status of 'secondary circulation', i.e. the case of books that were officially published, but subsequently withdrawn from sale, from libraries and from public circulation, so

---

19   A monograph by KIND-KOVÁCS, Friederik - LABOV, Jessie. *Samizdat, Tamizdat, and Beyond: Transnational Media During and After Socialism*. New York - Oxford: Berghahn Books, 2013 deals with an analogous issue in Soviet material.
20   In WÖGERBAUER et al., *V obecném zájmu* see footnote No. 10, pp. 1099-1223.

they played the same role as tamizdat, although this was not typographically evident. This issue is referred to in the article by Tomáš Glanc, whose contribution shares the interest expressed by Weronika Parfianowicz-Vertun's article in the media dimension of samizdat and samizdat that was not only distributed on paper, but also on other media including X-ray negatives that still showed traces of human bodies. This brings us back to the beginning – and to the present-day interest in samizdat, which is remarkable for its sensitivity to its fragile material nature, as well as to its movements, not only in the literal sense (i.e. the distribution of samizdat in the past between its physical mediators and its readers), but also in a metaphorical sense involving the interpretation of samizdat, i.e. shifts in its possible meanings.

The Semiotics of Samizdat

Miroslav Červenka

It is well-known that until recently literature existed in Czechoslovakia and other Communist countries that was copied out manually on a typewriter. (Use was not made of more advanced technology such as xeroxes until the last few years; a semi-mythical belief was widespread in the illegal culture that State Security did not go after anyone who for technical reasons was incapable of transcribing more than 10–15 copies at a time, i.e. anyone with no more resources than a typewriter, but that users of technologies that allowed for more extensive print runs were definitely open to prosecution. The first hectographed magazine was even believed by some to be a police provocation.) This did not just involve one-off works by dissidents, but an entire 'parallel' culture with numerous magazines, functioning publishing houses, publishing plans containing multi-volume collected works and carefully selected translations of both fiction and non-fiction. To achieve the status of literary culture this activity was primarily lacking a public, not so much due to the small number of addressees for any particular texts, but because of their disconnection, the fragmentary nature of the information that each individual received and the difficult feedback between readers and authors, while the standard functional distinction required for ordinary literary communication circles and expressible e.g. in structuralist terms in the dominance of the aesthetic function could not be achieved as part of the sum total of this communication.

The existence of this distinctive 'incomplete' literary culture is a serious subject for reflection not only among literary historians, but also with regard to their general theory. Our experience of samizdat re-clarifies several literary theory categories; in particular, those theoreticians who appreciate the relevance of communication theory to all philology may find that samizdat provides some very interesting inspiration.

In the next few pages I would like to demonstrate this in a semiotically conceived analysis of **publication**. The meaning of this key factor is to some extent provided by the normal operation of literary communication circles. Samizdat presents what is taken for granted here as a problem.

Let us proceed from an entirely banal fact. Only the oldest samizdat texts exist in the form of the ordinary typescripts that were submitted to publishers, for example, i.e. bundles of A4 carbon paper sheets attached together in one fashion or another. This kind of arrangement was only sufficient if the authors themselves wished to inform each other of what they had written that was new. Sometimes reading out loud served the same purpose as a manuscript. As soon as a broader circle of those involved entered the fray, and the publisher and the transcriber emerged (i.e. sometime around the creation of the Petlice [Padlock] series[1] before the mid-1970s), the samizdat distributors began to deal with graphic layout, hardback binding, title pages and very often illustrations, A5 book format (or quarto) and the like. This was not just a matter of playing at book publication. At the expense of difficulties and increased financial costs, these books – as objects sui generis – were provided with indicators of **definitiveness**: the standardly designed book conveys the author's instruction 'that is how I wanted it, and that is how it is. For now I do not wish, and nor am I even able, to interfere in what is being presented here – this and this alone is my book.' In contrast, a bundle of sheets, no matter how sophisticated the text, is still just a manuscript, a private document, work in progress, inviting the reader to wonder what might

---

1 The literal translation of the Czech word 'petlice' is more likely to be 'latch' however, we decided to use the frequently used term Padlock within all the texts included in this anthology. (Edit. note)

still change, rather than to continuously perceive and experience a completed work.

Another aspect of publication emerges if we refer to the same thing in this way: the layout of the book is an index of the way the text in question has completed the process of **designification**: nothing but those physical entities which have the function of signs is presented. After all, it is only signs, and not 'things' (e.g. a random defect in the paper), that can enter into literary communication. Again this looks like stating the obvious, but it only applies to texts that are normally imaginable in book form, i.e. texts that have been through proofreading. Anybody who has read samizdat publications that never got rid of their transcription errors or even their interlinear corrections knows how the communication process is disrupted by undesirable material elements left over. I, for one, find that reading a samizdat text is often a torture chamber of conjecture, with repeated attempts to restore the correct original version, i.e. which is free of anything that is not a sign.

One interesting case here is Bohumil Hrabal, who in contrast loves his original typescripts, churned out at a rate of five or six pages an hour, with all their typos and the confusions of the supreme moments of creation. Of course, what is elsewhere considered a material element left over, here becomes an independent sign in itself, at least for the author, as a reminder of the creative outburst, a record of the act (as in action painting) and it is not by chance that Hrabal speaks of his originals as graphic prints in their own way.

Another important semantic correlative of definitive book layout is that in compliance with the standard of western book culture it is accepted as an expression of **intent towards the public**. I shall clarify this with an example from literature, which is everything except samizdat-inspired.

Let us imagine that Anna Holinová (poet Jan Neruda's 'eternal bride') has received the famous verse from his *Kniha veršů* [Book of Verses] in a private letter:

Raděj bych však po ulicích žebral,
raděj kletby lidstva na se kopil,
nežli bych snad u sobectví podlém
lásku svoji v bídy blátě stopil.

Rather a street beggar I would be,
With folk pouring curses down on me
Than allow some abject selfishness
To mire my love in penury.

She will read it as just another fact in her painful erotic relationship and count it among the circumstances that are known only to herself and the writer. She will justify it causally, associating it with her lover's material circumstances, his character and intentions. It can be seen to match justified objections.

Disregarding the semi-folkloric legends, the readers of Neruda's cycle *Anně* [To Anna] will know practically nothing about it. They will take the meaning of the quoted verse to be like a marble in the mosaic of thematic elements, stylistic approaches, intonational structures and compositional components from which as far as they find it possible, they create an impression of the speaker, the lyrical subject. This is a construct that varies from reader to reader. The relationship between this construct and the 'real' Neruda is one of entire indifference at the given level of text perception, and many a fact from this sphere would only obstruct the reader's creation of this construct. An understanding of this verse does not require causal connections, but the connections involved in the reciprocal motivations between elements and parts of the work, i.e. its overall intention.

At the seam between the two situations described, i.e. communications with the addressee of the letter and communications with the reader of the poem, there is the act of publishing the work. It is at this moment that the causal connections involved in the text expire to be replaced by the intentional motivation associated with the fact that the work creates a new previously inexistent reality. It is at this moment that the communicators, aware of the objective context of the communication and for the most part engaged in it, recede in favour of people of a quite different ilk – people lacking this information, but who nevertheless are able and willing to re-create the meaning of the work and to use all and nothing but those signification and referential systems that are public property (and which remain too unspecific for the poet's intimate circle). Notice that following this decisive act, motifs, words and sentences acquire a completely different meaning: '*bídy bláto*' [penury / mire] with its alliteration and inversion would have sounded bombastic in a private letter even in Neruda's time, while in a poem it is a normal element with a somewhat rhetorical overtone, which brings the speaker closer to a standard rather than drawing attention to some real (or exaggeratedly pretended) exceptionality in his experience.

Hence due to this shift from one reality to another the work does not behave passively. By means of the sign systems which it uses and the sets of knowledge which it demands for comprehension, it postulates its public, the group of readers whom it primarily addresses. It 'wants' these readers, who know the entire situation and are capable of applying this knowledge. The work is able to literally create its own public, which previously did not exist, through the form of its language, its signifying articulation of the world. The Czech-speaking intelligentsia emerged in the 19th century inter alia through being brought to life by texts, which to communicate about matters that were of importance to people (any people at all) at that time, made use of the basic literary code, i.e. natural language in its Czech form.

Let us notice here that publication in this sense is never actually absolute, for the public identified by the work is always in some way restricted. Even though a great work always has a tendency to transcend these boundaries, the original project of the work relates to a particular culture and a particular nation. (Hence the work as a complete sign may come to be a collectively conceived identifying mythical sign with the meaning of 'we' – just like some prominent building, historical memorial, flag and the like. Compare the operation of cultural legacy in such situations as the Nazi occupation of Bohemia and Moravia.) For a text to be accepted as coherent, a quite specific set of objective knowledge and reading skills is often required. Output that is only comprehensible to friends and lovers is thus just one extreme point on a scale, at the opposite end of which – as an ideal but no less extreme construct – is the absolute public represented by 'all humanity'.

The samizdat text always appears to be tempted to place its addressees closer to that private, intimate pole than ordinary literature. What kind of public is addressed by a speaker debarred from the public? Can carbon transcription of a text in fifteen copies be considered to be publication? How can we deal with the fact that between a set of author's sign systems and the set of sign systems available to the potential reader an increasingly wide gap opens up between their mutual isolation?

Of course, we can refer to similar cases in the past, and say that the completed act of publication is not the main thing, but the heart of the matter is the intention towards the public that is imbued in the text. However, the existence of literature over the long term is quite unthinkable without a response from its readers, without the grace of their distortion, polish and unexpected enhancement through contacts with unknown life experience and the desire for unknown beauty, yes and without the banalization that enables a literary text to exist in public. And here the public is by definition associated with their numbers.

It is also associated inter alia with the number of people who, as we have said above, must be ignorant of many things in order to apply the semantizations that circumstances allow them: e.g. ignorant of what remained before the watershed of publication, and whatever was brought into play after this event acts improperly as an ad hominem argument in academic disputes.

In this respect the narrow public of samizdat readers is also handicapped by the fact that a large proportion of them are people who know each other personally, so they may have a tendency to understand a friend's text as a personal document; there are even texts that cannot be fully understood without the biographical details. In contrast, of course, thanks to their professional training, many of these people endeavour to adopt the appropriate textbook-defined interpretational approach towards their reading: 'When you are creating a coherent meaning you may use all possible codes that could be of relevance to the communication in question, but only if they are codes that are socially effective.'

Under these circumstances whereby publication is drastically limited, texts somehow stand out in a vacuum, demonstrating the unused capacity for literary experience that potential readers are deprived of by force. With their own absurdity, they document the absurdity of society, which in its extreme penury allows its sources of creativity to remain unnoticed. The literary work as such is a model for human communication in general: the semi-published samizdat text is a signifier of the fragmented communications of those times, and the more artistically intensive they are, the more successfully they accomplish their thankless task.

When facing these circumstances, authors may adopt various attitudes, which make themselves manifest in their treatment of the sign systems, and thus have a considerable effect upon the work as a whole, its form and its content. Let us consider several kinds, without forgetting that in reality they do not occur in a pure form.

There were few texts whose authors had consciously given up on public communication and accepted samizdat as direct communication within the narrowest of circles only. Samizdat generally fostered a certain standard which downplayed the implication that objective knowledge was only available to a small group of people. The exclusion of readers who were unable to create a coherent meaning from the text due to their simple lack of this knowledge would have led to hermeticism, and to a particular microculture, but then even without these extreme consequences the distinctive character of the anticipated public had an effect on the content and style of the samizdat works in the sense that they became more and more intellectual, and the proportion of essayistic, philosophical and 'philosophical' contemplations in them increased.

At the other extreme there are the authors who chose an international public instead of the nationally defined public that was forbidden to them. Samizdat presented their Czech originals for translation into world languages. They come close to something that Barthes once described as '*the zero degree of writing*'.[2] Here we have to deal with stylistics of a kind: the language is a transparent layer of the work, disowning the hard-to-translate effects that derive e.g. from utilization of the level of sound alone, the stylistic differentiation of the national language, plays on words, domestic cultural allusions and so forth. On the other hand, at other times there are interpolations and explanatory notes that put off the domestic reader. In this way entire horizons of possible meaning are eliminated; the authors supply them more in a discursive form (including metalinguistic considerations on the meaning of this or that Czech word) than by means of a literarily specific means of expression.

The third type of attitude that authors had towards samizdat can be considered fundamental. The fact that not everything could be published was not consciously taken into consideration, and the texts are conceived as if they were addressed to the normal public in normal communication circles. The overall communication issue surrounding samizdat, as we mentioned above, is not internalized in the text, which is why, paradoxically, it comes to the forefront of attention. This approach has all the characteristics of tragic heroism and absurd Sisyphean efforts. And yet there is nothing all that exceptional about this: a large amount of modern art developed involuntarily for decades in the ghetto[3] and its presentation of assertive forms and content was only accepted within a narrow public circle. In

2   See Barthes, Roland. *Writing Degree Zero*. London: Jonathan Cape, 1967. (Edit. note)
3   Klee, Paul. '*Uns trägt kein Volk*' – Quotation used in the *Jeaner Rede* lecture (1924). (Edit. note)

the case of samizdat this isolation is of course also enforced on texts geared towards the broad reading public.

And there is another paradox. This work stands or falls on its artistic complexity and individuality, and only through them can it carry on along the path of art. However, the question remains as to whether at least in those acts of perception which are granted, this core value remains the centre of attention. The reader is often gripped not so much by the individual message of the work as by the general circumstance shared by all that a text of that standard is not allowed to be published. The complexity of these creations becomes something the readers quickly skim over in favour of the general connotations: as if all the texts refer to the same thing, i.e. the fraught circumstances of their creation and the intransigence of their author.

The rapidly changing face of communications turns into an incentive for a new definition and self-definition of literature. The fourth kind of samizdat author bases his efforts on this point. His chief concern is not to preserve but to change literature based on active reactions to the circumstances surrounding communications. The situation of free literature in a totalitarian system is systematically internalized in the work – as well as in its subject, style and particularly its genre form. Texts appear that modify unliterary forms of written communication and auto-communication – diaries, correspondence, autobiography, memoirs and dramas for living-room performances. These creations may carry on the strong tradition from Mácha [1810–1836] to Kolář [1914–2002] and Hanč [1916–1963]. A literary journal was created by bringing together submitted copies on the spot: each author submitted so many copies until eventually each one received a complete 'copy'.

Of course, publication is an essential requirement for this to make sense even in these cases, but the genre is a better match for the particular circumstances behind defective publication, disregarding the fact that the creation of a new genre is always a proposal that can be taken advantage of by the literary genre system, be integrated into it or initiate a further innovation in it. The intimate and documentary features in confrontation with standard literary systems become generators of unusual combinations. They are also bearers of a semantically complex communication gesture that can be transcribed in terms of 'bearing witness'. Such works can only fully operate on condition that they do not make up the majority, so they can show up as a backdrop to the predominant works, which do not go beyond the boundaries of traditional literariness. For readers who are unaware of the circumstances and realia of the dissident world, these circles provide them with motifs such as distinctive metonyms and synecdoches, just as the Silesian realia of Petr Bezruč [1867–1958][4] once did for Prague readers. If this analogy applies, then time will one day turn these metonyms into metaphors and symbols. Meanwhile they are fragments of an unknown world intimating the wholeness from which they have been excluded. With normal publication these days the cognitive function can easily get to the core of their operation. What clearly distinguishes these texts from those samizdat publications which give up on the public (our first category) is the capacity to create meaning on several fronts, both for the 'initiated' and the 'laity'. The latter do not perceive unknown spaces as the emptiness of mere incomprehension, but instead the semantic construction integrates them as fragments, references and bearers of mystery.

---

4 A regional author of social ballads from the Moravia-Silesia region. (Edit. note)

Two Notes
on Samizdat

Miroslav Červenka

[...]

When the creator of samizdat transcripts makes sure that the lay-out is decent, the binding is firm, the format is A5 and so forth, he is not just playing at making books. This treatment is a signal of his intentions towards the public, providing a necessary sense of definiteness: 'this is the way I wanted it' is the message of a bound book from its creator, 'and I do not wish to and indeed cannot interfere in what is presented here'. This communication, conveyed at the expense of considerable sacrifice of time and a bundle of typescript (in contrast to a sheaf of loose leaves in a folder, which is still a manuscript, work in progress, tending to invite readers to consider what might yet be changed, rather than act as a spontaneous and ongoing perception experience), is drastically disrupted in the absolute majority of samizdat typescripts by imprecisions, inaccuracies and hence the incompleteness of transcripts.

Each of these errors is a stumbling block that trips readers up as they follow their linear path of text perception, deflecting them from their true perception task, i.e. evaluating and putting together semantic complexes of varying orders, back to banal graphic and designative matters, through which in appropriate circumstances (and of course presuming graphic artists are not being artistically used in some way) they simply proceed as directly as possible to higher levels. I, for one, find that reading any samizdat text is more than anything else a torture chamber of conjecture, as I repeatedly have to try to restore the correct original version.

For the most part these are all the upshot of incorrect transcription, as in my experience the author's mistakes do not figure as prominently in all this with regard to graphic accuracy, particularly the punctuation and the evergreen issues of Czech spelling. However, every book clearly shows that it did not go through the normal process of editing, which in the good old days we often used to curse, but whose very absence now makes it look like an essential element of publication. Writers are simply not attentive and above all systematic enough to get by without a language editor, but we can hardly do anything about that.

However, what urgently requires specific attention is the lack of a proofreader and proofreading, as transcriptions these days are not even able to appropriately fulfil the role meant to be played by each duplication in one or several copies, i.e. that of ensuring the continued physical existence of a text even if the original or some copies of the work have met their end.

What can be said of the fate of a translation whose author spent hours recreating the rhythmic structure of the alexandrines and whose transcribers then added or subtracted a syllable here or there – yes, that is all it takes for the fragile structure to fall apart like a model made with skewers and veneer. And the same naturally applies to prose that is worthy of the name; while the syllables might not be so important, it has a similar fragile structure that is only effective when undisturbed, e.g. involving the intonation of sentences and their parts, not to mention objective precision and correctness.

If I now come to consider what is to be done about all this, I do so in the awareness that I am making demands on people who selflessly spend their evenings on hard work that nobody is going to appreciate in public, while often exposed to pressure from outside. However, they should also consider that just a relatively small amount of extra work can act as essential insurance against the risk that the results of their efforts will ultimately be devalued.

Textological discipline and culture naturally begin with the **authors**. If they value their work enough to want to protect it, so that the readers get hold of what the authors have actually written, then they have to focus concentrated attention on the original text that is to be transcribed. Even when printed texts are being published, the author's definitive manuscript, the master copy for the first edition of the book, has a privileged position as proof of the author's 'so be it!'. Perhaps decades later it will still enable corrections to be made to errors in the first edition, which unnoticed by the author (authors do not make good proofreaders: they often think they are reading what they once wrote, not what is actually there on the page), are subsequently reprinted from one edition to the next. The master copy for transcription should have several carbon copies (it cannot be replaced by several consecutive typescripts, because they will differ from each other), which the author should proofread as carefully and identically as possible without leaving any of them out. The author ought to indicate on them that they are the definitive text of a particular work, date them and attach relevant information on the creation of the work. If the master copy is being drawn up by someone else for a deceased or incarcerated author, an editorial note is required to explain which authorial sources the publisher has relied upon and what has been done with them. One corrected carbon copy of the master, or ideally several of them, should be securely stored away as a guarantee of the continued existence of the authentic version of the work. If the work is ever officially published then this master copy and not some samizdat transcription is the only acceptable source.

The policy that I am noting here can only be adhered to with difficulty, and any strict observation of it might slow down the distribution of samizdat texts, and yet it is enormously important and should not be breached out of indolence, as often occurs, but only if there is really no other way. The principle is basically that any other transcripts, foreign reprints and the like should only be made on the basis of these master copies, prepared, proof-read and verified by the author himself, i.e. we have to presume that even with the best possible checking, some of the transcription errors will always remain uncorrected, so that chain transcription means errors increase as in a game of Chinese whispers. It just needs three or four consecutive transcriptions without checking the original and we have a cruelly distorted text in front of us. Moreover, it should be a rule that each subsequent editor has direct contact with the author for other reasons too, as we shall see.

Another person (and role) involved is the one that arranges the transcription and preparation of the samizdat book, who for lack of a better word shall be called the **editor**. Ideally, he or she performs the tasks of a publishing editor, making various comments on the content and form of the work, including the language aspect. (Perhaps it need not be said here, but all changes made at the behest of the editor must be reflected by the author in the other carbon copies of the original, ideally in such a way that they can later be identified as editorial.) As for the textual culture, the editor should always check to make sure that the original is clear and unambiguous enough for the transcriber. In all contentious cases the author should be consulted. The editor is the only link in the samizdat chain facilitating feedback between the source and the publication – feedback that is normally provided numerous times when a work is being published.

As already noted, there is no proofreading in samizdat, and that is a highly unfavourable circumstance with regard to reliability at the textual level, as it exacerbates beyond critical level the task of the **transcribers**, increasing their responsibility. Clearly, the transcribers are the weakest link in the process we are dealing with. They cannot and must not work other than mechanically, and yet ideally they should perform elementary proofreading as they write. The best corrections in samizdat publications are those in which the differences between the original and the emerging transcription are removed before the page in question is taken out of the typewriter. Deletion or tippexing of an erroneous segment of text and insertion of the correct version, if only between the lines, might spoil the neatness of the transcript, but that will be spoilt even more if the correction is carried out later, and what's more, the correction will have to be inserted separately into each carbon copy. In comparison with this manual insertion, throwing out an A5 page that has too many errors and replacing it with a new one saves considerable energy.

More on the subject of neatness: A smooth typescript with the errors left uncorrected is like a household that looks well-swept from the outside, but which has its drawers and cupboards in a shameful mess. Nicely typed out nonsense is still nonsense.

We are getting to the stage where the completed typed transcript is returned to the editor. It should not be disorderly, i.e. all the carbon copies of the same page should be together, as the next stage is perhaps the most important for the textological culture of the text. It is absolutely essential that the author and the editor check each copy of the transcription independently of each other and correct all the errors, swapping their findings and comparing their results. However, if this checking work only involves reading the transcription then it cannot come near to performing its task, at least in the case of the editor, and as a rule in the case of the author too, unless he or she has a marvellous memory. For this to happen, it should be in the nature of **collation**, i.e. comparison with the author's original. If we merely read, then as a rule we only detect typos like 'she threw her arms round his meck', which ultimately disrupt the integrity of the text least of all, while we can neglect the omission of entire paragraphs. At the very least it is essential for the checkers to have the original to hand and to keep consulting it.

Even in the case of printed books, correction slips are often attached to imperfectly performed proofreading, e.g. 'Page 10, line 8, *neck* not *meck*.' It is useful in practice for the author and the editor to draw up a similar list, which will then serve as the basis for either of the two to transfer the corrections to each copy of the transcription. This stage completes the checking work, which is devoid of meaning without it. It is an unforgivable transgression to only make corrections in some carbon copies and not in others. Moreover, one list of errors should be attached to the archive carbon copies of the original.

Of course, the same procedure must be undertaken for each new transcription and set of carbon copies, even if as part of a single

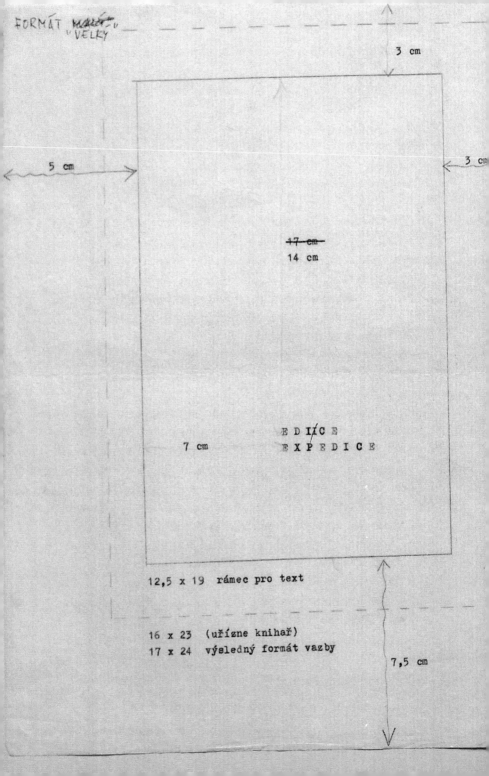

FORMÁT ~~MALÝ~~ „VELKÝ

3 cm

5 cm   3 cm

~~17 cm~~
14 cm

7 cm   E D I/C E
              E X P E D I C E

12,5 x 19 rámec pro text

16 x 23 (uřízne knihař)
17 x 24 výsledný formát vazby

7,5 cm

'edition' more copies are being produced than the typewriter's capacity permits, so that several transcriptions are being made. This should result not only in accuracy, but also in totally identical transcriptions distributed to readers. Only when this is assured are carbon copies of the same page separated from one other, bound together in a single book and so forth.

As stated above, any subsequent chronologically or geographically remote transcription should again be based not on a transcription, but on an original master, and the above checking procedure including the collation is likewise naturally essential, even if a new author had to perform it while liaising in difficult circumstances with the author. If the author has changed something in the text between individual transcriptions, it should be indicated in the new transcription that this is a new version dated such and such a year.

Most of those involved in samizdat will probably find this scheme appears optimal but unlikely. Our requirements focus on the minimum conditions for the cultured publication of samizdat texts. At the same time I reject the possible objection that this note is just the outcome of a philologist's *déformation professionelle*, simply applying the principles of his own trade. I am not basing myself on philology, but on the existence of samizdat as one of the primary phenomena of contemporary culture. Perhaps I might have said 'parallel' culture, but that epithet does not seem to me to do justice to the circumstances under which the traditions of Czech literature are legitimately carried on in typescript publications, whereas printed literature – at least in the case of original fiction – wastes its back matter and typographic resources on producing marginal products that hang in the air devoid of all tradition. One of the Czech tradition's attributes is that the language is fostered, developed and differentiated along with its literature. By taking on the task of upholding and developing the legacy of Mácha, Neruda, Vančura, Čapek and Čep in the gloomy

◀ Editor's notes for typists of the samizdat books 'published' in the Expedice series

circumstances at the end of the millennium, samizdat authors, editors and transcribers have thereby also taken on this (only seemingly) marginal and burdensome obligation. If these specific requirements, derived from nothing but this obligation, sound like something paradoxical, it is not their fault but a consequence of the paradoxical status of samizdat as a whole.

Another way of looking at it is that in view of the culture that we are all eye-bulgingly on our knees and at pains to provide, I simply suggest that in the interests of internal consistency my colleagues include this one little additional absurdity to the total absurdity of their activities.

Samizdat

Josef Jedlička

We have already noted that a new magazine called *Dialogy* [Dialogues] entered samizdat literary circulation. This is further evidence of the qualitative changes that were taking place in unofficial Czech culture, confirming the trend that for several years had started taking vague shape. When the first substantial literary texts appeared around 1970 and began to circulate in typescript carbon copies, they were for the most part works written for the ordinary book market, which did not meet the censor's demands which had suddenly become more ideologically rigorous. After several 'merciful years' there was a return to tried and tested practice. Throughout the 1950s, texts appeared that had no hope at the time of being brought out by a normal publisher, even though they were very much in demand. These weren't only original works, but often also translations. Older witnesses will surely recall that back some time in 1953 the manuscripts of *Zbabělci* [The Cowards, 1970] and *Konec nylonového věku* [End of the Nylon Age] were circulating round Prague, both signed by a certain Errol[1], while in those days many who are now fifty years old used to pass round some fascinating stories about these weird 'palaverers', to which a romantic legend was attached that they were written by some kind of defrocked lawyer who now worked at a scrap yard. Just a few copies of the Mánes edition of *The Castle* passed through hundreds of hands, but it was not only the highly suspect Kafka who was reliant at that time on private distribution, but from the start of the post-1948 period even Yesenin and Shklovsky. At the time it felt like a stopgap solution to bridge the worst of times, with some justification as it turned out, because most of the original sock-drawer literature had

---

1   Writer Josef Škvorecký. (Edit. note)

to wait until the mid-1960s to be published as books some ten or fifteen years later, to the irreparable detriment of the authors. The situation at that time ought not to be idealized. The works of several Catholics, surrealists, Trotskyists, structuralists and neo-gnostics did not even get through the loose net of the 'Prague Spring', even though conditions were indisputably more relaxed, so there was no need to spontaneously distribute unauthorized works or to specially organize or institutionalize this distribution, never mind defining it as a unique cultural phenomenon.

During the 1970s, however, it soon became evident that previous practices would not be sufficient. Unofficial publishing activity which adopted Soviet samizdat methods without ever explicitly identifying with this term began to seek at least some minimum defensible legal platform to protect the distribution of unofficial and non-conformist texts from direct persecution. Because this did not (at least at first) involve the work of unauthorized debutants hiding away in anonymity, as was the case at the end of the 1940s and the beginning of the 1950s, but texts by authors who were more or less already well-known, established and in recent years often famous, it was clear that this literary activity would soon start to be considered an equal-valued element of national culture, albeit at a considerable disadvantage.

As the conformist and non-conformist creative paths increasingly diverged each year, it was only a short step from there for this DIY-distributed literature to start being considered the best alternative, i.e. with more rather than less justification, as the authentic literary reflection of social reality. A considerable shift in this self-creating and self-aware process was brought about by increasing official and subsequent police pressure, which activated the defensive strength of the alternative culture, vitalizing it with specific political controversies. The Petlice [Padlock] series, the most famous and productive activity involved, simply had to include particular samizdat 'genres' in its publication programme for reasons of self-preservation, such as the open letter, the public complaint, the topical feuilleton and the legal document. To add weight to its arguments, the direct reactions were also countered by the specialist memorandum, the expert analysis and with implacable logic the philosophical disquisition, which could not avoid defining its basic worldview if it was to remain authentic and credible.

Charter 77, which was in any case directly triggered by another stream of alternative culture, i.e. the music and songwriting scene, was a further developmental stage in the original DIY culture. Here culture begins to appeal explicitly to its socially creative role, growing from its realist mental experience to knowledge of the true state of affairs. It begins to stand up for the right to meaningfully intervene in these affairs, in a way that is distinctive to culture and a way that is common in our national tradition, which sanctifies it.

So what could be more natural than that the chartists' documents be collected in anthologies, while accompanying texts are written seeking to place their initial standpoints and effects in context, and while the prime stock of the literary inventory, originally fiction, has begun to branch out into other types and genres, which might not yet have burgeoned, but which testifies to the viability of the organism, as well as its uniqueness and legal capacity. It is surely not by chance that Jirous's coinage *second culture* appears in *Dialogy* at just this time. *Dvanáctka* [Twelve], *Spektrum* [Spectrum] and *Patočkův sborník* [Patočka's Anthology], to randomly name just some of the magazines, are not merely external evidence of the variety of this *second culture*, but also its most prominent embodiment, as they bring about that qualitative change mentioned earlier. As this second culture has now worked its way up to be organically viable, it no longer intends to just make do with its role as a polemical device to defend against specific acts of political, intellectual and personal persecution and discrimination. With an increasing self-confidence based on the facts that they were producing top-rank works of value, the leading intellectuals in various fields were now joined in solidarity, and they were being granted a hearing and recognition elsewhere in a world that now took their high professional standard for granted. They wished to appropriately confront the Czechoslovak social breakdown in its totality. Hence they increasingly turned their attention from current affairs to the timeless, from the transitory to the fundamental, from trivialities to human issues. They were interested in man and his purpose, not only as a duty, but as a natural requirement of real culture. If this ever lent them arguments and strengthened their defensive capacity, then it was meant to internally transform them further until they realized that they were deeply and utterly incompatible with totalitarian power.

Question Marks over Unpublished Literature

-n [František Kautman]

A book is normally considered to be a *'printed work with a substantial number of paper sheets bound together as an independent unit'*[2]. Of course, this is a very imprecise definition. Firstly, we do actually consider manuscript books to be books, because there were no other kinds before the invention of typography. Secondly, 'a substantial number of paper sheets' is a rather vague expression, both because those sheets need not be made of paper and because a 'thick magazine' might have several hundred pages but still not be considered to be a book, whereas a brochure with just a few pages undoubtedly is one. It might well be appropriate here to at least refer to a book's lack of periodicity, which regardless of its size would differentiate it from a magazine, which *is* characterized by its periodicity, regardless of its size.

However, we do not wish here to delve into bibliological terminology, which we shall leave to the experts. What we have more in mind is the sociological aspect of the origins and existence of what is known as *inediti* [literally 'unpublished', here underground and all spheres of unofficial] literature, which readers first became aware of in the form of *samizdat*.

The term *inediti* has not yet become established, and many intellectuals do not even know what it is actually intended to mean. If we

---

2 PROCHÁZKA, Vladimír. *Příruční slovník naučný* [Reference Encyclopedia], *Vol. 2*. Praha: Ústav pro českou literaturu, 1963, p. 518.

have the 'real socialist states' in mind, where this kind of literature first took root, then the term *neoficiální* [unofficial] or *nelegální* [illegal] *literatura* is used more often, (culture in its broader meaning is referred to in a similar way). However, both these terms are inappropriate. As regards the first one I go along with Fidelius's standpoint expressed in *Kritický sborník* [Critical Review].[3] However, the term *nelegální* is fundamentally flawed (State Security units evidently distinguish two categories: *nelegální*, the content of which is supposedly harmless, but which cannot come out in this country for one reason or another, e.g. because of the author's identity, and *ilegální*, which is supposed to be literature with harmful content), directly contradicting the position adopted by *ineditní* authors, as they consider their activities to be perfectly legal, since there is no law in this country prohibiting you from transcribing your work several times and lending it out to acquaintances. So nothing unlawful is taking place.

The term *ineditní* is definitely not above criticism either. To begin with, such a manuscript is only 'underground and unofficial' in this country, while it can be published abroad (and indeed some of them are from time to time), secondly, as an 'unofficial' term it draws a sharp line between published and unpublished literature, and thirdly, it is only appropriate for literary work, i.e. from the parallel culture (which is also an imprecise term), while it is unable to include apartment drama performances, exhibitions, music performances and so forth, which in any case are not 'published' as such.

Otherwise, however, the term is fairly clear and precise, because it covers all the literary works that cannot be published in this country for various reasons, whichever fields of art or knowledge they come under, whether they are works by domestic authors or translations of foreign works, living or dead, publishable or not, for there are authors who may publish some works but not others (Seifert and Hrabal), and there are authors who can be published, but who do not

---

3 FIDELIUS, Petr. 'Kultura "oficiální" a "neoficiální"' ['Official' and 'unofficial' culture], *Kritický sborník*, No. 3, 1981, Vol. I., pp. 71-89.

wish to be. There are also cases where a work exists in two versions, one *editní* [official] and the other *ineditní*, which can substantially differ from each other.

Hence from the terminological standpoint it would appear that we can accept the division of literary works into *editní* and *ineditní*, so long as we rule out the axiological aspect and we do not forget that even an officially published [*editní*] author could come up against obstacles and restrictions as he is bringing his book to press, including compulsory changes to the text, publication delays, drastic limitations on the print run, distribution difficulties, gagging in advertising media and so forth.

Nobody invented *ineditní* literature; it is not the bizarre whim of some individual or literary group, or a symptom of the exclusivity of future literature, as Rozanov thought, when he opined that future literary works would only be distributed as manuscripts within a broad circle of specialists. By coincidence, 'samizdat' (i.e. literature published by the authors themselves without intermediaries, i.e. without publishers' editors and censors) also emerged in Russia, but definitely not because its creators had any doubts about interest among the masses of readers in their works. In one sense *ineditní* literature was brought into existence by the regime, whose strict control network over publishing production (both on content and authors, which was a novelty compared with classic censorship, focusing on the texts alone, not on their creators) excluded a considerable proportion of intellectual output involving advertising. Of course, strict Stalinism did not permit any non-conformist literature at all to appear, even in manuscript form. It was not so long before that Soviet poets kept their unpublished poems solely in their memory and perhaps only recited them to trusted friends without witnesses somewhere deep in a forest. This should not surprise us, considering the heavy punishments visited upon authors of various pamphlets, privately written magazines or even injudiciously formulated sentences in private letters.

Hence samizdat could not emerge until Khrushchev's era after Stalin's death, when it achieved considerable growth and expansion (nowadays it seems to be on the retreat and limits itself mostly to politological, sociological and historical texts, while fiction appears more rarely).

From the standpoint of democratic countries, 'unpublished' literature must be a phenomenon that is hard to understand, as a typewriter is a typical American invention that originally served to speed up commercial communication, and for many decades it did not occur to anyone that it could compete with Gutenberg, especially considering that nowadays there are several other reproduction techniques apart from classic typography that can quickly and quite inexpensively duplicate any text or image in any quantity. Without other reproduction techniques a typewriter can only be used to write letters and short texts or drafts for printing (so most professional writers these days use typewriters).

Hence samizdat literature is extremely impractical: its costs are high, its legibility is for the most part poor and it has a short lifespan, which to its detriment distinguishes it not only from printed literature, but also from old manuscripts, which might have been expensive, but were highly legible and for the most part also of aesthetic value. (Moreover, *ineditní* literature has its bibliophile prints, particularly in this country, albeit hitherto only to a limited degree, because the associated costs are rising to a dreadful extent as consumers of this literature are not as a rule an affluent readership.)

These circumstances imprint a special character upon *ineditní* literature, which distinguishes it from published literature: the role of the economic element in literary production was fundamentally changing. Indeed the practice of almost the entire 19th and the first half of the 20th century was being stood on its head. To be sure, typography was a cultural pursuit from the outset, but for the most part it was a profitable one. Of course, the authors quickly and justifiably started attempting to gain their share of the profits, for 'the labourer is worthy of his hire'. In the 19th century the majority of countries had legislated for the printing and publishing trade, while providing copyright protection, first at a national level and later internationally. Authors were released to some extent from subsistence worries, which was a plus, but at the same time commercial pressure on literature intensified, which increasingly compelled them to be successful rather than good, which are rarely the same thing, and very often are not. Socialists liked to attack publishers' exploitative practices towards authors and promised that this would change after the revolution. It did change, in such a way that the author is indeed no longer exposed to the pressure of the capitalist market in 'real socialist' states, but instead is exposed to the relentless pressure of exclusive ideology and cadre repressions. If an author wants to be successful under capitalism he often has to meet the demands of readers who are behind the times. Under socialism he has to meet the demands of the regime and succumb to the pressure of an editor who is often considerably behind the times. Both the former and the latter are unfree, the difference being that under capitalism authors of integrity can publish their unpopular works at their own expense in extreme cases, whereas the same authors cannot publish such works under socialism. However, there are enough publishers in capitalist countries who are willing to publish unpopular works at least once in a while, both in the interests of their reputation and in view of the competition, because 'you never do know'. Under socialism there is no competition, because of the back-room collaboration between the few central publishers with similar profiles, and no editors are going to work with an author whose cadre profile is unverified or not even screened.

Even in the West there are obviously authors who do not publish their books, because they cannot find a publisher, and they do not have enough money to publish anything at their own expense, but then it is all up to their own free will. I do not believe any author is so poor as to be unable to have his work transcribed or to transcribe it himself and then use some reproduction technique to duplicate at least a hundred copies. Hence the phenomenon of *ineditní* literature does not exist in the West. (One of our critics believes that western countries such as France or Germany ought to study our samizdats simply because a time will come when real literature there will only be 'published' underground.)[4]

Underground literature negates the entire commercial basis of the contemporary publishing business. Nobody ever grew rich by producing 'unpublished' literature and indeed nobody has even made the most modest living. Authors have come to take it for granted that they are not going to receive royalties for their work, regardless of whether it is a two-page article or a thousand-page novel or philosophical treatise based on many years of work. In this way they have certainly lost much, but they have also gained something: a creative freedom that literature has never previously had anywhere, for not only are they no longer under the supervision of any censors, so they can rid themselves of the last remnants of self-censorship, but they are released from any economic pressure exerted on them by editors: for if authors do not accede to their demands then editors can threaten not to publish manuscripts, and so deprive authors of their royalties. And how many people are robust enough to resist such pressure?

If expenses for a manuscript included not only the costs of materials, transcription and the binding, but also a fee, albeit a very low one, for the author, the price of the manuscript would be so high that it would be practically inaccessible to ordinary mortals.

With its attitude towards banned authors the regime has thus achieved two unexpected and inconvenient results: it has liberated their work, and at the same time it has lost the control over them that it could have exercised even over non-conformist authors who have to negotiate with the editors and censors over their manuscripts.

This all places 'unpublished' literature in a favourable light: free and selfless, it is written by authors of integrity out of honourable motives.

It is free insomuch as its authors have eliminated their own self-censorship. It is also selfless, even though some authors might

---

4   See also NĚMEC, Jiří. 'K Zapomenutému světlu Jakuba Demla' [To *Zapomenuté světlo* by Jakub Deml], *Kritický sborník*, No. 2, 1986, Vol. VI., pp. 29–37.

The Gulag Archipelago by Alexandr Solzhenitsyn

be accused of writing for their own self-aggrandizement, i.e. out of vanity, or of being graphomaniacs, whose obsessive writing would never be printed by anyone anyway. Such cases can indeed be found, but they are isolated.

The high standard of unpublished literature, particularly in this country, is also often mentioned. It is true that the best works of Czech literature during the 1970s came out in the Petlice, Expedice and Kvart series [Padlock, Dispatch, Quarto], though not thanks to unpublished literature as such, but simply because after 1969, the 'normalized' regime excluded most of the best authors, philosophers, historians and journalists that we had at that time from any publicity. At the same time it made any publishing initiatives by energetic new authors too difficult, thus frequently forcing them to join the 'unpublished authors'.

Let it not be said, however, that everything in the unpublished literary realm is of a high standard, whereas all published literature is shoddy. *Ineditní* literature comes out much less and it is easier to survey and map out, while percentage-wise it includes more high-standard works than the bloated figures on newly published titles that the regime likes to quote particularly abroad to document the extensive development of contemporary Czech literature. However, there are equally good and indeed outstanding works of literature that are published, as well as weak and substandard *ineditní* works. It is just the grey average, making up a high percentage of published literature, which is much less frequently represented in 'unpublished series'. Hence this average is the typical product of commercial pressures, whether from undemanding readers or from official ideology. As a rule the average author does not have any great talent, but he has learnt the writing trade and intends to capitalize on it appropriately. But this is only possible in the realm of published literature, where royalties are paid.

However, underground literature also has its dark side and its serious issues, because it lacks a definitive stage at which the manuscript is edited, which can only be done in marginal proofreading. No matter how much the author polishes his manuscript, it is still just a manuscript, i.e. a fairly open text whose incompleteness and indefiniteness, by always allowing for more additions and corrections, actually acts as an incentive. A printed text also looks different to a typescript – which is something of a psychological mystery, but some defects in a manuscript cannot be seen by the author until the text is set.

Then there are the harsh restrictions on advertising and thus the number of readers. To be sure there are exceptions, where an underground text has as many readers as the author would obtain through publishing in bulk (e.g. Seifert's *Morový sloup* [The Plague Column, 1979]). Moreover, the number of readers for each manuscript copy is much higher than for a published book (purchased copies of books are normally put on the bookshelf and will be read 'when there's time', which can be five years later or sometimes never, while a manuscript borrowed for a week has to be read immediately), but this only partly makes up for the lack of copies available to readers. A large number of those interested do not actually gain access to unpublished texts at all.

The situation with critical response is even worse. Authors occasionally get to hear their friends' opinion by word of mouth, which of course is not too authoritative, because it is hard to criticize somebody to their face. With few individual exceptions (Václav Černý, H. Rak and L. Dobrovský) there was practically no written criticism during the 1970s, at least in this country. This was the obverse side of the unlimited creative freedom enjoyed by unpublished authors, and they never actually found out what their readers thought of their work. Indeed this was also an advantage of a kind, but to a large extent it was conditional. It is actually much more of a drawback: the author stews in his own juice, and his text is neither interpreted nor reflected upon. The author is held captive by his own self-reflection, which is deceptive: sometimes he is spoilt, convinced by turns of his own ingenuity (and lack of recognition – which collocates so nicely – unrecognized genius!), while then succumbing to nihilistic moods and becoming firmly convinced that his work is worthless. Indeed it is possible to write for nobody at all, but this does not guarantee literature that is truly viable.

Unpublished authors might also stop feeling any solidarity with a particular national literature, or to be more precise, they still feel it, but only nominally. Some authors live entirely on their own, with practically no contact at all with other authors. To be sure they are the exception, but then other unpublished authors only associate with narrow circles, bound more by ties of friendship than any uniform creative objectives, as used to be the case in creative literary groups. Contacts are only rarely maintained between published and unpublished authors for understandable reasons, because unpublished authors are often subject to supervision by security forces, so this indiscretion may lead published authors to lose their right to publish their books at the very least.

Like it or not, two separate social phenomena have come into being here – published literature and unpublished [*inediтní*] literature.

There are definitely also unpublished authors who believe they are victims of a temporary anomaly and that their manuscript will be published sometime somewhere, hence they consider their current state to be some kind of provisional arrangement, even though it has lasted over ten years. If only that were the case! But then what if unpublished literature were a new literary phenomenon which in line with Rozanov's ideas anticipates a constantly restricted number of readers while book printing costs continue to rise?

In America contemporary book culture is predicted to come to an end in the 1990s to be replaced by microfiche for utilitarian economic reasons (a microfiche of a thousand-page novel will fit into a small matchbox and will cost just a few cents instead of tens of dollars). What will remain alive of *ineditní* literature at that time will simply be put on microfiche – who would still risk laboriously producing a book first? Of course, there will always be bibliophiles who are willing to undergo privations in order to pay a very high price for a classic printed book, so as to add it to their library, but they will be increasingly few in number and like bibliophiles today they will focus on classic, time-tested, shorter texts and curiosities.

However, let us leave futurological forecasts to one side. For the time being, *ineditní* literature plays an important role in this country: it preserves the continuity of development of our thinking and literature with the national culture of the past, and if it is up to the task it attempts to do so in a worldwide context. This task is so important and honourable that it is worth the effort and the risk associated with the creation and distribution of *ineditní* literature.

The Forgotten Question Mark over 'Unpublished' Literature

-pf- [Petr Fidelius]

A strange custom has recently caught on in this country, whereby all samizdat literature is called *ineditní* ['unpublished', hence 'unofficial' or 'underground']. It might be just a passing fashion, but if it is the result of seriously intended efforts to definitively resolve those long-drawn-out terminological difficulties associated with describing the free, independent literature that emerges beyond the purview of official supervision in a late totalitarian Communist-style regime, then it should be pointed out that this usage of the term *ineditní* is not only inappropriate, but quite nonsensical. When an article appeared in *KS* No. 4/82 entitled 'Question Marks over Unpublished Literature'[1], I expected the author to point this out, but alas he did not. Although amongst other things he basically deals with the terminological appropriacy of the new term, surprisingly he forgets the main question mark: having carefully considered the various pros and cons, he comes to the conclusion that '*otherwise it is a fairly precise and clear term*'. Now this could only be agreed with if the term did indeed with some precision and clarity express the exact opposite of what it

---

1 -n [KAUTMAN, František]. 'Otazníky kolem ineditní literatury' [Question Marks over Unpublished Literature], *Kritický sborník*, No. 4, 1982, Vol II, pp. 56–72. See also the previous chapter and the Commentary at the end of this book. (Edit. note)

is meant to. However, if it is adopted to such a broad extent then this clearly testifies to the fact that the writer indeed (unintentionally) hit the bull's eye when he expressed the view that '*many intellectuals do not even know what it is actually intended to mean*'.

Hence should we wish to improve on our mother tongue willy-nilly with this foreign word, let it at least be clear in which sense it can be used. Translated into Czech *ineditní* quite simply means 'unpublished', so *ineditní* refers to those manuscripts that have hitherto remained in the bottom drawer. Hence as soon as a manuscript is brought out it ceases to be *ineditní* and becomes *editní* [published] (you may improve on Czech in this way too if you will). At most the word 'ineditní' might appear on the title page of the *first* copy to inform readers they are looking at a text that was *previously* unpublished. (However, editors usually just resort to such practices in the case of posthumous publication.) And that just about exhausts the options for legitimate usage of this adjective. Anything else is just thoughtless overuse, which is basically just as absurd as if we still called meat 'raw' after it was cooked.

Now many people might well object that of course they know all this, but all the same if a text is typed out on a typewriter and brought out that way in samizdat then that is different to, indeed completely incomparable with, a publishing house bringing a work out in print in a correct and standard manner. Of course, this is something quite different, but is it really *incomparable*? Let me ask: what are we actually doing with these manuscripts in samizdat if not publishing them? And why on earth are we using the word for series *edice* (in Edice Petlice [Padlock series], Edice Expedice [Dispatch series] and so forth)? And is it not true that if we are to be consistent in this respect then we should not even use the word *sam-izdat*? Still, those who support the title 'ineditní' evidently do not ask questions of this kind at all. This can be seen from the fact that they quite spontaneously utter expressions like *ineditní edice* [unpublished publication], as in the example of the aforementioned *KS* article. Sure, this is acceptable as a poetic oxymoron, but unless I am mistaken, we are actually concerned here with giving a practical name to a particular reality.

It might help us a little if we clarify the meaning of the actual term *vydání* (or *edice*) *rukopisu* [publication of a manuscript], as the question is, to what extent does this term also cover our samizdat practice?

If we understand *vydávání* [publication] of texts in the broadest sense then we can distinguish two aspects: let us call them the technical and the creative. As far as the technical aspect is concerned, I see no reason why the term *edice* should necessarily be limited to the use of typography or the size of the print run. It is true that the number of copies published has an effect on the 'publicness' of the text (in the sense of its dissemination among the public). So it is obvious that samizdat literature, as the author of the aforementioned article mentions, is characterized by '*the harsh restrictions on advertising and thus the number of readers*'. However, this is no reason for us to call it *ineditní*. After all, we do know that even in a free society a large number of printed items (both private and bibliographical) were brought out with tiny print runs, yet we never doubt for a moment that this involved regular publishing activity. Disregarding the fact that 'publicness' conceived as the 'number of readers' is by no means directly proportionate to the print run amount, from this standpoint printed matter that is truly mass-produced might have tiny 'publicness', as in the case of the Marxist-Leninist classics, which Czech publishers tirelessly poured out perhaps merely in order to ensure an uninterrupted exchange of materials between the pulp mill and the printing press. This is definitely needless and futile activity, but clearly still 'published' after all. On the other hand it is obvious that from the technical standpoint samizdat is not once and for all basically restricted just to the typewriter: this limitation is dictated by current power relations. Where conditions permit, samizdat also extends into typography, as was once the case for example in Poland, and as is (at present) the case in Hungary.

However, what is determinative about the term 'publication' is the *creative* aspect. What I have in mind here is the irreplaceable role that is (or at least should be) played in this process by the editor. A good editor is almost as important a factor for the author himself and for the development of his talent as a good literary critic, indeed from one point of view editors are even more important, because it is collaboration between an author and an editor that creates the final form of the work that subsequently comes before the critics. And that is not even to mention the considerable responsibility that the editor has towards the readers.

Now how does the current situation concerning samizdat appear in this regard? Even from a very sober and indeed sceptical viewpoint, I do not think it can escape our attention that following an initial period of rather extensive growth, there has been increasing concern in Czech samizdat for the quality of *editorial preparations* of published texts. For example, let us recall (at random) the publication of Patočka's *Opera Omnia*, a paperback translation of *Sein und Zeit*, a reedition by the Kvart [Quarto] series and of course, last but not least, our own dear *Kritický sborník* [Critical Review]. Can there be any doubt at all that these accomplishments are achieved by honest *editorial* work? I believe it is only a fair statement of facts to say that, generally speaking, an awareness of the irreplaceable creative role of the editor in Czech samizdat has slowly but surely been gaining ground over the last few years. Here I see gratifying signs of a complete turnaround from a more or less non-committal amateurism to responsible design work. I do not believe the time is so far off when it will in general be taken for granted that a samizdat typescript should be edited in such a way that it can 'immediately be printed' if the need arises.

The question still remains as to what to call this unofficial publishing activity (as well as the literature published in this way). I really do not know why we should refrain from using the established term *samizdat*, as out of all the names that are concurrently used, it is the only one that nobody can object to on the grounds of precision or appropriateness, and that is entirely free of any intrusive or misleading connotations. I think this word best expresses the essence of the matter: samizdat is basically self-help publication of anything that cannot be published at establishments subject to state supervision, while we can look at this self-help activity from two different standpoints. From the material standpoint it is of course a last resort, an extraordinary and abnormal approach that has been forced on us by extraordinary and abnormal conditions; an expensive and ineffective procedure which must look like a fantastic waste of physical and mental effort from the standpoint of normal conditions. But then on the other hand, from the spiritual standpoint a hopeful spark of normality can be seen in this phenomenon, as here we have a real chance to preserve for future generations (albeit to a very limited extent) not only the theoretical idea, but also a *practical sense* for what is called a free autonomous cultural institution.

If it is at all possible to object to the term *samizdat* then it might only be in the name of linguistic aesthetics: for this typically Russian abbreviation is somewhat redolent of all those *kolkhozes*, *politruks* and the like, which truth to tell, do not look all that good in Czech. But if after all we have accepted such monsters as *khozrashchot*, an expression that might best be compared to a pig's snout in terms of aesthetic appeal, how can we deny rights of residence within our native language to the undoubtedly more mellifluous expression *samizdat*? And that is not to mention the fact that it is only fair and proper this word should forever remind us of the pre-eminence which the Russians have by rights gained in this field.

Censorship and Literary Life beyond the Mass Media

Jiří Gruša

[…]

The term *samizdat* has the advantage of being internationally well-established, its impactful Soviet short form is very practical, reflecting self-starting personal initiative, but then the highly important activity behind the creation of 'unbooks and unmagazines' refers over-specifically to Russian conditions. That is its basic disadvantage. For however much the existence of this literature everywhere is the product of Sovietization (and this needs to be remembered in spite of our admiration for it), it is actually very different outside Russia, and indeed serves a different role. Historically, Russian samizdat is a Russian creation, whereas in societies outside the Soviet Union it operates as the only continuum for lean and suppressed historicality. Hence it is more than just oppositional… indeed in one sense it could be called the only possible place for metalanguage, cultural memory and the polis to be preserved.

Terms such as *persecuted*, *prohibited* and *unofficial* again highlight the act of the 'other side' – while the term *ineditní* [unpublished, unofficial, underground] literature overlooks the fact that it covers works or texts that actually are edited – and of course it does not take other non-paper genres into account. Another term frequently used – *nelegální* [illegal, illicit] – is practically contiguous with official terminology, which is also 'evaluative', conducting its evaluation from the same standpoint, albeit with different labels: (offensive, diversionist, seditious, libellous, slanderous and the like), regardless of the fact that the concept 'lex' is basically absurd in circumstances where the law boils down to pure and simple administration.

Perhaps the most precise adjective would be non-mass-media, as this depicts the situation in a purely cartographic manner. Because the fact is this literature (and culture) lies beyond the mass media of the Stalinist state. Withdrawing from mass media mechanisms, rejecting their 'language', or as Havel puts it, their 'Ptydepe', means opening up to the possibility of providing at least some *information*, and not just parroting some cliché or other. Although it is the task of all literature to provide the information that seeps through the filters come what may (i.e. it is a defence of speech and its semantic weight against entropy as such), under the circumstances of a totalitarian state this task also includes the need to confront the deliberate background noise. The adjective non-mass-media would also enable us to include another aspect of such conduct, which will perhaps soon be widespread, i.e. its possible future application to literature outside 'real socialism', which will increasingly have to deal with the pressure of the mass media operating on the market principle. This will cause overproduction of 'news', and thus from another angle it will contribute to its standardization and sterilization. Here, too, even outside the mass media it may ultimately be necessary to avoid what we have summed up in the expression 'semantic weight'.

The first meeting of the re-Stalinized Writers' Union as it were definitively launched the era of this non-mass-media literature. The three year period in which literary institutions and instruments were entirely eliminated was a sufficiently long time for a community of this kind to bring itself together. When the new literary overseers eventually counted up their numbers they found they had around 175 people available (at a very liberal estimate, as they were often mostly qualified outside the literary sphere), i.e. in their 'hard core'. From the standpoint of a carbuncle, any other body is unhealthy. Some 400 people remained beyond the wire, renounced as writers. Our statistics here are supported by our own, i.e. Brabec's Dictionary (in its

Prague version), as well as the official dictionary of writers published by Bílek (the latter being inspired by the former).[1] Hence the ratio is 3:1, and it is not possible even in Bílek's official dictionary to overlook authors who suffered unmentionable victimization (e.g. Holan, Hrabal, Seifert and Mikulášek). Perhaps we could describe the official report most precisely as a list of those authorized. We shall leave equivalent calculations for others (e.g. the situation in America) to the diligence of those who know the scenes in question, but let us just point out straight away that calculations of this kind enable us to see the Czech figures in their greater context, which is sometimes not irrelevant if we wish to identify what is actually going on in the Soviet sphere.

Basically, any Czech who has lifted a pen in the last 35 years without resolving to recognize the '*chief task to be actively and creatively taking part in building a better tomorrow for our homeland and in raising a new Socialist Man*'[2] has had a 75% chance of being gagged, imprisoned, exiled or killed.

On the other hand 1969–1972 was also a period in which Czech self-publication was slowly coming together, as well as a time when it was finally realized that stopgap arrangements and self-help were a permanent fixture, the only possible means of expression and indeed mode of existence. Then the degree and level of writers' participation in non-mass-media literature depended on the extent to which

---

1 BRABEC, Jiří – GRUŠA, Jiří – HÁJEK, Igor – KABEŠ, Petr – LOPATKA, Jan. *Slovník českých spisovatelů. Pokus o rekonstrukci dějin české literatury 1948-1979* [Dictionary of Czech Writers: An Attempt to Reconstruct the History of Czech Literature, 1948-1979]. Toronto: Sixty-Eight Publishers, 1982 (the first official publication in Czechoslovakia under the name *Slovník zakázaných autorů 1948-1980* [Dictionary of Prohibited Authors, 1948-1980]. Praha: Státní pedagogické nakladatelství, 1991); BÍLEK, Petr. *175 autorů. Čeští prozaici, básníci a literární kritici publikující v 70. letech v nakladatelství Československý spisovatel* [175 Authors. Czech Prose Writers, Poets and Literary Critics Publishing in the 1970s in ČS spisovatel Publishers]. Praha: Československý spisovatel, 1982. (Edit. note)
2 GOTTWALD, Klement. *Spisy* [Writings] *XIV.* and *XV.* Praha: Státní nakladatelství politické literatury, 1958 and 1961. (Edit. note)

the system had 'settled in', or its ability to control, or rather defer its crises. From the outset, however, it still appeared that the post-invasion Establishment would stick to the 'Husákian model' (with reference to Kádár as a parallel of sorts, more as an assumption than established by any sober assessment of the situation), and this appearance also played a certain role in the thinking of those who advocated or brought about reform. Although instructed in military fashion, they still believed in carrying on with remedial efforts of some kind, albeit to a very limited extent.

When expectations of this kind turned out to be empty, they had to decide either to move closer to the regime, or to stick to their now purely personal viewpoints. However, persisting with their views or even pure silence automatically brought them one way or another closer to the undesirables. It should be pointed out that the great majority of them were not actual converts; indeed the new situation compelled them to at least actively formulate their lack of desire and in special cases even to express their now unideologized feelings and views. Otherwise the police and other authorities at the time we are speaking of were only just refining their techniques, so that dozens of people were still gathering for readings among friends at apartments (the most prominent activities being those of Ivan Klíma), whose fortunes and paths were soon to diverge (e.g. Holub, Šotola, Hrabal and numerous others who hadn't yet had to make the existential (and existentialist) decision, i.e. editors at publishers still active here and there, artists in different fields and the like). By 1972 this activity had become so regular that one could speak of monthly semi-public readings with a set programme and accompanying discussions on the recited texts (for example Kohout, Klíma, Vaculík, Havel, Hrabal, Pochop, Gruša, Sidon, Kriseová and others read or agreed to read). This regularity and fairly broad participation (with an average of 30 attendees) meant that by the end of 1972 the authorities had decided to move in on them.

Attendees were vetted, intimidated and blackmailed so much that it eventually made more sense just to abandon the broad project entirely. However, the manuscripts involved got into the hands of attendees in the form of transcripts (still mostly in the classic A5 'reading' format at that time), and thus emerged the first circulating literature – at this stage still quite similar to the wave in the 1965–1967 period. However, the first books in the Petlice series, as it was subsequently called, do not appear as a product of self-help procedures until the end of 1972 and not on a regular basis until spring 1973.

The name 'Edice Petlice' [Padlock series] was thought up in the summer of that year (by Ludvík Vaculík, alluding ironically to edice 'Klíč' [Key series], whose normalized titles had begun to appear around that time in bookshops). The name gradually caught on both at home and abroad until it served as a simple term not only for the books actually published in the Petlice series (referring to Petlice books, Petlice editions, Petlice authors and Petlice people), but basically for any books brought out outside the mass media, as other series of a similar kind also addressed readers quite soon afterwards.

The most famous include Havel's Expedice [Dispatch] series, Vladislav's Kvart [Quarto] series, *underground* titles, (unspecified) publications in Brno, in Ostrava (by author Jaromír Šavrda), other titles that we might give the working title of 'special-interest print-runs' (philosophical, historical works and publications of a scholarly nature appearing with some regularity without actually being firmly anchored in any regular series) – and lastly, most prominently and most efficiently with regard to the duplication technique, Catholic publications (typed in the Moravian village Radíkov). Also worthy of note are the unrecorded and perhaps hitherto unrecordable publications of anthologies and works by young people brought together by music groups – only semi-tolerated or directly suppressed by the regime (Psí vojáci [Dog Soldiers] etc.). Then there are the Slovak initiatives, however sporadic.

Clearly, then, numerous actors and activities are involved that are noteworthy for their broad range and high standard, but they are also found worthy of note by the police. Each of these series has had its victims. It is generally the case that the more unprotected (e.g. by international popularity), the more isolated and the more one-off the initiative, the harsher is the police response. 'Nacht und Nebel' [By night and fog] and work in hiding are the order of the day here across the board. Those who for one reason or another seem to lack the necessary publicity from international mass media are 'prioritized' for persecution if Security manage to 'decode' the personnel behind a series, the fates of Jiří Gruntorád (with the Popelnice [Dustbin] series), the Šinogls (Moravian publications), Jaromír Šavrda (Ostrava) and Ivan Martin Jirous (the *underground*) in particular are conspicuous proof of this.[3]

We cannot calculate precisely how many books were published, so we have to resort to a conservative estimate, but we can still verifiably say there were around 350 titles brought out between 1972 and 1979.

NOTES ON INDIVIDUAL SERIES

Petlice

Originally created by the reform-minded, i.e. by those from the old Union of Writers who had played an important role in reform attempts, and whose primary creative impulse to work outside of propaganda was still of decisive importance. Half of the first twenty Petlice titles can be categorized this way (Klíma, Vaculík, Kohout, Šotola, Trefulka, Pochop, Klánský, Čivrný and Šiktanc). These people brought the last as yet 'unexcluded' element of Czech literary life with them into the sphere of self-published expression, so that in parallel with its fate, literature outside the mass media could be definitively established as a permanent institution, guaranteeing viability and real continuity. Authors of this kind also help most effectively to highlight the ravages of Czechoslovak normalization at an international level, they contribute their own extensive political

---

3 All of them were exposed to physical and psychological brutalisation not only at large, but also during their incarceration, which lasted several years. (Edit. note)

and organizational experience (in the case of Kohout and Klíma) and their strong personal 'engagement', which they also testified to in the 'legal' sphere (in Vaculík's case), not least, as an important element in their previous legal existence, as well as their 'legalistic conception' of Czech samizdat, at least as it appeared in the period under discussion.

What is meant by this? Basically, insisting on the right to speak to one's own nation through one's works, to speak directly, and to distribute them not merely as 'unknown, anonymous' transcripts, but to endorse them with one's own signature. This 'legalism' was most pronounced in the Petlice series, basing itself inter alia on the 'legal' vacuum, as there is no law prohibiting authors from making their own working copies of a text, so that it can subsequently be assessed by a circle of specialists or friends, and in view of Czechoslovakia's now notorious international image, there was unlikely to be one. Hence the authorities were reduced to roundabout punishment methods (using sections on incitement, slander, illicit business practices, obstructing supervision, moral outrage, enrichment, abuse of equipment in the Socialist sector and the like). This was both a slower and a more variable procedure. During the second period of Sovietization, it did not appear opportune to prosecute literary activity in itself, even though this was attempted. Besides, the disadvantages might have outweighed the advantages. This odd loophole in the law eventually came to be their living space from a legal standpoint.

Supposedly the authors were publicly handing over their books in manuscript form to a narrow circle of interested people and describing the nature of their works in a statement on the first page or the flyleaf, where it was simply not permitted to mention 'duplication of the work', i.e. the creation of a substantial number of copies, for which state authorization would obviously have been required. In other words, the typewriter was technically supposed to be the only way to produce these books. During the first year some of the new manuscripts were actually first offered to publishers, and only when a letter of rejection was received (or anticipated) did the authors get their works into Petlice circulation. Although the prohibition on transcription was 'explicit', at the same time it was entirely unmonitorable, and the road led from a narrow group of friends and those interested to regular subscribers and readers.

However, the series gradually opened up to other aesthetics, and as it increasingly received a positive response (it had the most stable subscriber and supporter base, as well as Vaculík's management experience), a readership of sorts crystallized, working on the 'optimum minimum' principle. It was based on the conviction that various aesthetics and world views could be upheld side by side, and that the primary criteria were the text's semantic weight and whether or not the publisher would publish it in different and better circumstances (which no one could properly remember in any case). This naturally led to fragmentation and imbalance, particularly with regard to genres, but the objective of the series – to restore authentic publishing life in some form – was accomplished. Editors and lectors, often identical, worked orally without written assessments, and the 'publication' of a work simply meant the text was accepted for at least one transcription at one of the Petlice 'workshops' – and this transcription was included in the catalogue of self-published books that was compiled on average for every fifty titles and was then published even abroad.[4]

Petlice 'workshops' should indeed be understood in inverted commas, as these were nothing but the apartments of the people who put themselves forward to transcribe or bind books, often exposing themselves to greater risks than the authors (as in the case of Šinoglová, Zmatlík and not least Erteltová, who handled practically the first two hundred Petlice initial transcripts).[5] This subscription

---

4 A 'rejected' author could have his manuscript transcribed himself, the dissemination of the text being decided exclusively by whether or not voluntary transcribers could be found, or people for whom the 'information' contained therein was of such exigency that they wished to expend energy in its acquisition.
5 Drahomíra Šinoglová and Jan Zmatlík were sentenced to one year and two and a half years in prison respectively for transcribing samizdat texts, which was found to entail the criminal acts of sedition and subversion of the state. Zdena Erteltová was falsely accused of prostitution and forcibly detained for 14 days

base was typical of Petlice, as a book's independent life began among the subscribers, and subscription enabled the critical period, particularly at the beginning, to be bridged, as books could not be sold for any profit due to that most welcome of legal sections: unlawful enrichment. Acquisition costs per transcript were high, because the subscribers took up *all* the titles without distinction. They actually operated like founders.

The small number of copies, the acquisition costs and the labour intensity did not come cheap. The price per individual copy was fairly high, and the calculation of the bare costs ran approximately as follows:

transcript / @ 3.50 – 4.50 Kčs per standard A5 page /
    for 100 pages of text, 14 flimsies .... 450 Kčs
paper / pack of office paper and pack of flimsies
    approx. 36 Kčs for 100 pages of text x 3 .... 108 Kčs
carbon paper / pack @ 12 Kčs for 100 pages x 2 .... 24 Kčs
binding / dependent on quality but
    at least 50 Kčs for 14 copies .... 50 Kčs
minor expenses / retouching, correction fluid and the like
    approx. 5% of costs .... 15 Kčs

Subtotal .... 647 Kčs

The subtotal is used to calculate the value of individual copies, i.e. 647 / 14 = 46.2, which is then added back to the subtotal, as even the cost of the archive copy was carried over to the subscribers.

Archive copy .... 46 Kčs
total for 13 copies .... 693 Kčs
i.e. for each copy .... 53.10 Kčs

---

at a VD clinic in one of Prague's hospitals. She was subjected to long-term psychological pressure. (Edit. note)

Hence it can broadly be said that 100 pages of self-published text cost the readers 50 Kčs.

Taking into account the average Czechoslovak salary (2,200 Kčs at that time) and the circumstance that typescript text consumes more space than printed text, i.e. that a 200-page novel published in a Petlice version came to practically double this amount, i.e. 400 pages, then pricewise it came to around 15 Kčs for a printed novel and 200 Kčs for a self-published copy, we find that readers of non-mass-media literature, who wanted to not only read a book, but also to own it, were charged around (and at least) ten (or indeed fifteen) times as much as they would pay at a bookshop for a single copy.

This information, derived from experience at Petlice, can be applied with greater or lesser precision (with a tolerance of plus or minus 15%) to other series; these differed far more in the way they were managed, produced and distributed, rather than in their acquisition costs, for whether or not the acquisition costs actually became the price (i.e. if the book was being sold), or (in a number of cases) if the work was successfully covered from other sources, it was still the case that 50 Kčs needed to be paid for the work and materials involved in 100 pages of a Petlice or any other self-published text for a single book.[6]

Expedice

Approximately the same conditions applied as for Petlice with regard to the production method and the price range. The most important difference was in the emphasis on the personal choice of titles, or the more personal choice, which was also manifest in the fact that

---

6 Binding costs also varied widely. Books bound at TOMOS [a Prague binding company] kept to the above price range at around 12 Kčs for a hardback. It should be mentioned that a large proportion of titles were 'officially' sent to be bound in this way, with the risk of being reported. Again the logical consequence of the 'legalistic' approach and at the same time a defence of sorts, as the overseers were meant to be kept thinking that they had an overview of the situation. However, new titles that any rapid response would have been effective against were bound by private operators. This trend became increasingly evident along with growing pressure from the political police.

Czech Writers' Dictionary by J. Brabec

authorization was assumed by Václav Havel. '*Further transcription prohibited*', accompanied by the signature of the author in question, was replaced here by the statement '*Transcribed by Václav Havel for himself and his friends*'. Hence the 'optimum minimum' principle did not apply here, and the series endeavoured to achieve a higher profile. After Václav Havel was imprisoned, the management was taken over by his wife Olga and his brother Ivan, while Daňa Horáková was involved in the initial stages of organizational arrangements.

Kvart

A different emphasis again, with key figure Jan Vladislav, who was involved in the series not only as its editor, but also as its producer (based on his previous bookbinding training), with a characteristic square format, proportionally lower production costs and the focus on literature in translation.

Underground

This highly imprecise term covers a broad range of activities that might be characterized as arising for the most part out of creative circles critical of the now prohibited Union of Writers, its line of thought, bodies and media. Because it included authors who did not have such a high media profile, there is an appreciable focus here on anthologies of authors and joint presentations or presentations on behalf of a particular group (e.g. Jirous), as well as an emphasis on unartificiality (or authenticity – e.g. Lopatka), emphasis on a particular aesthetic considered to have been initiated either in the past (Klíma, Deml and Hanč) or in the present (Bondy). Less expensive pricewise, based more on self-help and assistance, often in A4 format.

Moravian titles

This category includes extensive and varied initiatives in Brno, Ostrava and South Moravia without any precise records (no 'list of titles' was published), hence the 'legalistic element' was to a large extent subdued. There is a (more frequent) variation in format, a lack of a single key figure to gather around (as Petlice centred around Ludvík Vaculík for example, Expedice around Václav Havel and Kvart around Jan Vladislav), but also a broader spectrum of prominent individuals (e.g. Trefulka in Brno and Šavrda in Ostrava) working more on a one-off basis than in a series. The smaller emphasis on the legal aspect led to more systematic attempts to criminalize the activities of these initiatives (Šinoglová and Šavrda are a particularly cruel example of this). Their own publishing 'policy' included several newly discovered authors (Kratochvíl, Vašinka, Kotrlá) and many authors were also taken from other series.

Special-interest print-runs

This term might be used to cover occasionally published titles: minutes of debates, lecture notes and special-subject anthologies not linked to any particular series: limited primarily to specialists (e.g. historians, philosophers and sociologists).

Catholic titles

This publishing activity began fairly late (at least in concentrated form), as if first prompted from elsewhere (Charter 77 or the Polish

Pope), and from the outset it was resigned to 'legalism' in traditional mimicry. The initiators worked with efficient duplication equipment. In comparison with other series it actually looked mass-produced in nature. It is estimated that some 400 translated titles were published, totalling 80–100,000 copies overall. However, the proportion of original specialist literature and fiction is quite small, and the titles brought out were often distributed through other series (e.g. Rotrekl, Palouš and Zvěřina).

'Moving' titles

The movement of individual titles is both vertical and horizontal, i.e. between series and also between mass media and non-mass media literature, as well as movement outside – to Czech and foreign-language publishers, and movement from outside back home, as some émigré texts have recently been transcribed, particularly for 'magazine' purposes. In our opinion it is not possible to speak of literary journals in the true sense of the word until 1980. Initiatives in this field – *Spektrum*, *Obdélník* [Spectrum, Rectangle] and the like – have had the character of 'irregular journals' or anthologies – thus ranking them among the 'special-interest print-runs'. It is only in the last two years that the situation has changed, see such periodicals as *Profil*, *Obsah* [Profile, Content] and *Kritický sborník* [Critical Review]. The only exceptions were information bulletins like *Infoch* [Charter 77 Information] etc., whose news-related nature takes them beyond what is understood by the term literary magazine.

Movement within the publication series has the character of re-editions or narrower selections. Works that were replaced and republished were most frequently of a kind that were standard for a particular series, and of course works that were successful with the readers, as even non-mass-media literature had its 'bestsellers'.

However, the most notable phenomenon is the 'movement' between 'permitted' and 'prohibited' literature. After the authors of some non-mass-media works (Frais, Šotola, Hrabal, Holub etc.) decided on some form of coexistence with the authorities, or when the importance of some authors (Seifert, Skácel and Mikulášek) could no longer be passed over in silence, they were simply taken up by the official publishers. The same applies to initiatives that compelled the Czech authorities to react to the situation by publishing their own 'polemical' compilations, e.g. the dictionary of writers.

No less noteworthy is the gradual shift towards self-publishing made by those authors whose existence and work of any meaningful kind in associated professions, e.g. translation, was made difficult one way or another (Wernisch and Kriseová). This also applies to debutants and young writers for whom the straitjacket of authorized writing was unacceptable (Třešňák, Zajíček and Benýšek).

However, this entire complex migration from one sphere to another is just proof of the hitherto lively, unsilenced and probably unsilenceable voice of Czech literature – regardless of how the authorities have categorized it and whether or not the author accepts his 'categorization' from the outset. In 'authorized literature' it is also important to distinguish the authors from the overseers, who are either halfway towards being the police or manufacturers of kitsch for the powers-that-be, pogrom organizers and the like. The largest proportion of Czech writers, and possibly the most important with regard to talent and probable 'output', belongs to this grey zone between the permitted and the prohibited. In recent times this area has also covered the 'officialized', who have become part of the police-bureaucratic-ideological team (whose actors are more or less well-known and whose organizational spider ought to be described and preserved before it is forgotten like the one in the 1950s). Another increasingly strong prominent group of new writers should also be added here, who have not yet had to resort to self-publishing, because their talent has placed them beyond any 'thematic taboos' and there has been nothing (yet) to object to in their biographies.

In any case it is at this literary level that self-published literature is best known, and this 'competition' provides the primary yardstick for literary 'output'.

Readership

The valuable discovery made by anyone who has some practical familiarity with the phenomenon of unauthorized literature is that the scope of action of these 'unbooks' is by no means as numerically restricted and elitist as is generally supposed. One transcript (or the aforementioned 14 copies) can be said to be read by approx. 130–150 readers. However, since practically no title has ever been transcribed just once, we can speak of titles that have been classified as 'special-interest' with a potential reach of some 300 readers, which – as anybody who has ever dealt with official special-interest print-runs (see the Nové knihy publishers' catalogue: lecture notes, textbooks and the like) surely knows – is actually still quite acceptable.

As for poetry, we can speak of a reading community that is twice as large, both because transcription is less demanding and because the popularity of this genre is traditional. Experience during the interwar First Republic and in the West with print-runs for poetry collections is not too different from these figures (600–800).

Prose works have a broader fluctuation range, but the lower limit more or less matches the results for poetry (i.e. 3–5 transcriptions with a potential of 500–700 readers), while most prose titles exceed this number of transcriptions (the number of transcriptions actually equals the 'print-run', while the number of readers equals the number of 'copies sold'). Hence we can speak of 1,000–1,200 readers, while in the case of 'bestsellers' (with up to 30 transcriptions) some 4,000 or more readings.

As for Catholic publication, its overall character has already been described here along with its specific features, but as far as fiction is concerned the results will not differ from those achieved by prose in other series.

It should also be stressed that these estimates are conservative and based more or less on experience with transcripts found. Other publications (with transcripts outside Prague), especially those most important here, i.e. the secret ones, could not be taken into account and it was not possible to make any records of them of a permanent nature. Hence all other distribution methods (xerox, roneo and pho-tocopying at less well-monitored workplaces) cannot be considered, while the relatively numerous readers in and associated with the po-lice (amongst whom the texts now and then circulated) cannot be taken into account either!

Plus and minus

The Soviet-style one-party police state in Czechoslovakia scored a notable success the moment unauthorized literature was defini-tively established here, but at the same time it has had to pay a high price for it, as the authors of self-published series are not monitor-able in the most efficient manner, i.e. through licences. Entering the unauthorized world simply means not going via the censor, whereas every movement in the authorized world means fearing for your li-cence and fearing the censor. Fearing for your licence means fearing for your livelihood and your royalties. In the other realm, however, royalties are ruled out as an incentive, and indeed as an inducement to write. Although that is a palpable blow, paradoxically it is also a reason in itself why some people find writing worthwhile. The eco-nomic aspects, the market and agency (state, union, organizational and institutional) pressures are relaxed, so the usual, subconscious endeavour to adapt to what is expected of the author gives way to a similar endeavour with regard to the public and one's own sentiments.

The downside is that life is gradually being ghettoized. The fact that the reader indeed exists but is very chimerical places the work in special seclusion. Criticism is made in an atmosphere of solidarity, which is necessitated under pressure from outside and feels itself to be more or less indispensable, even if it is only indirectly made. There is a palpable lack of European and worldwide literary compe-tition, which leads to an increasingly obdurate insider mentality and a type of 'authentic' writing, i.e. a no longer literarized stress on the 'semantic weight of the text' (unsullied by the literary craft), with-out being able to distinguish whether such an excessive emphasis deprives a text of the capacity – as essentially new information – to penetrate *all* filters. In a word, it is life in an exceptional state, which has become a permanent state without ever being able to become essentially more comfortable.

[…]

Independent Literature and Freedom of Thought 1970–1989[1]

Tomáš Vrba

TERMINOLOGICAL HESITATION

The definition of the topic itself is fraught with considerable terminological difficulties. After long reflection I have decided in most cases to reject the term *samizdat* for summary descriptions of independent literary output, both because it is a Russism and hence unintendedly tainted, and because of its weak denotative capacity, not to mention

---

1 The following chapter will attempt to rapidly survey the extent of territory that still needs to be thoroughly explored at the first opportunity. It does not claim by any means to be comprehensive, so it deliberately provides a partial picture only. If it dwells on some facts and events, but not on others, then I am aware that it is not being fair to the latter. In the final edit I decided for the sake of clarity to divide up the text into something resembling dictionary entries. However, this layout is meant neither to create the impression of an exhaustive list of various literary phenomena or extraliterary aspects of literary output, nor to comprehensively describe publishing circles, series and periodicals. Here I would refer to Jiří Gruntorád's laudable bibliographical work for Libri prohibiti, as well as the work for the Institute of Contemporary History at the Czech Academy of Sciences in Prague, the Documentation Centre for Independent Literature in Scheinfeld and other literature. My selection is inevitably subjective and guided by several considerations that are not differentiated in any detail. I have endeavoured to mention phenomena that I consider to be of basic importance and to describe the situations and events that strike me as typical or of interest.

the misleading historical context.[2] The term undoubtedly has the advantage of being a single word that is easy to decline in Czech, and above all, its meaning is directly associated with publication. The entire issue of publishing and publication is central to free literature. When an author puts a work into circulation either himself or with other people, taking all risks into account to present it to the public, he is publicizing both himself and his work. He is placing both himself and his work at the mercy of criticism and appraisal. He is emerging from his privacy even if the text preparation and book production processes do not entail the 'usual' thoroughness. Official 'bricks and mortar' publishers over the last half century have for the most part had a long way to go before attaining truly free output, but they maintained and cultivated a traditional and almost invisible art or craft, namely that of the editor. Many a grey state employee by day turned into a free editor of independent books by night. The high quality of editorial work at the old Odeon[3] is a thing of the past. Many book entrepreneurs these days find that working with texts is something quite alien to them.

Rather than using such semantic miscarriages as 'unpublished publication', which are all the buzz among the portals of *academe*, when I speak of publication then I am thinking of publication at an established or clearly declared, albeit unofficial, publishers. While fully aware that doubt can also be cast on this concept, I do not consider authors' texts at the manuscript stage to be 'publications'. Of course,

---

2   Original Russian samizdat fulfilled its particular function, which differed from that of free Czech literature. It was more solemn in a way in its choice of subject, and it was more collectivist. It tried to be consensual, so everything in it was preceded by endless debates. With exceptions, e.g. the literary almanach *Metropol*, it did not deal all that much with fiction, in contrast to unofficial Czech literature, but it primarily focused on the social sciences. In this respect it has something in common with some of the Marxist-oriented Czech literature.
3   Odeon, a fiction, music and art publisher, was created in 1966 out of the original State Fiction, Music and Art Publishers established in 1953. It was one of the most important publishers in Czechoslovakia focusing on domestic and foreign fiction, as well as a selection of theoretical works on music and art. (Edit. note)

manuscripts usually came in the form of typescript, and in special cases two works, one a manuscript and one a publisher's title that has already been brought out, might only differ by the single word that indicates the publisher. Then again, the deletion of another two words, i.e. the author's first name and surname, can turn a manuscript into anonymous material for study or informative purposes. Presumably, this has occasionally happened on security grounds, and the author's name was only given orally to a reliable reader. The various forms that an 'unpublished' text can take include the author's unedited manuscripts, anonymous typescripts and unauthorized, unedited transcripts of a text already published in a different form by someone else, as well as hectographic and duplicated copies. This kind of independent literature with no particularly prominent subdivision might appropriately be described as *samizdat*, which in this meaning would keep to the original attributes of self-service and namelessness.

Hence while remaining fully aware of the disadvantages involved, I tend to use the looser term *independent literature*, which some may find rather too elevated. The somewhat archaic term *písemnictví* has the advantage for our purposes that it overlaps to a large extent not only with the semantic field of the English *arts,* but also with the French *lettres*, and so includes not only literature itself, but also the humanities, literary studies and art, as well as philosophy in a broad sense; for independent philosophical activity is indeed one of our concerns here.

Like other 'fields' of alternative culture, independent literary output in the 1970s and 1980s can be seen in two different ways: as a cultural phenomenon, i.e. more in terms of cultural history – and here we can refer to the fairly extensive compilations, catalogues, libraries and literature – and as a social, indeed a sociological, phenomenon. Hence any future attempt at description from this standpoint will take into account the environment that gave rise to independent publications, its internal relations and its interactions with the surroundings.

The heyday of independent book and magazine output was characterized both by its long duration and by its multidisciplinary nature, two factors that turned the original network of practical contacts into substantial interhuman relations.

I only refer to the actual content of independent book output during those decades on occasion, and I only set out a specific typology of the genres that appear in publishing plans as an example of several publishers at home and in exile.

Particularly noteworthy are those authors who did not give their permission to publish samizdats at home (e.g. Milan Kundera), and the exceptional cases of double publication, both in typescript and 'official' (Bohumil Hrabal, Jaroslav Seifert, and in the translation sphere Jiří Pechar)[4]. (Such ambiguity was not that exceptional in the case of artists like Olbram Zoubek, or photographers like Jaroslav Bárta. In any case it was cases like these that revealed the absurdity of the situation even more tellingly than a monotonous series of clear prohibitions.)

[...]

RAPPROCHEMENT WITH EXILE

One, two or three? Cautious disputes were waged at the end of the 1980s, even in the official literary weekly *Kmen* [Stem], over how many Czech cultures and Czech literatures there were. It was not until then that people dared in positive contexts to occasionally mention the

---

4   Bohumil Hrabal's journey from the underground to the world of state publishers and back is described in an unintentionally dialectical parable by the dedication to the prose work *Vita Nuova* from 1985: *'Dedicated to my friend Karel Marysko, who for over forty years has printed one samizdat work each year and distributed it to his friends, which makes him the champion of covered courtyards, a star and world grandmaster'*, together with a note: *'Because it has been ordered as the second volume in a trilogy, the original and first copy of this manuscript is for the Československý spisovatel publishing Director Jan Pilař. The copies are for readers and opponents. HB.'*

now world-famous Milan Kundera, not a line of whose was allowed in print at home, of course.

Quite unimaginable by both sides for entire decades, a unique meeting took place in summer 1989 between delegations of the official Union of Writers and participants in an open forum arranged regularly under the auspices of the lay organization Opus bonum by the former (and future) abbot of the Břevnov Benedictine Monastery in Bavaria (Franken), Jan Anastáz Opasek. The good work of literary diplomacy at this time opened the door ever so slightly to the possibility of substantial words being uttered both from home and abroad, but we did not achieve a catharsis: events then took too rapid a turn and there was no time left for missed debates once the regime had fallen.

Relations between Czech exiles and their homeland were never too close or cordial. Before 1968, their poverty and frostiness were reinforced by generational, world-view and psychological barriers, and after the shock of the Russian invasion the new emigrants spent their first few years primarily engaged in efforts to establish or reconstruct their lives. The decades of demonization had their effect on the émigrés, and anyone who moved away appeared to have never existed. (Efforts made by the regime's media to hush up sports results were tragicomic: the more successful tennis players Martina Navrátilová and Ivan Lendl became, the more the boycott became obdurate). The latest wave of émigrés, albeit in six figures, were strongly individualistic, never formed any politically relevant representation, and although they were quite well-educated and economically successful, they did not show any willingness to support the few elements that could have associated them with with the post-1948 emigration, i.e. émigré magazines and publishers.[5] An unsentimentally grotesque typology

---

5   Even an important publisher like Sixty-Eight Publishers had its concerns: although Josef Škvorecký attempted to make his subscriber's catalogues touch the consciences of his fellow Czechs living in the free world by offering them the entire year's output for the price of a bottle of Jack Daniel's whiskey, the equivalent of one or two hours' work at the minimum wage, subscriptions rarely

of Czech émigrés, as well as an unheroic herbarium of the quasi-intellectual community at home, was collected by Josef Škvorecký in his novel *Příběh inženýra lidských duší* [The Engineer of Human Souls, 1984], simultaneously disturbing several wasps' nests.

During the early 1970s the one link between the older and more recent waves of émigrés and the Czechoslovak public, which for a long time was one-way only, was radio broadcasting. While the BBC and Voice of America stations provided mostly reliable news reporting in both languages, Radio Free Europe was the chief target throughout its existence of regime propaganda and more or less effective signal jammers, but also provided a strong emotional connection, whether in the form of commentaries by Sláva Volný or songs by Karel Kryl. The need for foreign broadcasting remained, and indeed grew, but three or four years after the occupation, publishing activity gradually increased in importance, both as the first wave of domestic samizdats and as the activities of Czechs and Slovaks abroad.

After 1945 hundreds of Czech and Slovak magazines were published in exile. A catalogue of them that was commendably compiled and published from available sources by Libri prohibiti has a respectable 1093 items, though naturally with highly varied specific weights.[6]

Most émigré magazines arose out of, and were sustained by, the natural need of individual groups for communication within the local

came to more than one or two thousand. See ZACH, Aleš. *Kniha a český exil 1949-1990* [Book and Czech Exile 1949-1990]. Praha: Torst, 1995.

6   FORMANOVÁ, Lucie – GRUNTORÁD, Jiří – PŘIBÁŇ, Michal. *Exilová periodika* [Catalogue of Émigré Magazines], Praha: Libri prohibiti and Ježek, 1999. The list contains a number of ephemeral magazines that barely survived one or two issues, as well as publications with a tradition going back half a century: single-sheet leaflets and inch-thick volumes, highly political periodicals and religious or club bulletins, real émigré broadsheets and several Eastern European compatriot magazines, clerical and Communist publications and indeed several fakes courtesy of the Prague StB [State Secret Police]. Czechoslovaks primarily emigrated to Western Europe and North America, but the catalogue also includes such exotica as *Zápas o duši* [Struggle for the Soul] from Jakarta in Indonesia, *Sokolský občasník* [Irregular Sokol Publication] published during the 1950s in Casablanca and the Venezuelan bulletins *Náš vzlet* [Our Ascent] and *Orlí peruť* [Eagle's Wing]. We find Czech and Slovak magazines from 33 countries on this list.

community (even if it covered an entire continent as in the case of Australia). Only a small proportion aspired to intercontinental coverage and even fewer attempted to make direct contact with home. Journalistic and technical professionalism were very much the exception, as most of the émigré periodicals looked more like utilitarian samizdats, and many titles were merely hectographed typescripts.

Some émigré magazines were carefully edited to a high standard (e.g. *Studie* [Papers] in Rome and *Rozmluvy* [Conversations] in London); the broadest distribution, reception and influence in Czechoslovakia was enjoyed by the quarterly *Svědectví* [Testimony], published from 1956 by Pavel Tigrid, first in New York, then in Paris, and by *Listy* [Sheets], a bimonthly established in 1971 by Jiří Pelikán in Rome and moved in 1989 to Prague, where it has been published ever since. (*Svědectví* stopped production in 1992.) These two magazines succeeded to a large extent in achieving what Czech political émigrés had never hitherto been able to, namely to create a social space both for the liberal and the socialist-inclined opposition, both at home and abroad. Contributions from home were accompanied for some time (until about 1986) by the protective formula '*Published without the author's knowledge*', and this publication space was subsequently considered quite correctly to be permanently acquired territory. It was the removal of this two-way taboo and the lively exchange of texts over the previously impervious border that allowed not only for 'peaceful coexistence', but also for collaboration between circles around such different people as Tigrid and Pelikán. During the 1980s the two magazines even provided each other with texts. At home collaboration between different opinion groups assumed the form of Charter 77, so both cases were temporary victories over the seemingly innate patterns of Czech small-mindedness, which were to make a comeback, of course, soon after freedom was restored. As for the end of the 1970s and the 1980s, both magazines were collaborating and the two most important émigré publishers – Sixty-Eight Publishers in Toronto and Index in Cologne were collaborating with authors who were 'forbidden' at home to such an extent that émigré literature began to organically knit together with free literature at home. Neither branch could have existed without the other, at least not in the form we know it today, and in many respects the differences between the two began to disappear entirely.

Of course, the fortunes of the authors both at home and in exile had always been and still remained varied.[7] Some of them merged in perfectly with the new cultural milieu, adopted the language and assimilated, e.g. Gabriel Laub and Ota Filip in Germany, Viktor Fischl (Avigdor Dagan) in Israel, Pavel Kohout in Austria, František Listopad in Portugal (though in his case things were more complicated: he acts on stage in Portuguese as Jorge Listopad, but writes poetry in Czech as František). Some stopped writing, while others suffered constantly and never settled down in their new home.

Most of those émigrés with a background in underground or alternative culture took up ordinary occupations in civil life and only engaged semi-privately in occasional concerts (e.g. the Nachtasyl club in Vienna was well-known) or publication work (see also the underground quarterly *Paternoster* edited by Zbyněk Benýšek in Vienna, while Jaroslav Hutka, a musician, operated his one-man music publication house Fosil in Rotterdam).

Michael Konůpek, who for a short time before his departure had provided the dissident and alternative music community with great

---

7   Hundreds of artists left Czechoslovakia straight away in 1968. With the possible exception of leading musicians, their existential choice was even more difficult than in the case of doctors, engineers and architects, who generally integrated very well in their new homeland. As a rule this exile was borne worst of all by those whose primary creative tool was their language, i.e. authors and poets. During the 1970s dozens more authors, songwriters and artists were driven out of their native land. How did they manage to transition into the context of their new homeland? If we do not take into account such internationally recognized artists as Milan Kundera, Karel Ančerl, Miloš Forman, Petr Sís and a handful of others, who despite their commercial success abroad remained de facto 'alternative' at home because they were prohibited, there aren't many examples of prominence elsewhere: perhaps a few rock musicians (Ivan Kral with Patti Smith), while a couple of songwriters worked for non-Czechs (Jaroslav Hutka). However, several writers who first found success in Czechoslovakia went on to make it abroad, e.g. Ivan Klíma and Václav Havel.

assistance as a driver, distributor and organizer, became a successful Norwegian writer five years later. Libuše Moníková did not start writing and publishing until she got to Germany, while the bilingual Czech-American writer Jan Novák lives in Chicago.

But Fate was preparing a rather unfair test for the Czech émigrés. Although they had all been looking forward to the fall of the Communist regime at home, they could not have known that making the decision to go back would be as practically difficult as the decision to leave. Choosing your homeland again and again is all too much for one human life. Some returned for good, while others remained abroad, and most come and go quite freely.

Publishers came back along with their authors. Alexander Tomský continued work on his *Rozmluvy* for a short time in Prague, while the last issue of Tigrid's *Svědectví* came out at Melantrich in Prague. Jiří Pelikán died, but *Listy* carries on to this day.[8]

Josef and Zdena Škvorecký decided to stay in Canada. They wound up the publishing house Sixty-Eight Publishers in early 1994 after the final 'farewell volume' publication came out. The 227 titles which

---

8 Noteworthy are the twists and turns in the lives of several who returned: Daniel Strož, who published a beautiful, praiseworthy edition of Poezie mimo domov [Poetry Abroad] in Munich, surrounded himself with such nasty pro-regime pieces of work as Karel Sýs and Miroslav Florian, as if he felt compelled to atone for the good he had done in the past. A 1960s tearaway, who was later abandoned by all in California, Ivan Sviták, came back home, threw himself into setting up the radical Marxist Left Bloc, offended anybody and everybody with his political activities, and did not stop complaining until his death at the way he was being censored, by which he meant that his books, no few of which he published, mostly in Ostrava, were not being published in large print runs by any famous Prague publishers, as he did not realize that state publishing companies and politically determined publishing schedules had long vanished into the past. On the other hand, another firebrand, Egon Bondy, went into exile and maintains his position from Bratislava as the shaman of the next Czech underground generation. His apocalyptical indictments of greedy capitalism at least uphold his reputation as a prominent thinker among the intellectual left. His gestures are meant to be wrathful, but also express despair. Bondy's departure from the Czech Republic is not just a protest against the division of Czechoslovakia and the victorious hydra of the market, but also an escape from his own scarred past. Still, Bondy the poet has been forgiven by the Plastic People.

they left behind are a cultural achievement that could not have come about without the marvellous melancholic quixoticism with which Josef Škvorecký provided a connection to world literature in his talks on Voice of America.

The émigrés themselves did not have enough weight to provide the opposition at home with sufficient moral support. Fortunately, western politicians and intellectuals started to get far more openly involved after 1975. For many years collections made at the instigation of Czech émigrés in Swiss Protestant parishes served humanitarian and cultural ends at home. However, credit also undoubtedly goes to the cultural émigrés, who played a protective role at a time when nobody believed they might live to see the fall of Communism. Sixty-Eight Publishers, Index, Rozmluvy, Arkýř, *Listy*, *Studie*, *Svědectví* and a number of other publishers and magazines in exile published literary manuscripts, political analyses and testimonies of police repression. Thanks to them nobody would ever again be able to say that they did not know what was going on in Czechoslovakia. Some of the print runs were clandestinely transported across the border, and some émigrés became systematically involved in collecting testimonies of the national memory, such as the Czechoslovak Documentation Centre for Independent Literature run by historian Vilém Prečan at Schwarzenberg Castle in Scheinfeld (Germany). Fortunately, concern for the archiving and documentation of Czech independent literature increased, and some publishers ran their own archives even before the practice of sending 'legal deposits' across the border by various means was established. (One untiring organizer was Jiřina Šiklová, and the couriers even included some courageous diplomats. Perhaps the largest quantity of literature was transported by Jan Kavan, albeit on a commercial basis and despite a number of unpardonable excesses.)

Despite the personal animosities and the varied nature of cultural exile, the end of the 1950s saw the establishment of the Czecho-Slovak Society of Arts and Sciences. This was no small or easy victory: the alternative culture both at home and in exile ultimately demonstrated that they were able to come to an agreement.

BESTSELLERS AND EVERGREENS

As is normally the case, entertainment has more success than essays, to the frustration of all ideals. Of course, popular reading has its place in the history of literature, and indications of commercial attitudes towards books appeared even in samizdats. There may have been no more successful title than Miroslav Švandrlík's *Černí baroni* [Black Barons], and no other inspired such truly popular initiative when it came to transcribing. An identical subject – the 1950s in the Czechoslovak army and the new Švejks' passive resistance in the face of a more rotund obtusity than is customary in other armies might have ceded second place in the reading hit parade to Škvorecký's *Tankový prapor* [The Republic of Whores, 1994], which incidentally aroused four times more interest among fellow countrymen than any other Sixty-Eight Publishers output. A similar genre, a satire on the powers-that-be, was represented by *Kronika místodržení v Čechách* [Chronicle of Governance in Bohemia] by Jiří Hochman, which was a successful Index title from Cologne after it had very much done the rounds at home.

This does not mean that *Tankový prapor* is a bad book. It only means that the broader public has a need for a certain type of story – at that time a dose of vengeance plus laughter. Some superlative stories of this kind were delivered by Bohumil Hrabal, so the archive copies of his book typescripts have been very well-thumbed. Hrabal could be used as a small token of gratitude for the dentist, but Havel hardly. As for Seifert's poems and memoirs, he was considered a grandmaster even by those who did not read very much. The total free print runs of *Všecky krásy světa* [All the Beauties of the World], a book that was not only editorially challenging, but also difficult to produce, were relatively high. (However, the reader almost always also had a rare autograph from the Nobel prizewinner.)

An entirely different case of a successful samizdat, albeit purely of a commercial nature, is what might be called the well-being trade, i.e. the unedited advice of healers, herbalists' recipes and anything with the tawdry smell of mystery, the miraculous power of Fate or the Orient. Nowadays, of course, we have bookshops full of all that.

And then there are the titles that have survived down the years and which keep coming out. *Tajný život Salvadora Dalího* [The Secret Life of Salvador Dali, 1942] – translated way back in the 1950s. There is also Arthur Koestler's *Tma o poledná ch* [Darkness at Noon, 1994] and George Orwell's *Zvířecí farma* [Animal Farm, 1945] (*1984* came out much later). These three books at least were circulating as far back as the 1960s, as were transcriptions of Karel Čapek, e.g. *Proč nejsem komunistou* [Why I am not a Communist] and surely there were more.

BIBLIOPHILIA

Although nowadays even old samizdat bestsellers have their collector's value, their true counterparts are titles that came out in a single edition, often in a microscopic print run: some were unique items, spiritually akin from the very outset to Josef Váchal's experimental books (i.e. several surrealist collections), while others came out as two, three or four copies (e.g. in the Půlnoc mini-volume series), so if they survived at all they were extremely rare. It is particularly in these cases that doubts emerge over the extent to which we can call them publications, or to which they were just deliberately esoteric private activities within a close circle of friends.

Czech independent literature can still provide specialists and collectors the many pleasures of discovery: it has its manuscripts, its incunabula, its irredeemable losses and curiosities, and it keeps adding to its bibliography.

Although a number of titles (but by no means all!) were published in the 1990s to greater or lesser acclaim, the original typescript editions retain their charm and very often their exceptionally high aesthetic standards as well. Moreover, during the 1970s and 1980s both individual works and entire series were brought out deliberately as bibliophile editions. The imprint in Seifert's 1981 poetry collection says: '*The* Ruce Venušiny [Venus's Hands] *anthology has been transcribed in fifty copies. Every copy includes a page with the poet's handwriting and a photograph,*' together with the copy number. The *Betlém 1980 (škola české grotesky*) [Bethlehem 1980 – School of the Czech Grotesque] collection compiled by Josef Kroutvor includes texts and signed graphic art by Karel Nepraš, Michael Rittstein, Jiří Sopko and Jiří Šalamoun. Oldřich Hamera brought out not typescript but printed bibliophilia (e.g. Ladislav Klíma's *Cholupický den* [Cholupice Day]) and occasionally one could find an unofficially printed poetry collection financed by the author (Jiří Rulf: *Polední příběh* [Noon Tale], 1983).

Unsurprisingly, these literary rarities have increasingly drawn the attention of collectors, i.e. people with a background that is for the most part remote from alternative culture, which they have exposed to the test of market demand. In the early 1980s, Hrabal's, Kundera's, Škvorecký's and Vaculík's books published up until 1969 started to be discovered at meetings of curio collectors, where typescripts were discreetly bought or exchanged in back rooms. Classified ads appeared in newspapers saying '*Wanted: All the Beauties of the World by Seifert*' and there was almost as much of a scramble for Zadrobílek's editions of hermetic literature as there was for Štyrský's *Erotická revue* [Erotic Review] from the 1930s.

POETRY

A surprisingly large proportion of free literary output comprised poetry, both original and in translation. I mention this not because I consider it more important than other genres, but simply because it can serve as an example of the literary, intellectual and generational variety of independent book production. Poetry came out in traditionally compiled author's collections, as well as underground anthologies, which naturally often went far beyond more conservative readers' ideas of poems and poetry.

This output also included song lyrics. It turned out that even without their musical accompaniment the lyrics to songs by the Plastic People of the Universe (with Egon Bondy and others), and particularly lyrics by such song-writers as Jaroslav Hutka and Vlastimil Třešňák, intellectual cabaretiers like Jan Vodňanský and later younger generation radical singers like Filip Topol and his band Psí vojáci [Dog Soldiers] provided a notable commentary on the times.

Several independent publishers dealt with poetry, sometimes exclusively. At first the Expedice series only rarely included poetry, but the amount and frequency gradually increased until it eventually came to 54 titles, almost a quarter of the entire catalogue. Thanks to its founder, poet and poetry translator Jan Vladislav, the Kvart series was destined to become a poetry publisher of importance. In addition to translations of great poets from the past (from Tu-Fu to Guillaume Apollinaire) and the present, it also published poetry by several Czech poets, e.g. Seifert's collections *Morový sloup* [The Plague Column, 1979] and *Deštník z Piccadilly* [An Umbrella from Piccadilly, 1983], both actually in several editions that were fitfully and urgently supplemented by the poet. (Seifert's writings were edited by Dr. Marie Jirásková: it was fine work, but by no means easy.)

Although the Petlice [Padlock] series mostly focused on prose work, it also included several dozen volumes of poetry. Jaromír Hořec's Česká expedice [Czech Dispatch] samizdat publishers ran several series of poetry, while almost one third of titles in Vladimír Pistorius's Krameriova expedice [Kramerius Dispatch] series comprised poetry. Antonín Petruželka also ran a series called Kde domov můj [Where is my home?] consisting of nothing but poetry.

BIBLIOGRAPHY

Bibliographical listings compiled by independent publishers had a multifold purpose. They primarily played the role of stock catalogues, while the music samizdat listings of tape recordings that were going around Czechoslovakia had a similar function, e.g. the alternative music scene catalogue that was disseminated by Mikoláš Chadima. Émigré publishers' catalogues were also in circulation and the latest information on the independent book market was provided by reports in *Informace o Chartě* [Charter 77 Information] and other magazines, but it was not until the quarterly *Kritický sborník* [Critical

Review] came out that book and magazine output started to be reported systematically in its columns *Co nového v samizdatu?* [What's New in Samizdat?], *Knižní zpravodaj* [Book Bulletin] and *Periodika* [Periodical]. On the other hand, demand was covered by *desiderata* listings, i.e. lists of orders left with the publishers' colleagues, associated second-hand bookshops or the usual distributors.[9]

In addition to this information service, bibliographies also played a documentary role, both for conservation purposes and for studying. Listings of *prohibita* served in the same way, including bibliographies of important magazines during the latter half of the 1960s.

The third reason for bibliographical listings was a festively cheerful one: bibliographical activity provided all those taking part in compiling individual editions with satisfaction and encouragement, acting as a strong stimulus of proud self-affirmation. The list of the first hundred, and later the first two hundred titles of the Petlice series was cogent proof of the victory of free will over the inert matter of expropriated Czech culture. The Expedice series planned to compile an exhaustive bibliography of its output to date as its jubilee 300th volume.

PROHIBITA

A debutant underground publisher who decided to use a list of prohibited literature as a publishing plan would have been disappointed. Inventories of 'harmful' literature in the early 1970s and

---

9   There were public libraries of a sort on the Czech alternative culture scene, which were for the most part, of course, private collections run by individuals who in some cases provided those closest to them with a list of titles in writing. Some books were loaned for very short periods, as a rule 'for a night', but if the borrower promised to produce his own samizdat copy, which was to be returned with the original, then the loan period was extended for the required period of time. It was even said that in some of the more affluent circles of the establishment middle classes at that time, samizdat books were borrowed for a fee. The Hrobka [Sepulchre] underground library hardly loaned out any samizdat books, but usually just trash literature, and it was run by two professional librarians, husband and wife team Olga Stankovičová and Andrej Stankovič.

similar catalogues from the first decades of the Communist regime are made up of heaps of ideological ballast and pure trash. The criterion for prohibiting books was neither that of their high literary quality, however tempting that might be for a Manichean explanation of the world, nor necessarily their content, but primarily the political assessment of the author and secondly the aim of airbrushing history. If the 1972 list of *libri prohibiti* includes the marvellous-sounding title *Let Us Make the Plzeň Region an Indomitable Bastion of Peace and Socialism*, it was definitely not so that some young enthusiast could transcribe them night after night, but simply because the author had meanwhile fallen out of favour. Former chief ideologue Václav Kopecký's mentality suited the neo-Stalinist revanchistes just fine, but his idiosyncratic memoirs *ČSR a KSČ* [Czechoslovakia and its Communist Party] were a bit too chatty – hence the decision came down to airbrush all trace of him out and to 'write off his book in the usual way' in the 'outdated books section', rather than actually prohibit it.

Purges at public libraries were similar in scope and thoroughness to those in public and cultural life. After 1968 their aim was similar to that of the 1950s, to remove inconvenient people entirely from public awareness, to make them into 'non-persons' or to use the apparatchik-informer label 'ex-persons'. Books were rejected if the author was an undesirable person, but sometimes it was enough if the translator, the foreword writer or the editor was. Naturally enough, the regime was not too interested in publicizing its prohibition. In 1960 the Supreme Press Supervision Authority at the Interior Ministry, i.e. the censors, published a serialized catalogue of 'harmful' literature in a limited quantity of numbered copies designated 'TOP SECRET'. This 277-page catalogue included around 10,000 titles of fiction, political, technical, agricultural (!), occult, freemason's and even children's literature. The children's catalogue includes 702 titles and in itself is a remarkable little work. Under the category of 'Závadná dětská literatura' [Harmful Children's Literature] *Kája Mařík* disappears into the pulp mill along with half of Karel May's work (*Winnetou: The Red Gentleman* was fortunately spared), *Božka jde do primy* [Božka in the First Year], *Věra vede kvartu* [Věra Heads the Fourth Year], *Prázdniny studentky Jáji* [Student Jája's Hols] and *Kulihráškova abeceda* [Kulihrášek's Alphabet]. *Marbulínek a Kašpárek* [characters' names] did not make it either, not to mention *Tulínek a Bulínek*. The prohibition on the softbacks by Jan Hostáň applauding Masaryk comes as no surprise, but there would also be problems with this notorious applauder in the early 1970s, when he overzealously renarrated the biographies of Lenin, as well as Kája and Béďa [Charlie and Freddie], alias Marx and Engels in *Jak Voloďa přemohl zlého cara* [How Voloďa Overcame the Wicked Tsar] and *Dva věrní přátelé* [Two Faithful Friends].

If we try to get into the minds of the censors at that time (sometimes their explanatory notes actually help us here), we see several external enemies: the Scouts, the Legionnaires, Masaryk and Beneš, the Western resistance, Russian emigrants, 'clericalism' and Nazi collaborators. (The last category was also vigorously pursued by all the democracies in Western Europe that had experience of them, e.g. note the fates of Ferdinand Céline and Knut Hamsun. Hence the writings of Emanuel Moravec and Felix de la Cámara indeed were left to rot in hell, while *Árijské pohádky* [Aryan Fairy Tales] by Květoslava Fialová, also on this list, might well have been awful trash). Over the years, these were joined by internal enemies. The show trial of Rudolf Slánský and company and other purges led to more and more blacklisted Communist authors, so that by the 1960s even Stalin and Gottwald were quietly disappearing from the library bookshelves. After 1968 it was the 'revisionists and rightist opportunists' who were public enemy number one.

The second listing is undated and was transcribed by a courageous librarian from a secret order that was received by the previously vetted library managers in 1972. It includes itemized instructions on how to proceed with library 'whitewashing'. It reads as follows:

Removal
- letter Z for '*Závadná literatura*' in the acquisitions list. Do not record in the losses book. The manager has the district library lists in his safe.
- remove from all catalogues, apart from the working catalogue, to which readers have no access – deal with index cards separately, they do not need to be destroyed.
- proceed in line with the Ministry of Culture Directive of 31st May 1972, lists are available to this day – 'Printed matter with anti-state content'
- also remove works with a harmful afterword (and the like)
- deadline 31st May 1973
- properly justify lost books

The list of books earmarked for removal has 404 items, but the exact number of titles cannot be accurately determined. The restored regime was in a hurry, so it handled the matter with a sweeping gesture: '*The CD sign after the author's name indicates removal of the author's entire work*'. There are 145 such 'diplomats' on the list, including Jaroslav Foglar, who was banned in the 1950s on account of just two juvenile works. The great majority of those affected were native authors. The foreigners amongst them included three 'revisionists': Zygmunt Bauman, Ernst Fischer and Roger Garaudy, two 'traitors': Anatoly Kuznetsov and Aleksandr Solzhenitsyn, and faithful foe André Gide. About a half of the entire list is made up of fiction, Ludvík Vaculík, Ivan Klíma and Karel Pecka, almost the entire future Petlice series, and of course the writers in exile, while the other half is made up of social sciences, political literature and historical works in an apparent attempt to spruce up the history of Communism after the fiasco of 1968.

These determined deletions by the authorities affected hundreds of Czech authors. Logically, prohibitions could only affect those authors who had already been published, hence in the case of the first catalogues those who had published before, during or shortly after the war, and in the case of prohibitions under normalization, usually those who were able to publish during the 1950s and 1960s as more or less 'official' authors. There could be no prohibition on those who had not yet published anything, but many only made their debuts in typescript magazines or publications during the 1970s and were not referred to again until the dictionary of 'prohibited Czech writers' was published by Petlice and Sixty-Eight Publishers in Toronto.

Likewise all book and newspaper consignments from abroad underwent censorship. Dr J. R. [Jan Rous] from the Museum of Decorative Arts recalls that several times he discovered an item in the museum or the Municipal Library that had been sent to his home address from abroad. The book had been confiscated and never arrived, but in the most fortunate cases it might still serve in some way after all. More often, books sent from abroad simply disappeared without a trace. Censorship was also carried out by Dilia, the literary agency monopoly. For example, three years after an application was made for the mediation of optional rights on Graham Greene's work *Ways of Escape* and an editor's copy, Dilia informed the Odeon publishers on 24th May 1983 that the book had 'harmful content'.

Surprisingly, the magnificently illustrated magazine *National Geographic* was distributed almost without restrictions, just so long as somebody somewhere subscribed to it for a Czech citizen. It was said that the foreign distributor contractually imposed high fines on mail delivery services for lost consignments. It was also possible to order a very limited range of foreign newspapers and magazines through the newspaper mail service monopoly, so that every issue of *Newsweek* or *Le Monde* that made it across the border passed from hand to hand almost as much as *Svědectví* or *Listy*. Even 'fraternal' Communist papers like *L'Humanité*, *l'Unita* and *Morning Star* had increasing difficulties with the increasingly paranoid censors. Subscribers (mostly schools or official institutions) received ever more detailed slips announcing that such and such an edition had been 'withdrawn from distribution'. The British Communist daily was confiscated from 1977 to 1979 so regularly that readers received barely half of them and sometimes just two or three issues a month. When they even started confiscating *Moskovskiye novosti* after Gorbachev came to power, the end was clearly nigh.

PUBLISHERS

From the most primitive level at which an author is no more than a writer and distributor who *privately* gives somebody his text to read, which does not actually amount to *publication*, Czech independent literature has developed into a cultural institution bringing together a number of professions and linking up entire chains of people into structured communities. I would like to draw attention to the fact that mature independent publishing (because at this level, it was publishing, regardless of the number of copies) underwent two cycles for each title – the editorial cycle (author, reader, publisher and editor) and the production cycle (transcription, proofreading, binding and distribution). One important but sensitive factor was the financing of book production and private publication, and particularly the sale of completed books. Publishers were encouraged by all aspects of feedback, whether involving demand, statistics or readership estimates and literary criticism in samizdat magazines. Of crucial importance to publication, of course, were those 'invisible' professions such as the typists, graphic designers, bookbinders and above all the editors, many of whom in practice assumed these roles themselves, including that of publisher, as editorial work and in particular the work with the text itself, although hidden from public view, most fundamentally distinguishes purposeful publishing from raw samizdat.

TYPING POOL

From about 1978 to 1985 the usual rate for typing work was 5 crowns per standard page (1,800 key depressions), exceptionally (and subsequently) 6–7 crowns and in extraordinary circumstances (for express work, transcription from a tape recorder and complex graphic design) up to 10 crowns. Interestingly, the price at samizdat typing pools was identical to that quoted in official rates, and like them it did not change over the long term. There were never enough top-notch typists. Moreover, those who were well-known for the quality of their work (some had even taken part in typewriting competitions) actually came with a certain risk, i.e. if the secret police had wanted to, it would not have been difficult to follow them and check to see if they were taking part in independent publishing activities. This was one reason (alongside economic need) why many publishers rejected professional typists' services and transcribed their works using their own resources. The typists (primarily women) were themselves usually interested in regular work, preferably with periodicals or larger independent publishers, even though with the exception of pensioners and young women on maternity leave they combined samizdat writing with some 'official' employment or order.[10]

Regular collaboration had its advantages for both sides. A good typist provided the publishers with a substantial improvement in quality and output, while the typist acquired certain 'social benefits': e.g. not only a gentlemanly rounding-up of incomplete pages (e.g. at the end of a chapter) and supplies of paper, but also if it was in the publisher's interest that the tone did not vary then the perks also included a repair service[11] and sometimes even the purchase or loan of a new typewriter.

Typists on the Petlice series had their own personal cipher, namely a unique version of the protective warning code on the back of the title page. Contemporary witnesses testify that the Petlice publisher

---

10 A suitable defence against various denunciations was also to have a commercial order in your drawer alongside a culturally dissident work: on summer weekends, the monotonous rapid fire of a typewriter could be heard from a high-rise block window by the entire estate.

11 Editors also sometimes handled security matters with regard to typewriters. Small flexions in a letter lever or small alterations to some letters with a fine file made it impossible to clearly identify a typewriter. However, as a rule editors only resorted to such measures if the typewriter had been 'contaminated' by typing political documents with a higher risk level, not for transcribing ordinary fiction.

Ludvík Vaculík had a perfect overview of all activity in the series until 1979, but that subsequently Petlice transcriptions were made by the authors themselves off their own bat and thus without the typist's 'seal'.

DESIGN AND DESIGNERS

As experience was increasingly gained, so the artistic standard of independently published books and periodicals rose. For the most part the graphic design and the selection of illustrations and binding was undertaken by the publishers and editors themselves. The straightforward but logical and consistent graphic regulation of *Kritický sborník* made use of simpler typograms, the point of which was not only to establish a fixed order in the division of the features, but also to provide a binding framework for the self-service dissemination chain, on which distribution of the magazine was based. A faithful hard-copy-based transcription delivered to the primary parent cells could not only guarantee the same visual transcription quality, but also facilitate checks on text completeness (e.g. based on the final word on the page). Of course, not all copiers were disciplined enough to think of maintaining quality standards: evidently they often considered feature headings to be needless decorations and ignored them.

The deluxe review *Spektrum* [Spectrum], three editions of which came out between 1977 and 1979, was typographically quite original. As far as I know, it was the first and last time that a professional with a strong creative bent was asked to do the graphic design. Jaroslav Krejčí, who was known primarily as a photographer and teacher, decided to take full advantage of the opportunities offered by a typewriter and to turn its shortcomings into something positive (for example, by using the black and red ribbon to achieve a two-tone effect at least on the original transcription. He drew up an entire swatch of possible title types and an initial draft of single-column and three-column 'compositions', he worked with various line-spacing densities, used vivid headings and provided the editors with various ways to retain and simultaneously further develop this dynamic style. Details such as pagination were carefully planned out: the original idea to use a paginator or a large steel stamp with automatically changing serial numbers was rejected, so the page number was written by the poor editor with a sharpened soft pencil in the bottom left-hand corner on the back of the page, which meant about 16,000 entries for each edition. The design of *Spektrum* was based on the best traditions of modern Czech typography in the 1960s and associated artistic phenomena at that time, which contrasted the artistic quality of the script with the literal and symbolic meaning of the text that it carried.[12]

The opulent typographic treatment in *Spektrum* contrasts with its austere binding made from burlap with long flaps loosely set between the end-sheets. Vladimír Pistorius chose an entirely different approach for his Krameriova expedice series. Individual titles are written in the simplest way, without any special typographical features (the A5 format shared by most volumes does not leave much space for free typography), but the binding is dealt with in a distinctly artistic manner, usually with photography, sometimes with a tinted base, occasionally with script designed as a negative or in colour, sometimes with three-dimensional effects achieved by cutting or cross-sectioning the front cover.

It is because of its high graphic and artistic standards that Czech *samizdat* differs so much from the output of independent publishers in Poland, who managed huge print runs, but the form of most duplicated or even printed publications was subordinate to utilitarian need. Even the symbols seemed to support the surviving stereotypes that each neighbouring nation had of the other: the Poles traditionally have marvellous posters – a street medium that engages with people, but does not concern itself too much with

---

12   The 1960s were years of visual poetry experiments. At the beginning of the decade Jiří Kolář created the first typescript typograms, a collection of typograms was later published by Václav Havel, while letters and symbols were included in graphics and painting by Jiří Balcar and other artists, and Jaša David experimented with typographical calligraphy.

details, while the Czechs have their detailed work, which is somewhat impractical and going out of fashion.

PUBLISHING ECONOMICS: BUDGETING

All the unofficial Czech publishers worked entirely beyond market
principles, i.e. not for profit and in most cases for a loss. Their ac-
counting was all the simpler for that: they did not need to concern
themselves with items for author's royalties or editors' wages, and
most of the other work associated with making books was voluntary
and thus unpaid. Hence only a few figures needed to be watched,
and each forthcoming book comprised the price of the paper, carbon
paper, the typist's wage, the cost of binding, any photography and
other atypical material, and from time to time irregular costs such as
typewriter repairs had to be added. Losses were covered by the publisher, who in any case had to invest an amount in each publication
that was about equal to a month's pay at that time, unless the typist
was doing him a favour. Occasionally they could at least make up
some losses from small subsidies (or rather social support) provided
by foreign foundations, and a few were paid foreign royalties for their
copyright work, which they could use as core capital. It was not until
the late 1970s that two magazines were established on the subscription model – *Spektrum* and *Kritický sborník,* which was the only one
that could pay its authors a small but definite fee.

The twenty-eight or thirty gram carbon paper, which had to be
used for the number of copies to exceed ten, cost twenty-nine and
thirty crowns throughout the 1970s and 1980s. Carbon paper came
in two hundred sheets, each costing fourteen hellers, and a folder
twenty-eight crowns. A Consul typewriter cost anything from 1,600
to 2,350 crowns.

The cost of transcription rose gradually, as it did elsewhere in offices and institutions (remember that at least some typists had a day-
time job as secretaries or copy typists at competing state publishers)
and in the early 1980s it came to five to seven crowns per standard

page (1,800 key depressions). The price of binding also rose from what was originally a few crowns for soft binding and trimming to a settled price of ten to fifteen crowns for high-standard paperback binding and twenty to thirty crowns for cloth binding.

As a specific example let us take the production budget for the second edition of Hannah Arendt's *Krize kultury* [The Crisis in Culture] from 1984:

266 pages with standard layout in the Kvart series
(i.e. 26 lines, each with 63 keystrokes, i.e. 0.91 standard pages)
    = 242 standard pages @ 5 Kčs .... 1,210 Kčs
Original plus 11 copies = 12 copies = 3,192 pages,
    = 4 packs of paper @ 30 Kčs .... 20 Kčs
Carbon paper should be replaced after being used about
ten times, hence
320 sheets are utilized, i.e. 2 packs of 200 sheets
    to be purchased .... 56 Kčs
2 photographs, cost of materials only included
    (5 x 12 Kčs) .... 60 Kčs
Binding: book block stitched at home,
Softback cover with wallpaper from contacts
    @ 10 Kčs .... 120 Kčs

Total .... 1,566 Kčs

Costs per copy (1,566 / 12) .... 130.50 Kčs

Jiří Gruša[13] presents similar figures for the Petlice series. In spite of arithmetical errors in the calculation, he comes to almost the same result – about 50 Kčs for 100 pages of text, i.e. 100 bound pages.

---

13 GRUŠA, Jiří. *Cenzura a literární život mimo masmédia* [Censorship and Literary Life beyond the Mass Media]. Praha: Ústav pro soudobé dějiny - Čs. dok. středisko, 1992. The edited text makes up part of this publication - see previous chapter. (Edit. note)

According to purchase price figures that have been preserved, the Expedice series publishing calculations were almost the same.

If a publisher wished to reduce the necessary costs, he could proceed as follows: he might decide first and foremost to save money on the transcription, and transcribe the book himself. In that case each copy would come out at less than 30 Kčs. He might also use a donated package of paper or someone close to him might bring him paper from their office. In that case the cost might come down to around 17 Kčs. Of course, this could only be done in exceptional circumstances, and even adventurous spirits were aware of the risks involved. To ensure smooth publishing operations and a reasonable division of labour it was easiest to proceed as professionally as possible, that is, to pay the price of the services provided.

SUPPLIES

There were long periods when the required carbon paper was not available on the market, so prudent publishers had hold points or stores to hand – both to gain independence of irregular supplies from stationers and because supplies of a single production batch of carbon paper enhanced the aesthetic aspect of book production, as fluctuating paper colour and texture due to the use of several different batches resulted in an undesirable 'streaky' effect.

There were also difficulties involved in buying typewriters, not to mention maintaining old ones. Supplies were irregular and buyers were never sure if shopkeepers had an obligation to record purchases in some way or to report 'suspicious circumstances'. (They could obtain the customer's personal details when he filled out the guarantee form). There were usually no difficulties buying carbon paper or typewriter ribbon, but correction paper strips and local or East German correction fluid was of poor quality and in short supply, while Western products (Cores, Pelican or Tipp-Ex) were a welcome gift in every book workshop.

In addition to one-off financial contributions, material gifts of any kind were a great encouragement. Sometimes these came from abroad – Barbara Day tells the tragicomic story of an entirely impractical copying machine,[14] mostly from the ranks of sympathizers in the 'grey zone', while at other times they came quite unexpectedly (e.g. a substantial quantity of paper from the headquarters of the pro-Soviet World Trades Union Federation in Prague or a package of mimeograph stencils from the gallantly Voltairesque headmaster of a rural primary school – '*as a Communist I cannot agree with you, but here you are anyway…*'). For the most part they expressed messages of moral support, but they could not be counted on in advance and included in the production plan.

EQUIPMENT

The old Underwoods, Continentals and Remingtons were quite indispensable. They usually loaded the original plus twelve copies for the typist. The mechanism was robust and the typescript was pleasantly conservative.

Even though they were electric, East German Robotrons were not popular among underground publishers due to their distinctive and thus easily recognizable font. Moreover, they were very noisy.

To the credit of the local manufacturers of Consul office typewriters it should be pointed out that they served very well. The producers, a Brno Armaments Factory branch plant, were not exaggerating when Item 23 of their operating instructions stated: '*Its solid build and rugged design makes the portable CONSUL typewriter ready for the heaviest workload.*' There was a special demand for machines with a broad platen, which allowed for the use of non-standard paper formats, for instance, in the graphically demanding *Spektrum* review, in which A4 was used, albeit placed flat with long lines running lengthways.

For independent publishers, computers and copiers were truly a historic change, but they came towards the end of the ailing old

---

14 DAY, Barbara *Sametoví filozofové* [The Velvet Philosophers]. Brno: Doplněk, 1999.

regime. One of the first computer age pioneers was Ivan Havel, who performed the editorial work on his Expedice series on a computer at least in the last few years of its existence. Despite the initial difficulties, expectations of computers were high, and some experts saw the elimination of issues with Czech diacritics to be a matter of professional honour. Small groups of technicians worked as it were on two fronts simultaneously for leaner times: on software and on floppy disks with texts for the reserves, so that better times would find them well prepared. By the end of 1989 floppy disks were available with works by F. A. Hayek, Paul Johnson, Josef Pieper and Hannah Arendt, as well as documents on Catholics and transcriptions of entire issues of *Kritický sborník* and *Svědectví,* all in ChiWriter 3.10 format by Kamenický Brothers and PC Latin2 code. From 20th November 1989 and the very first days of Civic Forum's existence, their originators' computer skills enabled them to create and distribute an electronic version of the *Informační servis* published by the Independent Press Centre and various topical documents. Hence for a short time there was actually such a thing as an electronic samizdat, at least in a rudimentary form.[15]

---

15 Efforts by publishers to move up to a higher technical level occasionally led along unusual paths. At one out-of-the-way research institute in the late 1970s, V. P. [Václav Procházka] constructed an incredible monster. Himself a copious typist, he knew that the human hand gets tired and makes mistakes after much writing. Electric typewriters with memory were rare and in view of their low memory capacity (just a few lines) impractical for the requirements of samizdat. So he started thinking in the opposite direction and came up with an automatic hand, capable of writing any infinitely long text on an ordinary typewriter, though of course the machine had to be supplied by a human operator with prepared stacks of flimsies and carbon paper. This golden Czech hand, or rather claw, was controlled by a punched paper tape on which the text was encoded, while its 44 slender little fingers required hours of rapid sewing by the alternative editors' families, because it turned out that only elongated coils of scarce East German thread were suitable for their production.

From the early 1970s the professional interest of Czech computer engineers centred around the latest mainframe computer models. One peripheral CSAS institute had what was then a brand new IBM, whose penthouse-sized brain communicated with the outside world by means of a small printer with a replaceable ball head (various fonts and even several national alphabets

Whereas one obstacle to the complete computerization of editing work was the inadequate level of compatibility between word processors at that time and the clear reduction in typographic standards (most fonts were too 'technicist', and printing by 8-dot matrix printer was of poor quality), the transfer of carefully prepared copy to ordinary office paper by copying machines was increasingly popular. Strict supervision of copying at state enterprises and offices gradually decreased, and the first public 'xerox shops' even opened for business in large cities. The outdated and unaesthetic technology of hectography disappeared from samizdat production (smudged blue printing had previously served well for copying Hejdánek's *Dopisy příteli* [Letters to a Friend]), as did photocopying on special chemically treated paper (a method that was rather toxic with only short-term results, as the lettering disappeared over time). From the outset the revived *Lidové noviny* [The People's Newspaper] was xeroxed in print runs which from a Czech perspective were practically mass-produced (with hundreds and in 'self-service' thousands of copies, the two 'zero issues' being in autumn 1987 with regular output following from January 1988). However, the first to use xerox systematically (at

_____

could be selected). This began to greatly interest independent publishers, as mainframe operators secretly processed the results of unofficial sociological research converted into punched tape for them as a friendly favour. At the time the technicians were using the printer for production 'on the side', including all kinds of biorhythm charts and female nudes, although they did not wish to publish beyond that level of risk. It was only a few years later that the first PCs started to appear, but it soon became clear that they could not handle Czech. In the mid-1980s V. V. [Václav Vondráček] had good contacts with several groups of engineers, who were themselves interested in placing their equipment in the hands of independent publishers. Those in Brno were the fastest: one day they triumphantly announced that they now had several titles of primarily political literature transcribed on large-format disks. The editor found to his horror that they had got the better of Czech diacritics by simply ignoring them entirely, making the texts look like hundred-page-long telegrams. They later argued that this was actually just an old convention and that the readers would soon get used to it. The race against time to bring Czech software into operation on donated computers and all the associated hopes and disappointments are recalled in a book by Barbara Day, a British coordinator of unofficial lectures by foreign lecturers in Czechoslovakia at that time. See DAY, *Sametoví filozofové*, op. cit.

a distinguished Prague office!) was a paperback edition of the *'first Czech translation of the most important philosophical work since Plato and Aristotle,'* i.e. *Bytí a čas* [Being and Time] by Martin Heidegger. (The publicity quote on the cover was rounded off by a boastful, albeit self-ironizing slogan: !!ORDERS TAKEN AT ALL BOOKSHOPS!!). The group that brought out Heidegger then used the same technology to copy the monumental Collected Writings of Jan Patočka (the 27 A4 volumes in characteristic blue bindings have 7,423 pages!).

Here, however, xerox was being used as a technique to produce the entire print run of the first edition, which was rare. Otherwise all kinds of things were being copied, particularly when there was no time for transcription, for example, cuttings from foreign newspapers in many cases and where possible more sizeable texts, often printed rather than typewritten (the master could occasionally even be a first carbon copy). In particular, as far as I can judge, *Svědectví*, *Listy* and the excellent selection of translations in exile from the foreign press *150,000 slov* [150,000 Words]. (The name did not lie: it was not possible to transcribe it entirely on a typewriter, as each edition would have had 500 pages!) Technically, the duplication of a book by means of a copier was not a new edition, but only an anonymous reprint, if it was not authorized by the original publisher, as it often was not. Particularly in the case of magazines, it sometimes remained unbound as if *ad informandum* or as the original for subsequent copies.

Another rarity is the occurrence of classic photocopying (i.e. where a text is photographed on a negative and then reproduced on photographic paper in a darkroom); this was more labour-intensive and expensive than other techniques. It might have been used, for example, when a rare text was only borrowed overnight. The advantages included its documentary reliability and secure archiving (in particular, negatives can be discreetly concealed). However, a stack of photographs is difficult to bind and even worse to read. The lettering was usually reduced in size, so that a double page fit onto A5 paper. I do not know of anybody who compiled photocopied texts and put them into circulation in a systematic manner or in a substantial print run.

An essential condition for any publishing activity was access to bookbinding machines. Many publishers learnt the basics of book-binding themselves, though in the case of more sizeable titles the book block needed to be trimmed neatly. Fortunately, there were enough reliable bookbinder's workshops, and friends could be found who worked as nightwatchmen at stationery and printing establishments. Hence one midnight at an old factory on the slopes of Petřín in Prague, as poet P. V. [Prokop Voskovec] was testing the settings on an automatic guillotine he sliced up the columns of old telephone directories into vermicelli.

DISTRIBUTION

Delivering the freshly bound print run to the readers was the final, most risk-prone operation in the entire publishing cycle, an operation that was physically and mentally demanding, as well as time-consuming, particularly if it was associated with the collection of financial contributions for the production of the publication.

It need not be repeated here that for the most part the distribution was dealt with by the publisher and editor-in-chief all rolled into one. If he was supposed to sell a fairly attractive title as quickly as possible, he turned to his regular customers, and if he was lucky he would succeed with half of them. He could not make further headway so quickly, so he had to ask around, make offers and be persuasive: what was paradoxical was that on the one hand there was a hunger for uncensored literature, while on the other hand only a few people could afford to buy more than a couple of small books a year. Bare production costs were always very high, so even one copy of a fairly sizeable novel came to a tenth of a monthly salary. Selling a dozen copies and so getting a return on basic capital, which allowed for the production of more books, meant referring to and often personally visiting twenty to thirty potential customers. Many publishers lacked marketing skills, and it even took the Expedice series some time before it stopped offering poetry to natural scientists and found half a dozen poetry buffs among its customers, who were happy to relieve them of their idle stock.

From the distributor's standpoint the reading community here had a quite random and changeable make-up, while other times (according to the most common method of transcribing the 'original plus II carbon copies') it spontaneously organized itself into stable 'dozens', which was the dream of every distributor. This generally applied to periodical publication subscribers. Some circles of loyal subscribers actually turned progressively into self-service 'relay stations', who transcribed the original and redistributed it. The sociological profile of the readership groups also varied, depending on the nature of the literature involved. However, as in the case of Catholic samizdats, the *underground* and Eurocommunists, the basic conditions for long-term successful distribution were discretion, discipline and trust.

One special case was that of books that really were not intended for public distribution, even to the limited circle of readers that otherwise had access to samizdat output. These were for the most part special-subject and occasional anthologies for life anniversaries, when either the entire print run was taken up by the authors, or the individual contributions resulted in a single bound copy, which was ceremonially presented to the person being honoured. Where is the boundary here between publication and private printing for friends? Perhaps one clue is the size of the print run? What is the smallest amount of sand that qualifies as a heap? (Let us recall Bondy's Půlnoc series.)

If we include the various leaflets, informative material and minor texts among samizdats then indeed many of them were distributed en masse, particularly in the first weeks of Charter 77, when its introductory Declaration, together with other documents, was transcribed in bulk, so that the broadest public, whose interest had been aroused by the outsized campaign against the petition, could find out what was really going on. Hence the Charter texts were distributed at the time by all available means – in person, by post, in trains and to random hitch-hikers, as well as being pushed through random letter boxes in towns.[16] Later all subsequent documents were distributed in large quantities from Charter 77, the Committee for the Defence of the Unjustly Persecuted (VONS) and other groups defending human rights and the other civic and opposition activities that had progressively come into being within the 'grey zone', where many people were apprehensive of being exposed to direct contact with matters they considered too political. Especially popular were the feuilleton comments by Ludvík Vaculík and other well-known writers. This type of spontaneously transcribed and distributed samizdat focusing on short, at most several-page-long texts, existed all the time alongside independent series and magazines.[17]

The *Spektrum* review had a relatively high print run. Coming out in 66 to 88 copies, it was one of the most challenging independent literature projects: its distribution was organized in detail to some six or seven subscribed ten-member groups of readers. Hence each number had over 600 subscribers! The coded table with a breakdown of *Spektrum* distribution has been preserved, but none of the editors from that time would be able to decipher it today.

EDICE EXPEDICE[18]

The limited space of this chapter does not allow us to pay as much attention to each series as it deserves. It might well be possible to refer to each of them very briefly, but I believe the reader will gain more from a thorough consideration of just one of them.

16　Incidentally, this was one of the excuses recommended for interrogations: 'I found it in my mailbox'.

17　The chronologically arranged detailed *Informace o Chartě 77* [Charter 77 Information], also known under the apparatchik-style abbreviation of *Infoch*, was published by Petr Uhl and Anna Šabatová, primarily for readers closely associated with the Charter, albeit in a substantial print-run, which increased tenfold between 1978 and 1988 to 500. See POSSET, Johanna. *Česká samizdatová periodika 1968-1989* [Czech Samizdat Periodicals]. Brno: Továrna na sítotisk, 1991.

18　Dispatch series – see also the previous chapter 'Censorship and Literary Life beyond the Mass Media' by J. Gruša. (Edit. note)

The establishment and development of Edice Expedice (EE) [Dispatch series] has been described by Jan Lopatka[19] and an exhaustive bibliography was compiled and published by Jiří Gruntorád.[20] From the outset EE was friendly towards future researchers. Each volume comes with an imprint detailing the series name, volume number, title of the work, author's or editor's name and year (*Transcribed in 19-- by Václav Havel for himself and his friends*, or *....transcribed by Olga Havlová*, while the publisher's name was represented by the signature). Together with the uniform graphic layout and binding, this formula provides a significant watershed in the period classification of Czech independent literature, as it meant the end of 'wild', i.e. mostly anonymous samizdats, and a transition to regular publishing activity, albeit undertaken at considerable personal risk and in totally irregular conditions. The Petlice series, which was two years older, was stringently edited and not anonymous, and its publisher provided a similar guarantee (*Ludvík Vaculík had this transcribed for friends*) for some of his titles, though the series designation was missing, as was the volume serial number and the characteristic binding that would have unambiguously identified the series.

EE was established by Václav Havel in 1975. Together with his wife Olga and his brother Ivan he looked after it throughout, whenever he was not actually in prison. Together with the editorial board he also determined its publishing plan. EE output can be divided almost symmetrically into two halves. The first 119 titles came out in a 'black' series, and with just a few small exceptions the books were bound in black cloth, some with the gold embossed initials EE on the spine and the covers, while the others were in a 'white' or 'pale' series, depending on the shade of natural burlap used, with most of the titles having a textile label on the spine with the typewritten name

---

19 LOPATKA, Jan. 'O původu, vzniku a dosavadní historii Edice Expedice' [On the Origins, Establishment and Previous History of Expedice Series], magazine of the *Nové knihy* weekly, Winter 1990 and Spring 1991.
20 GRUNTORÁD, Jiří. 'Z bibliografie samizdatu: Edice Expedice' [From a Samizdat Bibliography: Expedice Series], *Kritický sborník*, No. 3 and 4, 1994, Vol. XIV.

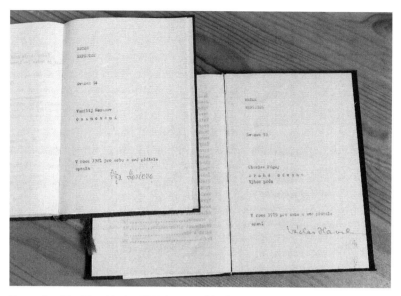

Transcribed by Olga Havlová/Václav Havel for himself and his friends

of the author and title of the book. The division between the two series was brought about in 1981 by the prosecution of Olga and Ivan Havel. During the enforced interval, several titles that had already been drafted in the Svíce [Candle] series were brought out. From 1983 EE came out again until November 1989, with several volumes even being distributed in 1990. The editorial board working at the end of the 1980s comprised Zdeněk Urbánek, Gabriel Gössel, Tomáš Vrba, Josef Danisz, Martin Palouš, Ivan M. Havel, Václav Havel and Jan Lopatka.[21] They came together for the last time on 17th October 1989, when they discussed whether they would manage to bring out the 300th title before the regime collapsed (the annual average was 18 volumes). The 278th work was meant to be *Pocta Magorovi* [In Honour of Magor Jirous] together with letters from his wife Juliana. The text was to be prepared by Jan Lopatka (each title had its guarantor – a designated member of the editorial board).

---

21   Ibid. No 4.

EE brought out a total of 232 volumes. The bibliography correctly provides a list of 279 titles, 47 of which never entered circulation for various reasons, either because they were published by somebody else, or the editorial work was too demanding or long, or they were confiscated in a police raid. Another point of interest is the statistical breakdown of the titles: a full two thirds (152) were works by contemporary domestic authors, while items accepted from publishers in exile were far rarer than those travelling in the opposite direction at that time – a mere 14 (6%). 18% or 42 volumes were translations, of which eight were from Russian and Polish. Twelve cases involve older works by Czech authors who were no longer alive (EE also included translations of Paul Verlaine, Roman Guardini and even Saint Augustine).

As for the genre structure, the largest group (67) comprised prose works (including memoirs and interviews), almost a quarter (54) comprised poetry and another quarter (53) philosophical, natural sciences and theological works, while 8% (19) were dramas and film-scripts (EE also brought out works authored by its publishers, e.g. Václav Havel's plays and the philosophical dialogues between Ivan M. Havel and Zdeněk Neubauer under the pseudonyms of Sakateka and Sidonius). Fifteen volumes are on literary criticism and art theory, while the rest are historical, politological works and twelve are for the most part special anthologies.

The print runs usually involved multiples of twelve, depending on the number of transcriptions. Most frequently there were just two transcriptions and the highest print run recorded of 72 copies[22] was only possible thanks to the xerox duplication of the original. In some copies a pencilled-in monogram has been preserved to identify the subscriber, as well as information on the price between 35 and 150 Kčs, while in addition to the number of pages, the quality of the copy (the eleventh and twelfth were at a discount) also played a role, as did the attractiveness of the title.

---

22 Ibid. No 4.

Samizdat Literature in Czechoslovakia during the 1970s and 1980s

Jiří Gruntorád

The term *samizdat*, commonly used both in this country and abroad, was inspired by the abbreviated forms much loved among Soviet propagandists. It is an ironic reflection of the Soviet state publishers' name *Gosizdat* (Gosudarstvennoe izdatel'stvo), which precisely describes the heart of the matter, i.e. self-publication. The term filtered through to the West in the 1960s together with the first samizdat products that Russian publishers in exile started printing. Of course, the phenomenon itself is older, indeed as old as the Soviet Union itself according to some sources, as the first samizdat text is considered to be a letter of protest written by the Moscow Orthodox Patriarch soon after the October Revolution and disseminated in transcriptions. There was also some illegal printing in Russia at the end of the 1920s. Varlam Shalamov's autobiography mentions that he was arrested at a secret illegal printing centre at Moscow University in February 1929.

The golden age of samizdat took place during the thaw that followed Stalin's death, when it also acquired its name. Many writers (including Alexandr Solzhenitsyn and Nadezhda Mandel'shtam) had offered their works for publication at Soviet publishers and the editorial offices of magazines, and while for the most part they were not published, thanks to the editors, their transcriptions started to be distributed spontaneously among the population without any constraints. Of course, the authors never offered their more politically sensitive texts for publication. As a rule their transcriptions were distributed anonymously or under a pseudonym. In 1969 the head of the KGB at the time, Yuri Andropov, published a 'Report on the emergence of samizdat', evidently for the highest state administrators, in which he named Grigorenko, Litvinov and Solzhenitsyn, and described academician Sakharov's 'Reflections on Progress, Peaceful Coexistence and Intellectual Freedom' as particularly noteworthy. By coincidence, Sakharov's article came out officially in Czechoslovakia at the same time. However, samizdat was not just limited to the Soviet Union. It existed in other Communist regimes and to this day can be found in Vietnam, Communist China, where it has a long tradition, and in Cuba.

Samizdat saw its greatest heyday in Poland, perhaps the only country where the word itself has never actually caught on. Here it is called 'second circulation' literature or underground literature. It has a very extensive tradition, as even in the 19th century under Russian rule the Poles were printing their *bibuly*. Some illegal magazines that came out under German occupation carried on their activities even after the Second World War, as their anti-Nazi content turned anti-Communist and anti-Soviet. This Polish opposition saw a real renaissance towards the end of the 1970s. Not only did numerous underground magazines appear, but so did book publishers with extensive technical facilities. Print runs of books in their thousands and offset newspapers and magazines in their tens of thousands were quite routine at that time. Meanwhile, samizdat in Bulgaria was just a matter for a few intellectuals, while in Romania, where typewriters were registered just like weapons, it was clearly a suicidal business.

Other names apart from samizdat have been used in this country for the phenomenon that we are about to deal with, e.g. unofficial, prohibited, parallel, underground, independent and unpublished literature. Authorities involved in criminal proceedings (i.e. the StB political police, prosecuting authorities and courts) also referred to illegal or illicit literature, unlawful or harmful writings and pamphlets. In broader contexts, reference was also made to the second culture or parallel culture, where some of the space was taken up by the underground. It was the rapid development of parallel cultural structures (not only in literature, but also in music, art and theatre) that inspired Václav Benda to publish his essay 'Paralelní polis' [Parallel Polis] in samizdat.

One of the chief characteristics of samizdat is the way it is transcribed, duplicated and spontaneously distributed. Of course, there also has to be some political censorship involved, which might not 'permit' the work, or to which in the circumstances of a totalitarian state the authors or publishers cannot or do not wish to submit their work. All that is then required is a typewriter and an urgent desire to express yourself, which has to be stronger than your fear of the reprisals that have always existed in even the most liberal of Eastern bloc regimes. Hence samizdat may generally be regarded as anything created under a totalitarian regime without the permission of the censors and then somehow distributed. Vilém Prečan considers *'self-published (i.e. samizdat) material to be any written work of a documentary or literary nature, written and duplicated in Czechoslovakia by individuals or groups of people, which could not be published or distributed through the official mass media in its own country due to censorship'*.[1] To this definition I would add the fact that in the circumstances obtaining at that time in Czechoslovakia, censorship did not necessarily apply just to specific works, as there were authors who were completely prohibited, i.e. there was a ban on all their works both past (which had been withdrawn from the libraries) and future.

This was the way that authors who had displeased the regime for whatever reason, either by emigrating or by signing *Two Thousand*

---

1   See Prečan, Vilém. 'Čs. dokumentační středisko nezávislé literatury' [CS Documentation Centre for Independent Literature], *Svědectví*, No. 78, 1986, Vol. XX, p. 402.

Words, or later the *Charter 77 Declaration,* were dealt with. Both the living and the dead were prohibited. Their work might have been politically neutral or Marxist in orientation, but what was of decisive importance was the authors' reliability rating. In March 1982, Charter 77 published 230 names in an incomplete listing of these authors. The actual number of banned authors in the 1970s and 1980s was around four hundred. Their works were not published by any Czechoslovak publisher, some of them were pulped after publication and previously published books were withdrawn from library bookshelves. Of course, the authors kept on writing and the only space left open to them was the world of samizdat.

In addition to literature and the written word in general, there were also samizdat tape recordings and videos. Their reproduction was substantially simpler than the transcription or copying of documents. These non-conformist recordings were even more common than written samizdat. Apart from concerts by musicians and groups, recordings were also used to disseminate the spoken word, e.g. foreign radio broadcasts, apartment lectures and seminars and readings of literary works. Samizdat messages could use such media as postcards, labels, posters, badges, printed bags or pieces of clothing, or even decorated Easter eggs. Another samizdat speciality was the leaflets that dogged the Communist regime from its beginnings right up to the 'velvet finale'.

Much has been said and written about samizdat literature in this country over the last few years. It has become a part of Czech culture; its authors are generally well-known and recognized. Since November 1989, its books have got onto publishers' schedules and the great majority of them have been brought out, often in large print runs. Literary scholars have paid them considerable attention and continue to do so, and they have their place in the textbooks. Samizdat literary publications are for the most part recorded and documented in bibliographies. Nevertheless, the samizdat phenomenon remains on the margins of research interest and there is much about them that we do not know.

The roots of samizdat in this country go back to illegal magazines and leaflet newspapers during the Nazi occupation. The same characteristics can be found several years later in 'illegal' documents with anti-Communist content, some twenty titles of which are known, and despite the harsh reprisals they kept appearing until 1956. Additionally, texts were copied for the needs of Catholics, and copies already existed of such literary works as Bondy's Půlnoc [Midnight] series, Boudník's Explosionalismus [Explosionism], collections of Seifert's poetry and surrealist anthologies. In the early 1960s Ivan M. Jirous transcribed previously published but quite inaccessible texts by Kafka and Breton for himself and several friends, as well as a manuscript by Věra Linhartová. During the liberalized late 1960s, samizdat activities were not the order of the day, and only a few anthologies came out this way, such as the last *Tempo I*, brought out by Jiří Kuběna in spring 1968.

Czechoslovak samizdat gained a new impetus after the April Communist Party Central Committee plenum in 1969 when Dubček and his supporters were deposed from power. The first political magazines appeared (e.g. *Fakta připomínky události* [Facts, Comments, Events] and *Pokrok* [Progress]) as well as literary and journalistic work by authors who were prohibited from publishing due to their anti-occupation stance. Various proclamations and appeals of a political nature started circulating in samizdat after 1969. Individual literary and journalistic works of all kinds – including translations – also began to appear.

Probably the first samizdat literary publication after 1969 was the Texty přátel [Friends' Texts] series from Olomouc, which Petr Mikeš and Eduard Zacha published under their own names in the early 1970s. They were later to be joined by Rostislav Valušek and others. This series branched out, expanded, intertwined and kept going in various forms until 1989. Some three hundred prose and poetry titles were brought out by this circle, some original works by Moravian authors and some adopted from old series published by Florian under the Austrian Empire and from elsewhere.

The first transcriptions of literary works started appearing among 'prohibited' Prague authors (Gruša, Havel, Hrabal, Klíma, Kohout, Kriseová, Pochop, Sidon and Vaculík) in 1972 in connection with their readings and subsequent discussions, which took place from the early 1970s at Ivan Klíma's apartment and elsewhere. At the same time feuilletons by Ludvík Vaculík, Pavel Kohout, František Vaněček and many others were also transcribed for thirty recipients, among whom they passed from hand to hand, while copies also went to Moravia and Slovakia.

Apparently the first literary text that was transcribed in this way was Klíma's prose work *Malomocní* [Lepers], followed by Vaculík's *Morčata* [Guinea Pigs, 1974] and dozens of others. All this was taken in hand by Ludvík Vaculík's transcription organization. The 'protective' statement: *'Any further transcription of this manuscript is expressly forbidden'* was written on the back of the books' title page in order to ensure the legality of this activity, as under the copyright act the author may deal with his work as he sees fit, i.e. he may even transcribe it. The authenticity of the transcription was guaranteed by the author's signature on the title page. The first letters of this statement in Czech (*Výslovný zákaz dalšího opisování rukopisu*) also stood for the working name of the series (VZDOR [Resistance]), which was never stated elsewhere. Vaculík named the series Petlice [Padlock] in summer 1973 as an ironic allusion to the Klíč [Key] series published at that time by the regime. This name did not appear in the books either, even though it came to be generally used over time as a generic term, e.g. a Petlice author, Petlice book, Petlice transcription and Petlice layout. By the end of 1989 over four hundred original Czech and Slovak prose and poetry titles had been published by Petlice, often in several editions. In its heyday, six transcribers were working there, using their own 'protective' statements on the back of the title page, e.g. *'This manuscript must not be retranscribed'* or *'Transcription of this manuscript prohibited'*. The most important and prominent transcriber was Zdena Erteltová, who handled most books. Without the transcribers, the artists and the bookbinders, literary samizdat in this country would not have attained the dimensions and standards that distinguish it from similar activities outside Czechoslovakia.

Other samizdat series operated on similar principles. Jan Vladislav's Kvart [Quarto] series had '*Manuscript! Transcription not permitted*' and the like on the back of its title page. These books were also signed by the author or the translator, as in contrast to Petlice, translations were also included. The same route was also taken in 1978 by Jaromír Hořec in his Česká expedice [Czech Dispatch] series, which actually included a declaration that the book was transcribed in compliance with Act No. 35/1965 Coll. Books without any prohibitive initials, carefully prepared and with professional graphic layout were published by Vladimír Pistorius. This series bore the name Krameriova expedice [Kramerius Dispatch].

New impetus was provided by Edice Expedice [Dispatch series], which joined the samizdat world at the same time as Kvart in 1975. In each imprint, publisher Václav Havel announced the series name and the sequence number of the particular title, as well as appending his signature to confirm that he wrote the book '*for myself and my friends*'. At that time this was rather a bold step. Publication of this type of book series could be prosecuted under several different sections of the criminal code. However, Václav Havel was ultimately prosecuted for completely different acts, and when he was in prison the book imprints were signed by his wife Olga. After the 'French caravan' was revealed in March 1981, a prosecution case was launched against her for publication of Expedice series books in the famous case of Jiřina Šiklová and company.[2] Likewise Jaromír Hořec was convicted of state subversion and imprisoned. This meant temporary suspension of activities for both series. By the end of 1989 Expedice had published

---

2   In May 1981 a residential caravan smuggling prohibited printed matter (*Svědectví* and *Listy* magazines, Western literature – books and magazines published in France, GB, Austria, Germany etc. and at Czech émigré publishers) into Czechoslovakia was detained at the Czechoslovak-Austrian border. Dozens of people were arrested as a result, eight of whom were remanded in custody for up to a year. (Edit. note)

over 230 book titles, while Česká expedice, whose books are some of the most beautiful, published over a hundred titles during its samizdat incarnation. After Jan Vladislav's involuntary departure abroad, Tomáš Vrba carried on publishing the series with some interruptions. A total of nearly a hundred titles were brought out by Kvart.

Specialist series were also launched. Poetry was spotlighted by the Kde domov můj [Where is my Home?][3] series, edited by Antonín Petruželka, while philosophy was dealt with by Radim Palouš's Nové cesty myšlení [New Ways of Thinking], philosophical translations were later brought out by Prameny [Sources] in Brno thanks to Jiří Müller, while the archive collection of works by Jan Patočka was brought out over twelve years by Ivan Chvatík and also worthy of note was Zadrobílek's Hermetická edice [Hermetic series], which was transformed after 1989 into the Trigon publishers. Some editors went to enormous efforts without ever giving a name to their activities, e.g. Sergej Machonin, Klement Lukeš, Milan Jelínek in Brno, who published some three hundred titles, and Jiří Müller, who managed the 'Brno branch' of Petlice, to name just a few.

Like other texts circulating in samizdat form, these book series and individual books were typewritten on carbon copies. Depending on the quality of the typewriter and the paper, the print run for a single transcription could be anything from seven to fifteen copies, the last of which was usually barely legible. They were transcribed by the editors themselves or by professional typists for a fee, which was reflected in the price of the book together with other production costs. The price of a 100-page samizdat in simple binding was around 50 Kčs, though this could be increased by photographs or other supplements. Simple calculations indicate that samizdat publications were at least ten times more expensive than officially published books, so it wasn't everybody who could afford them, even though demand very much outstripped supply. It often happened that one of the readers became a publisher, transcribing or copying a book for

---

3   The title refers to the lyrics of the Czech national anthem. (Edit. note)

his circle of friends. That is how what is nowadays known as 'wild samizdat' came into being. This involves unauthorized transcriptions made in amateur fashion from other transcriptions, often also unauthorized, and distributed by friends of friends or acquaintances of the original publishers. These transcriptions were then sent as gifts to friends of the transcriber, who bore the costs. Authors' editions of books were also distributed free of charge, often with a design and particularly with graphic supplements that increased their value, e.g. the aforementioned Texty přátel and the hyper-bibliophilia of Ludvík Kundera, sometimes typewritten, sometimes printed, but always with accompanying graphics. The anthologies that they compiled were so exclusive that the number of copies was usually the same as the number of authors taking part. Hence these publications did not manage to satisfy demand, but rather tended to serve the authors, who could at least show a narrow circle of readers that they were still active. To a large extent this also applies to Petlice and similar series with a print run of no more than several dozen. Higher print runs could only be boasted by Vokno [Window] and Půjčuj, rozmnožuj, rozšiřuj! [Lend, Copy, Distribute!], which roneoed several titles, and by religious samizdat series. Larger samizdat print runs were not possible until copying machines became available in the latter half of the 1980s, 'reprints' of Petlice and Expedice titles started to be made, and a reprint series of Proti všem [Against All] was created as well as the Prostor [Space] and Pražská imaginace [Prague Imagination] series brought out by Václav Kadlec. His publications, particularly some shorter texts by Bohumil Hrabal, are evidently the only samizdats that were able to get greater access to masses of readers, alongside newspaper *Lidové noviny* [The People's Newspaper], which incidentally also had its series.

Samizdat distribution is an interesting phenomenon in itself. The ways of samizdat might be said to be as inscrutable as the ways of the Lord. Religious samizdat, particularly in Moravia and Slovakia, had its well-organized distribution channels, which enabled relatively high print runs of these publications to get to the readers. Literary samizdat was distributed differently. The circle of subscribers for

Petlice was made up of 20–24 people, generally personal friends of Ludvík Vaculík, who to a large extent overlapped with the circle of Petlice authors. Other transcribers could then obtain the originals for their transcriptions from them, often indirectly. It was simpler to transcribe short texts, particularly feuilletons, which often commented wittily upon the current situation. Ludvík Vaculík's feuilletons enjoyed huge popularity. Some of them were brought out later in book collections. His feuilleton 'Řetěz štěstí' [Chain of Fortune] is a good guide on how to go about samizdat. It actually deals with the principle of a chain prayer, which you one day find in your letter box. The text concludes with a challenge: Copy ten times and pass it on! John Brown from London copied it and won a million dollars, Pedro Martinez from the Philippines did not copy it and was dead within the week. The Czechoslovak chain of fortune has sometimes had outcomes that were rather different.

In 1977 dramatist František Pavlíček received a suspended sentence for distributing Petlice books. Jiří Lederer was sentenced to three years in prison in the same case, which was known as Ota Ornest and company, for his book *České rozhovory* [Czech Conversations]. In 1978 Pavel Roubal and Jiří Gruša spent two months in prison. However, the expert report on Gruša's novel *Dotazník* [Questionnaire, 1982] showed that it was not inflammatory literature, finding it merely inept. A year later the Ostrava writer Jaromír Šavrda was sentenced to two and a half years in prison for distributing samizdat publications in his own series called Libri prohibiti. After he was released he carried on until he received another conviction, this time for 'just' two years. Drahomíra Šinoglová was also sentenced to a year in prison by a court in Znojmo for transcribing Petlice books.

In December 1980 Jiří Gruntorád, the publisher of the Popelnice [Dustbin] series, was arrested. In June 1981 Prague City Court judge Jan Rojt sentenced him to four years in prison and three years of protective supervision. He stated in his summing up that poems by Bohuslav Reynek were also transcribed in ten copies and continued: '*However, even a harmless text can be used for hostile propaganda against our socialist social order, as we saw in 1968. In particular, the landscape is described in the opening poem in the* Pieta *collection, in a very gloomy mood, as it is in the* Setba samot [Sowing Solitudes] *collection, with such poems as ‚Žalář* [Dungeon] *and ‚Krysa v parku'* [Rat in the Park].' With the events taking place in Poland at that time, the drastic judgement was undoubtedly meant to intimidate the opposition, but thanks to friends the Popelnice series continued to be published with some 130 books coming out.

Eight years later the judge presiding over the case at the Ústí nad Orlicí district court, Jana Faifrová, appraised František Stárek's publication activities with a sentence of two and a half years in prison and two years of protective supervision. Summing up, she singled out the articles printed in *Voknoviny*, stating: '*it was found to involve contributions attacking the state and social order of the Republic, especially criticizing and ironizing the activities of State Security bodies and national committees. In particular we cannot pass over the conclusion of the article ‚Povstaň, povstaň, veliké město pražské'* [Arise, arise, great city of Prague], *comparing the situation in 1939 to the events of 28th October 1988.'*

Of course, Stárek was not the only samizdat magazine publisher to end up in prison. The end of the Communist regime caught Jiří Ruml and Rudolf Zeman, the editors of samizdat *Lidové noviny*, in detention pending trial, while in Slovakia the publisher of *Bratislavské listy* [Bratislava Letters], Ján Čarnogurský, was also behind bars at that time. Hence he did not go to trial, which is just as well as he faced the same fate as Ivan Polanský, who was condemned in 1988 to four years in a Slovak prison for publishing anthologies on religious and historical subjects.

Hence the suppression of samizdat publishers, editors and distributors was of various intensities at various times. From 1977 the Committee for the Defence of the Unjustly Persecuted recorded at least fifty cases of trials and imprisonment, often for several years, and several times over in the cases of Jaromír Šavrda, František Stárek and Petr Cibulka. Paragraph 100 of the Criminal Code on incitement was often used to impose sentences of up to three years in prison. It was established that the perpetrator had acquainted at least two people with the seditious text. The preparations for a criminal act of this kind were themselves equally as criminal – it was sufficient just to own several copies of a 'seditious' text. What was known as subversion of the state could result in up to five years in prison, and if the activity involved or was largely associated with a foreign power, the penalty was from three to ten years. Any attempt to transport samizdats across the border normally entailed 'damaging state interests abroad'. The section on unlawful business activities, which actually sounded quite apolitical, was also much in use, e.g. in the case of Jazz Section representatives, who brought out their publications without the permission of state authorities. As early as in 1981, four Catholic samizdat publishers in Olomouc were sentenced for unlawful business activities. In similar cases use was regularly made of the section on what was known as obstruction of the supervision of church and religious associations, which was also applied to identified printers and distributors of Jehovah's Witnesses' literature. Their underground printing centres were very well organized and equipped. In December 1986 a total of some fifteen tons of various materials was confiscated at two illegal printing centres, including five thousand packs of paper and eight printing machines. Under Section 202 of the Criminal Code on breach of the peace, sentences were passed e.g. on Ivan M. Jirous, František Stárek and Eduard Vacek, particularly for publishing the *Vokno* magazine, where a couple of indecent words had been found. This section was also used in the notorious Plastic People trial, in which Vratislav Brabenec was also sentenced, even though his only wrongdoing was that he played the saxophone.

Despite all this harsh repression the space for samizdat expanded as new series and magazines kept coming out, particularly after Charter 77 came into being. The publishers were relying upon the right to receive and distribute information by all means irrespective of frontiers, i.e. guaranteed international agreements on civil and political rights, which were framed under Czechoslovak law in 1976. These magazines had varying duration and scope, while their readers were also from various walks of life. They were often not magazines in the true sense, but irregular anthologies that sometimes expired after one or two issues, whereas others turned into viable journals, e.g. the still extant *Střední Evropa* [Middle Europe], *Revolver Revue*, *Prostor* [Space] and *Kritický sborník* [Critical Review]. Groups of historians, philosophers, theologists, sociologists, ecologists, literary scholars, economists, journalists and so forth brought out their own magazines. By nature, some of these were bulletins for newly independent initiatives, while others were more regional in character and yet others had a special-interest focus. There were numerous music magazines that spotlighted particular genres or bands, ecclesiastical magazines, backpacker magazines (over sixty of which have been recorded) and not least, sci-fi fanzines. Here it is particularly difficult to set precise limits for the justified use of the term samizdat. We often find ourselves in a kind of grey area, when a Trade Union or Socialist Youth Union works committee or some club run by them publishes a magazine, but sometimes these facts are misleading in order to divert attention from real samizdat. Sometimes imaginary figures are even given for non-existent printing authorizations, places of publication are thought up, e.g. Geneva for the works of the Prague surrealists and Hradec Králové for *Prostor*, while antedating is also common.

This activity, at first unorganized and spontaneous, presently took on clearer outlines and was investigated not only by State Security, but also by the participants themselves. In 1978 one of the participants in the Charter 77 discussions proposed the creation of six to eight magazines to cover topics previously neglected, e.g. workers', students' and youth issues in general, Slovak subjects and literary criticism. He was interested in perfecting the information system that had emerged just after the creation of Charter 77 and actually represented a kind of hard-to-define space, subject to its own laws. This communication space might be likened in some respects to a kind of prehistoric internet. By knowing the addresses, i.e. the apartments of friends who trusted him, a participant might take advantage of this flow of information. Of course, priority went to anybody who returned a borrowed text with several copies within a short space of time. This way one was drawn into the game and became a participant in activities. One could comment on the transcribed text and respond to it with one's own text, creating extremely interesting discussions, one of which was brought up in a 1978 feuilleton by Vaculík entitled 'Poznámky o statečnosti' [Notes on Courage] and another in a 1984 Charter 77 document entitled 'Právo na dějiny' [A Right to History]. During the becalmed normalization period this exchange of views was like the water of life, helping to emancipate society, which increasingly realized that it was not just reduced to gardening at the weekend. Parallel structures conquered and occupied ever more space and little by little moved the boundaries of the possible with their consistent pressure on the regime from an initial state, i.e. what is not permitted is prohibited, towards the target state, i.e. what is not prohibited is permitted. A spirit of democracy and tolerance also survived in independent literature and journalism. In those abnormal conditions samizdat maintained and developed cultural continuity and also undoubtedly helped to preserve the language, cruelly trodden down by the regime's mass media. The role of samizdat in religious life also deserves a separate study.

At the turn of the 1970s and the 1980s long-standing Catholic samizdat activity began to elaborately diversify, thanks in particular to Oto Mádr, who set up a samizdat publishing house and launched its first series Duch a život [Spirit and Life] in early 1980. Its objective was to fill in the blanks in religious literature in the spirit of post-Council Catholicism. It addressed readers in various age categories and at various levels of sophistication. The books were printed on both sides of roneo paper, normally in print runs of 800–1000 copies. A total of 26 works were brought out in the series, if we include Bochenský's *Cesty k filozofickému myšlení* [Roads to Philosophical Thought], which actually came before the series, and *S dětmi o bibli* [Talking to Children about the Bible], which has no publication details, and Anzenbacher's *Úvod do filozofie* [Introduction to Philosophy], which marked the end of the publishing house's activities. The series also included a 'K' (for katechetická [catechetical]) subseries with four volumes (*S dětmi o bibli*, see above, which came out with the same design as the fourth volume and has similar subject matter, which can be considered to be a fifth volume, but it has no publication details. Another series is called Theologica. The first work was Josef Zvěřina's *Duch svatý: Dar a dárce* [Holy Spirit, Gift and Giver], while the second is *Malé církevní dějiny* [Short History of the Church] by August Franzen and the third is *Maria matka Pána – obraz církve* [Mary, Mother of God – Image of the Church] by Max Thurian. Another series from this publisher bore the name Přátelé [Friends], which can be considered to be a supplement to the Duch a život series. This also came out from 1980 with portraits of saints and other prominent modern-day Christians. The individual titles usually came together with an editor's introduction or afterword for Czech readers and a note on the author. These books were in A5 paperback format and printed in the same way as the Duch a život series. A total of 13 titles were brought out, some of which were published after 1989 by the Cesta [Pathway] publishers in Brno. Subsequently, 1986 saw the establishment of the Alfa-Omega series for young readers. If we include Marie Holková's *Tisíc tomu let* [It's Been a Thousand Years Now], which preceded these publications, a total of eight titles were brought out. The Orientace [Orientation] series came out at random intervals from 1982, with a series heading and sequence numbers as of the fourth book. This is a series of minor tracts dealing with subjects primarily of interest to Czech Catholics, whom it was meant to guide. These works normally comprised several densely written stapled sheets. From No. 23 they were also dated and came to resemble the periodicals that Orientace is sometimes ranked among. In any case like the aforementioned series, Orientace was roneoed in relatively large print runs. The series of texts was reprinted in *Studie* [Papers] in Rome. A total of 37 issues came out. In addition to original Czech texts, translations were also brought out. Contributors included e.g. Karel Šprunk, Miloslav Máša, Miroslav Kratochvíl, Alžbeta Sirovátková, Michaela Freiová, Dagmar Pohunková, Zdeněk Schauta and Eva Doležalová. The technical side was dealt with by Květa Kuželová, P. Radim Hložánka, Adolf Rázek and others. The Mádr publication distributors were Květa Kuželová, Adolf Rázek, Vladimír Fučík, Jana Stojánková, Michal Holeček and many others. These publications also included the periodical *Teologický sborník* [Theological Anthology], five of which were brought out, *Teologické texty* [Theological Texts], seventeen of which were compiled in samizdat form by these publishers from 1978 (and they are still coming out to this day), as well as *Charizmatika* [Charismatics], the *Psi* [greek alphabet] annual anthology published in collaboration with Petr Příhoda, the *Salus* magazine published in collaboration with Dagmar Pohunková and a book series of the same name. The books were distributed throughout Bohemia and Moravia, as well as to some parts of Slovakia.

I cannot fail to mention *Informace o církvi* [Church Information], which came out as a monthly between 1980 and 1990, when an unbelievable 113 issues were published in print runs of several hundred. The men behind the establishment of this magazine were Karel Dománek, Josef Kordík, Václav Vacek, Václav Malý, František Lízna, Pavel Michal and Josef Jakubec, while Jindřich Sirovátka, Václav Benda, Tomáš and Jiří Kopřiva, Vít Pelikán, Michal Mrtvý, Ladislav Nedvěd, Michal Holeček and many others also took great credit for its publication. *Informace o církvi* was also transcribed by numerous nameless activists in Bohemia and Moravia, and it got as far as Slovakia.

Another outstanding activist engaged in Catholic samizdat was Augustin Navrátil, who was active in Lutopecny in southern Moravia, where he published his open letters addressed to state representatives in large print runs, while between 1988 and 1990 he published the *Křesťanské obzory* [Christian Horizons] magazine together with the Knihovna Křesťanských obzorů [Christian Horizons Library] series, with 22 small-scale publications. Augustin Navrátil was also the author of a petition entitled *Proposals by Catholics to deal with the situation of religious citizens in Czechoslovakia*, known as 'The 31 points'. It was signed by over 600,000 people from all over Czechoslovakia, thus becoming the largest petition in any Communist bloc state. Of course, this would not have been possible without the existence of samizdat.

We should also take note of P. Jaroslav Knittl's work in Vrchoviny. After 1968 he was engaged in youth work, organized secret spiritual exercise sessions, wrote, translated and had high-standard Catholic literature translated. His collaborators were Vladimír Matějček, Stanislav Hájek, Vladimír Petráček and many others, including around a dozen translators. It was also thanks to him that some 350 book titles saw the light of day, as carefully transcribed typescripts which were distributed to other interested parties in samizdat form. From 1973 he published inter alia 55 issues of the sizeable anthologies entitled *Znamení doby* [Sign of the Times] and paid the price in 1989, when he lost state authorization to perform activities as a priest.

We have samizdat to thank for quite a lot, e.g. Charter 77 would never have come into existence without it, independent initiatives would not have emerged, and no opposition could ever have come together. We can thank samizdat not only for some noteworthy cultural assets, but also for their preservation.

In addition to cultural assets, whether literary, musical or artistic, samizdat has also preserved scientific works and, most importantly of all, journalism, the testimony of the times. This faithfully reflected the abnormal situation at that time, which was hard to understand for people who do not have any direct experience with a Communist regime. This testimony, which was often written under dramatic circumstances, with sacrifices that have only fleetingly been mentioned here, is now housed in several libraries, for the most part in American and European libraries. The largest collection in the Czech Republic is at Libri prohibiti in Prague, which has been built up since the end of the 1970s in the awareness that these assets need to be preserved for the future, as they are going to be the 'memory of the nation'.

Libri prohibiti contains more than nine thousand Czech and Slovak samizdat books, some titles in various editions and transcriptions, as well as another few hundred magazines and some minor samizdat texts. All in all there are millions of pages of text transcribed on typewriters. All this enjoys considerable attention from readers and researchers, although they are normally only interested in the content of these books and magazines – i.e. they read them and look up information in them. In this respect the library operates like any other. However, Libri prohibiti is also an ideal place for examining samizdat as a phenomenon and dealing with its sociological aspects. Here I have to regretfully point out that as far as I am aware no research has yet taken place in this area, so there are no works on the function, significance or influence of samizdat within society.

How Underground Authors and Publishers Financed Their Samizdats

Martin Machovec

Firstly the question arises as to whether there is any point at all in defining a special subgroup of underground authors and publishers in the context of samizdat literary output and distribution, i.e. authors primarily from the circles surrounding Bondy and Jirous, and the communities that had arisen in the 1970s around the Plastic People and the *Vokno* [Window] magazine, or in the 1980s around both *Vokno* and *Revolver Revue* magazine, where we can definitely refer to particular publishers. Our findings in this regard may clearly support the view that a definition of this kind is rather unnecessary, i.e. that *underground* authors, like authors within the broad range of 'dissident' authors, i.e. the entire unofficial literary and artistic scene in the totalitarian 1970s and 1980s, including individual groups of authors, individualizable, for example, on the basis of aesthetic or world-view orientation, age category, region or 'domestication' within a particular samizdat edition, generally shared the unwritten but basically universal laws of the samizdat jungle.

The basis is clear: it might well have been theoretically legal under the 'Copyright Act'[1] for authors to publish their own works in typewritten editions, but the interpretation of this act was subject to the

---

1   1965 Collection, No. 35.

representatives of justice in an undemocratic, usurpative state, so that samizdat authors could often have justified doubts regarding its appropriate application. Far more uncertain, however, was the interpretation of the law on what was known as unauthorized business, a simple consideration of which could lead to the tentative conclusion that if samizdat authors didn't want another allegation thrown at them they had to take painstaking care that their samizdat production and distribution really did not earn a single penny, or even better, that they made a loss.

Nor can it perhaps be too surprising that silence reigned over the economic aspect of samizdat production before November 1989, as it was, after all, a rather delicate matter, and discretion was required. One well-known exception here is Vaculík's *Český snář* [Czech Dreambook], which is actually based on the 'indiscretion principle' and moreover embraces both fiction and non-fiction. The author's openness with regard to the funding of his Petlice [Padlock] series not only illustrates this principle, but also de facto postulates one of those unwritten laws of samizdat publication, namely never earn anything from it, do not capitalize on demonized capital, but do make sure that the financial 'input' and 'output' is essentially the same, i.e. do not on any account gain anything material from your own efforts and contributions, as this should remain purely within the sphere of enthusiasts.

Otherwise it is clearly characteristic that the lack or rather the absence of information on the 'economic base' (as it were) of the samizdat business continued into the nineties and the recent past: plenty of biographical listings of samizdats have been published, but we would generally be hard pressed to find any information of this kind in them.

As we now present several examples of underground samizdat publication, we are well aware that any subsequent generalization should be rather circumspect; in any case we have no choice in the matter here as we have no time or space for a more detailed examination.

On the basis of the author's own research and personal experience, two approaches to samizdat production funding can basically be identified:

1) In the case of small-scale samizdats and out-of-edition transcriptions, i.e. 'wild' samizdats, which were prevalent during the 1970s at least in underground circles, the 'self-financing rule' applied. The means of production, i.e. typewriters, typewriter paper, carbon paper and binders were acquired by every transcriber-publisher from his own financial resources, i.e. with money that he earned from his civic employment, which generally had nothing to do with literature, let alone book production, and distributed the resultant product with pleasure and for free among his clients, i.e. his personal friends, who could themselves again repeat the entire process. Such was the case, for example, with perhaps the most prolific underground author, Egon Bondy (1930–2007), who indeed often repeated that he was not at all concerned with the distribution of his literary works, but in practice he always appeared to employ (for free, of course) two or three transcribers who basically 'operated' on this self-financing principle. During the 1970s and 1980s his most loyal co-workers included poet František Pánek (*1949) and musician Jan Schneider (*1955), as well as Martin Machovec (*1956) for quite some time. We hasten to add that Bondy immediately redistributed the supplied typescript, sometimes unfortunately so quickly that it was not even properly proof-read, and he never wanted a penny for it. Similar self-funding could also probably be found among other samizdat authors and it was common with regard to *underground* poetry collections. Hence, for example, Ivan Martin Jirous confirmed that the publication of the first collections of this kind were solely under his financial management, i.e. *Egonu Bondymu k 45. narozeninám invalidní sourozenci* [To Egon Bondy on his 45th birthday from the invalid siblings] and *Ing. Petru Lamplovi k 45. narozeninám* [To Petr Lampl, M.Sc. on his 45th birthday] (both from 1975); the same applied in the case of the publication of *Magorův zápisník I.* [Magor's Notebook I] (1980). In all these cases Jirous was the publisher, compiler, editor, transcriber and distributor all rolled into one.

2) Naturally, as costs rose and the technical challenges of samizdat publication grew, so the financial demands also increased. As regards

underground enterprises, the fact cannot be ignored that after 1977 when underground authors, musicians and artists generally joined the Chartists and the underground finally also started to be perceived from the outside as a kind of Chartist offshoot, they started to be noticed by publishers in exile, the Charter 77 Foundation[2] and various humanitarian organizations, e.g. Amnesty International, so that the underground eventually came to be a target group for occasional financial support. It should be added that this funding was primarily meant to provide 'minimum subsistence' for individuals in Czechoslovakia who were persecuted for their political opinions, or for the family members of those who had been put in prison, and any samizdat activities obviously counted towards this 'minimum', though of course in the circumstances it was quite absurd to ask for any itemized 'billing'. The most compelling published testimony to date of these matters is apparently the correspondence between Václav Havel and František Janouch.[3]

---

2   The first specific details about how much the Charter 77 Foundation contributed to Czechoslovak dissidents were published by its chief representative Professor František Janouch as early as 1995. JANOUCH, František. 'Stockholmská Nadace Charty 77 a podpora nezávislé literatury a jejích tvůrců' [The Stockholm Charter 77 Foundation and the Support of Independent Literature and Its Authors], in Česká nezávislá literatura po pěti letech v referátech, F. KAUTMAN (ed.). Praha: Primus, 1995, pp. 98-122.

3   Havel's correspondence with Janouch basically confirms the further quoted testimony from Stárek, Topol and Gruntorád. The financial support that came in this particular case from the Stockholm Charter 77 Foundation was irregular, not all that much and often really just aiming to provide the most basic material back-up, e.g. to the family members of imprisoned Charter 77 signatories, not targeted support for samizdat operations. This was the case among underground authors such as Ivan Martin Jirous and his wife Juliana Jirousová. For some time financial support of this kind was also provided e.g. to Jiří Daníček, Jan Lopatka, Lenka Marečková and Andrej Stankovič. Several of Havel's letters and one of Janouch's (e.g. HAVEL, Václav - JANOUCH, František. Korespondence 1978-2001 [Correspondence 1978-2001]. Praha: Akropolis, 2007, pp. 152-153) indicate that 'magnitizdat' publisher Petr Cibulka was also being financially supported. At one point (Ibid: p. 375) a somewhat vague reference is made to Egon Bondy (referred to in Havel's letter as 'Fišer', and in the index as 'Bondy'), which perhaps indicates that he received support of some kind twice a year before 1987. More specific comments refer e.g. to Vokno and Revolver Revue, which Havel had requested

Three examples follow of this 'Chartist-underground' samizdat production with greater mass appeal:

1) *Vokno* magazine, whose chief organizer or 'manager', so to speak, was František Stárek 'Čuňas', whom we can thank for the following information, began publication in 1979. Spirit duplicator and silkscreen printing were used for their production at first, followed by mimeograph from the seventh issue. The print run allegedly increased from the original 100 to 380 copies.[4] Stárek told the author that the first issue of *Vokno* was basically financed from the organizers' own resources and that subsequently the non-profit capital turnover principle actually applied, so the sale of copies was meant to cover the costs of the next issue. *Vokno* was said to sell at first for 20 Kčs and subsequently 50 Kčs due to its increasing size. However, Stárek also mentions that a not inconsiderable contribution to the budget was made by the proverbial '*misappropriation of property in socialist ownership*', e.g. *Vokno* supporters at work repeatedly **stole** mimeograph stencils, which during the 1980s could not easily be bought on the retail market. Sponsorship gifts were evidently quite rare until the late 1980s, when e.g. Pavel Tigrid donated a video camera and video recorder.

2) *Revolver Revue*, originally *Jednou nohou* [With One Foot] was established in 1985, i.e. in circumstances that were considerably more favourable, and in a situation where the underground-Chartist symbiosis was tried and tested and financial support from abroad was an established tradition. *Revolver Revue* was first printed in mimeograph, with the last two issues in offset. The print runs from the first to the thirteenth, i.e. the last, samizdat issue, increased from sixty to five

---

support for from Janouch since 1986, while support for *Vokno* evidently never reached its intended addressees (e.g. see Ibid: pp. 261, 264 and 289). The Charter 77 Foundation was more successful with *Revolver Revue*, whose editors received funding through Ivan Lamper (e.g. see Ibid: pp. 337, 340, 343, 345 – e.g. on p. 343 a figure of 6,000 Kčs is mentioned) and Beatrice Landovská (e.g. see Ibid: pp. 215, 219, 296 and 346).

4   RŮŽKOVÁ, Jana – GRUNTORÁD, Jiří. 'Samizdatový časopis Vokno' [Samizdat Magazine Vokno], *Kritický sborník*, 1999/2000, Vol. XIX, pp. 193-231.

hundred copies.[5] Jáchym Topol, one of the *Revolver Revue* founders and one of its most prominent authors, contributors and organizers, told the author that from the outset they were financially supported by the Charter 77 Foundation and that Timothy Garton Ash also contributed, and Václav Havel himself allegedly set up the first issue '*with several thousand crowns*'. Later dancer Vlastimil Harapes also contributed in absolute secrecy to *Revolver Revue*, while unidentified friends from Poland and Hungary supplied duplicating machines. The money was used to purchase paper and printing ink, as well as to concrete over the basement apartment where the leaflet printer was located at the end of the 1980s. Just like *Vokno*, *Revolver Revue* was on sale – with the exception of the first issue (or in today's terminology the 'pilot' issue). The price per copy varied according to its size and print run between 50 and 150 Kčs. However, the principle of only covering the costs of the next issue was applied by the *Revolver Revue* publishers just as it was at *Vokno*. No 'misappropriation of property in socialist ownership' supposedly took place in the preparation of *Revolver Revue*.

3) Although it is rather debatable whether or not the typescript samizdat Popelnice [Dustbin], established by Jiří Gruntorád in 1978, can be considered an underground community publication or rather a Charter 77 activity, his listing[6] indicates that underground literature was represented more prominently there than in some other 'established samizdat' series. At the author's request, Jiří Gruntorád went into greater detail over the information from this listing on funding: between 1978 and 1984 Popelnice was only financed from his own resources, and from 1985 he started to receive money from the Charter 77 Foundation. Gruntorád definitely does not believe that large amounts were involved. To illustrate, he refers to journalist Petruška Šustrová, who was tasked with distributing aid from abroad,

---

5   JEŽEK,Vlastimil. 'Revolver Revue (Jednou nohou)', *Kritický sborník*, No. 3 and 4, 1991, Vol. XI, pp. 63–79, pp. 67–80.
6   GRUNTORÁD, Jiří. 'Z bibliografie samizdatu: Edice Popelnice' [From the Samizdat Bibliography: Dustbin series], *Kritický sborník*, No. 2, 1992, Vol. XII, pp. 67–79.

Samizdat publication of fairytales and poems *Magor for Children* by I. M. Jirous.

i.e. primarily from the Charter 77 Foundation. She provided Gruntorád with a single contribution of around 1,500 Kčs specifically to buy a new typewriter. Unspecified support was also evidently forthcoming from Pavel Tigrid a couple of times. Gruntorád concludes by saying: '*I did make an effort to ensure it wasn't too much of a loss-maker.*'

In the margins of these notes on samizdat *underground* authors and publishers, a couple of lines should also be devoted to the publication of 'magnitizdats', i.e. the distribution of recordings including music by *underground* bands on tape and cassettes. The most important source of information on this publication activity to date is a thesis by Czech-Canadian Anna Vanicek.[7] Of all the magnitizdat distributors, Petr Cibulka was evidently closest to the *underground* authors, publishers and in this case rather the *underground* musicians, whereas

---

7   VANICEK, Anna. *Passion Play: Underground Rock Music in Czechoslovakia, 1968-1989.* A thesis submitted to the Faculty of Graduate Studies; Graduate Programme in Ethnomusicology, North York, Ontario: York University, 1997.

Mikoláš Chadima focused primarily on 'new wave' Czech rock music in the 1980s. Vanicek writes that Cibulka used to sell his cassettes for an average of 120–180 Kčs[8] and although he himself states that he did not make a profit on these sales, he was evidently quite often suspected of doing so by his colleagues. There was undoubtedly a black market element involved, i.e. in 'unauthorized business'. What was also problematic was the fact that Cibulka often published recordings against the wishes of the individual musicians concerned.[9]

However, the most famous *underground* authors, along with their publishers, approached samizdat as a necessity of life and self-preservation activity, while the economic and financial aspect of this publication, i.e. the fact that it involved everything but lucrative economic activity, was perceived as something unimportant and peripheral.

8   See Ibid: p. 126.
9   See Ibid: pp. 131-134.

The Group of Writers around the Půlnoc Series (1949–1955): A Specific Example of Underground Cultural Activities

Martin Machovec

Nowadays there is quite an extensive literature, comprising literary history, essays and memoirs[1] on the activities of the underground group of poets and prose writers who brought out their works in one of the first ever Czech samizdat series (discounting illegal works under the Protectorate) in the Půlnoc [Midnight] series and as separate associated texts, in individual volumes sorted by names,

---

1 BONDY, Egon. 'Kořeny českého literárního undergroundu v letech 1949-1953' [The Roots of the Czech Literary Underground, 1949-1953], *Haňťa Press,* No. 8, 1990; In English in M. MACHOVEC (ed.). *Views from the Inside. Czech Underground Literature and Culture (1948-1989).* Prague: Karolinum Press, 2018. BONDY, Egon. '2000', *Revolver Revue,* No. 45, 2001; BONDY, Egon. *Prvních deset let* [The First Ten Years]. Praha: Maťa, 2002; BOUDNÍK, Vladimír. *Z literární pozůstalosti* [From the Literary Papers]. Praha: Pražská imaginace – Pragma, 1993; HRABAL, Bohumil. 'Co je poezie?' [What is Poetry?], 'Made in Czechoslovakia', 'Blitzkrieg', in *Jarmilka. Sebrané spisy Bohumila Hrabala 3* [Collected Writings of Bohumil Hrabal 3, Jarmilka]. Praha: Pražská imaginace, 1992; JELÍNEK, Oldřich. 'Jak to všechno začalo…' [How It All Began], *Haňťa Press*, No. 14, 1993; MACHOVEC, Martin. 'Pokus o náčrt geneze a vývoje básnického díla Egona Bondyho' [Attempted Outline of

which were dated 1951–1955, but mostly written between 1949 and 1953. As the actual literary work that was brought out in the Půlnoc series has been preserved more or less in its entirety and was then mostly published[2] in the first half of the 1990s, the situation is now fairly clear.

the Birth and Development of Egon Bondy's Poetic Work], *Vokno*, No. 21, 1990; MACHOVEC, Martin. 'Šestnáct autorů českého literárního podzemí (1948-1989)' [Sixteen Authors from the Czech Literary Underground], *Literární archiv*, 1991, Vol. XXV; MACHOVEC, Martin. 'Několik poznámek k podzemní ediční řadě Půlnoc' [Several Notes on the Underground Midnight series], *Kritický sborník*, No. 3, 1993; MACHOVEC, Martin. 'Vídeňská bohemistika o Půlnoci (Česká podzemní literatura 1948-1953)' [Viennese Czech Studies on Midnight - Czech Underground Literature 1948-1953], *Kritický sborník*, No. 2-3, 1999, Vol. XVIII; MACHOVEC, Martin. 'Náčrt života a díla Egona Bondyho' [Outline of Life and Work of Egon Bondy], in *Bouda Bondy. Projekt Bouda IV.* [Czech National Theatre Summer Stage]. Praha: Národní divadlo, 2007; MAINX, Oskar. *Poezie jako mýtus, svědectví a hra. Kapitoly z básnické poetiky Egona Bondyho* [Poetry as Myth, Testimony and Game. Chapters from the Poetics of Egon Bondy]. Ostrava: Protimluv, 2007; PILAŘ, Martin. *Underground*. Brno: Host, 1999; TROUP, Zdeněk. 'Poezie totality' [Poetry of Totality], *Rozeta*, No. 1, 1991; TYPLT, Jaromír Filip. 'Dvě svědectví o Židovských jménech' [Two Testimonies of Jewish Names], *Host*, No. 3, 1997; TYPLT, Jaromír Filip. 'Absolutní realismus a Totální hrobař' [Absolute Realism and the Total Gravedigger], *Host*, No. 1, 2006; VODSEĎÁLEK, Ivo - MAZAL, Tomáš. 'S Ivo Vodseďálkem o letech radostného budování 49-53' [With Ivo Vodseďálek on the Years of Happy Construction 49-53], *Vokno*, No. 18, [1990]; VODSEĎÁLEK, Ivo. *Dílo Ivo Vodseďálka I., II.* [Work of Ivo Vodseďálek]: *Bloudění, Nalézání, Probouzení, Snění, Zuření*. Praha: Pražská imaginace, 1992; VODSEĎÁLEK, Ivo. *Felixír života* [Felixir of Life]. Brno: Host, 2000; ZAND, Gertraude. *Totaler Realismus und Peinliche Poesie. Tschechische Untergrund-Literatur 1948-1953* [Total Realism and Embarassing Poetry. Czech Underground Literatutre]. Frankfurt am Main: Peter Lang, 1998; ZANDOVÁ, Gertraude. 'Básník - svědek - aktivista: Poetický program a vydavatelský projekt Egona Bondyho v čase stalinismu' [Poet, Witness, Activist: The Poetic Programme and Publishing Project of Egon Bondy under Stalinism], *Česká literatura*, No. 6, 1998, Vol. XLVI.
2   This primarily involves the first two volumes of the nine-volume work of BONDY, Egon. *Básnické dílo Egona Bondyho I.-IX.* [The Poetic Work of Egon Bondy I-IX]. Praha: Pražská imaginace, 1990-1993 (collections of poetry 1950-1987); or, more recently *Básnické spisy I.-III.* [Collected Poetic Works I-III]. Praha: Argo, 2014-2016; as well as the first two volumes of the five-volume *Dílo Ivo Vodseďálka - Zuření* [Fury], 1992 and *Snění* [Dreaming], 1992 - see previous footnote. Also a volume of texts by KREJCAROVÁ, Jana. *Clarissa a jiné texty* [Clarissa and Other Texts]. Praha: Concordia, 1990; see also KREJCAROVÁ-ČERNÁ, Jana. *Tohle je skutečnost (Básně,*

Within the broad range of unofficial cultural activities which were originally given the avant-garde label and which existed at least in trace form after 1948 (hence leaving aside those writers who emigrated, fell entirely silent, were imprisoned or, of course, those who after 'victorious February' attempted to comply or join in one way or another, pride of place is taken by Teige and Effenberger's surrealist group, which carried on its pre-1948 activities almost entirely in isolation. Its most prominent talents were clearly Mikuláš Medek and Karel Hynek. Activities also continued in the 'Spořilov' group and among some members of Skupina 42 [Group 42], particularly Jan Hanč, Jindřich Chalupecký and Jiří Kolář. Entirely isolated from the other posthumous children of the Czech avant-garde was the Záběhlice surrealist group known as the Libeň psychics (librarian Zdeněk Buřil, 1924–1994, varnisher Jiří Šmoranc, 1924–2003, radio mechanic Vladimír Vávra, 1924–2005, and bookbinder Stanislav Vávra, *1933), whose 1950s work was as a whole considered lost or destroyed, so that it only very gradually penetrated the Czech literary context after

---

prózy, dopisy) [This Is Reality (Poems, Prose, Letters)]. Praha: Torst, 2016; as well as a selection from the samizdat volume by Svoboda, Pavel. 'Próza, Poezie, Korespondence' [Prose, Poetry and Correspondence], Haňťa Press, No. 17, 1995, and more recently another selection, including Svoboda's book of collages, in Revolver Revue, No. 93, 2013, and excerpts from a text by Born, Adolf – Jelínek, Oldřich. 'Urajt', Haňťa Press, No. 17, 1995. Bondy's complete translations of Morgenstern from 1951 have been published in a single volume: Morgenstern, Christian – Bondy, Egon. Galgenlieder / Šibeniční písně [Gallows Songs]. Praha: Labyrint, 2000. Bondy's 'novel' '2000' from 1949-1950 has been published in Revolver Revue – see previous footnote. Two books of collages by Vodseďálek remain unpublished to this day. A different problem is presented by Karel Žák's literary work, which might well have been 'passed down orally' by other Půlnoc participants, but which never actually appeared in the series. A couple of fragments from this work from between 1947 and 1955 were collected in 1979 by Ivo Vodseďálek in the samizdat volume Hra prstečků mých neklidných [Game of My Restless Little Fingers], from which again only a couple of small samples were presented in the ninth issue of Haňťa Press (1991). A curious second samizdat edition of Vodseďálek's Trapná poesie [Embarrassing Poetry], 1952, richly illustrated by Adolf Born and Oldřich Jelínek in a single hitherto unreproduced samizdat copy is now awaiting publication.

1989.[3] However, as early as 1948 the former avant-gardistes became aware of Vladimír Boudník, with his first 'explosionalist' manifesto on 14th August 1948. Bohumil Hrabal (and evidently Hrabal's 'neo-poetist' associate Karel Marysko, 1915–1988, who made a living as a performing concert musician) apparently got to know Jiří Kolář back in 1946, although awareness of Hrabal's watershed 1950 texts, which were so highly rated decades later[4], only got through to this very limited 'public' some time afterwards, perhaps around the mid-1950s. Skupina Ra [The Ra Group] entirely ceased its activities. Of those mentioned above, Teige and Hynek died shortly afterwards and none of those remaining were able to obtain a vocation relating in any way to literature at least from 1949 until the mid-1950s. Most of them were engaged in working-class occupations. Kolář, who from 1948 to 1951 eked out a living at the Dílo co-operative and then at the Propaganda

---

3   With regard to the Záběhlice (or Libeň) group see the memoir article by Stanislav Vávra: 'Záběhlická skupina surrealistů – Libenští psychici' [The Záběhlice Surrealist Group – Libeň Psychics], *Jarmark umění*, No. 2, April 1991, where extracts are also published from original work by Z. Buřil, S.Vávra and contemporary fellow-travellers O. Rubeš and J. Sobotka. See also *Haňťa Press*, No. 10 and 11, 1991; also extracts from original work by S. Vávra and J. Šmoranc in *Haňťa Press*, No. 14 – No. 17, 1993–1995; and an interview: VÁVRA, Stanislav – TYPLT, J. Filip. 'Ukázat pramen a podat pohár' [Show a Source and Pass the Cup], *Iniciály*, No. 17/18, 1991. The fictionalized memoirs of S. Vávra present a testimony that is rather late and highly stylised. (VÁVRA, Stanislav. *Zvířený prach* [Swirling Dust]. Praha: MČ Praha 8, 2004). Of great value are three volumes that give some idea of the work by the 'Libeň Psychics': VÁVRA, Stanislav. *Muž v jiných končinách světa* [A Man in Other Corners of the Earth]. Praha: Pražská imaginace, 1992; VÁVRA, Stanislav. *Snovidění* [Dreamseeing]. Praha: Pražská imaginace, 1992; and ŠMORANC, Jiří. *Děti periferie* [Children of the Periphery]. Praha: Pražská imaginace, 1996. It was not until after the death of V. Vávra in 2005 that his younger brother S. Vávra managed to reconstruct from his surviving manuscripts an anthology of texts by the 'Libeň Psychics' lost in the 1950s. This anthology was published under the title *Libeňští psychici. Sborník básnických a prozaických textů z let 1945–1959* [Libeň Psychics. Collected Poetic and Prose Works from 1945–1959]. Praha: Concordia, 2009.
4   HRABAL, Bohumil. *Bambino di Praga – Barvotisky – Krásná Poldi* [Bambino di Praga – Color Prints – Beautiful Poldi]. Praha: Československý spisovatel, 1990; see also *Sebrané spisy Bohumila Hrabala*, Vol. 2 – *Židovský svícen* [Jewish Candleholder] and Vol. 3 – *Jarmilka*. Praha: Pražská imaginace, 1991 and 1992.

Section of SNKLHU [State Literature, Music and Art Publishers], was imprisoned from 1952 to 1953, and did not go back to work when he was released. Other 'maladjusted individuals' in similar straitened circumstances during the first half of the 1950s included Josef Škvorecký, Vratislav Effenberger, Vladimír Vokolek, Ladislav Dvořák and Jan Zábrana, while repudiated Czech literary grandmasters Vladimír Holan, Jakub Deml, Bohuslav Reynek and a large number of other authors were totally isolated with no hope of publication. Subsistence issues of a similar kind also affected all the members of the group whose work was brought together in the Půlnoc samizdat series.

The initiators, creators and most prolific authors of the series, Ivo Vodseďálek (1931–2017) and in particular Egon Bondy, actual name Zbyněk Fišer (1930–2007), were in a certain sense the 'renegades' from Teige's and Effenberger's surrealist group. Bondy made his samizdat debut, for the first time with his Jewish pseudonym, in what was still an entirely surrealist anthology *Židovská jména* [Jewish Names], which came out in early 1949 with Vratislav Effenberger, Karel Hynek, Oldřich Wenzl, Jan Zuska, Zdeněk Wagner, Jana Krejcarová and others[5] all represented under other Jewish pseudonyms. To a large extent, in spite of their manifesto for a radical schism with the poetics of surrealism, as documented particularly in the programme collections *Ich und es: totální realismus* [Ich und es: Total Realism][6]; *Egon Bondy* (samizdat 1951)[7] and *Trapná poesie*[8] [Embarrassing Poetry] (I. Vodseďálek, samizdat 1950). It is also possible to include their work from the early 1950s, like that of Hrabal at the same time and much of Skupina 42 (Kolář, Blatný and Kainar) among the work of those who repeatedly insisted on matching themselves with the surrealist legacy. In the case of Bondy and Vodseďálek there remained

---

5   M. Machovec (ed.). *Židovská jména* [Jewish Names]. Praha: NLN, 1995.
6   For this and other cited texts from the 1950s see Bondy, *Básnické spisy I.-III.* see Footnote 2.
7   Dtto.
8   For this and other cited texts from the 1950s see Vodseďálek, *Dílo Ivo Vodseďálka I., II.* See Footnote 1.

the poetics of the *objet trouvé*, the idea of dreams being equal to life (and of course life being equal to dreams!), admiration for the poetics of horror and the *roman noir*, the requirement for 'purity', 'nakedness', the linkage of the unlinkable, the drasticity of testimony *pour épater le bourgeois*, the stylization of 'childish naiveté', the inability to hierarchize values, and in particular dogmatic 'leftishness', faith in the socialist revolution (albeit of a Trotskyite anti-Stalinist kind) and resistance to 'religious obscurantism'. Some of these traits are more evident in Bondy, others in Vodseďálek and still others in Krejcarová, but all of them can be pointed out in the Půlnoc series texts as a whole. What was radical, however, was the retreat from metaphor and imagery in poetic language, the drastic 'purification' and 'de-aestheticization'. Key works from the Půlnoc series, some of which were to be of crucial importance to the aesthetic orientation of the 1970s *underground* include Bondy's poem *Jeskyně divů aneb Prager Leben (Pražský život)* [Cave of Wonders or Prager Leben, Prague Life] (1951), the poetics of which are notably similar to those of Hrabal's *Bambino di Praga,* which was written around the same time, even though Bondy and Hrabal did not know of each other. In other respects it hints at Bondy's future development as an implacable critic, a regular firebrand and a dogmatic 'wielder of the truth'. Also of importance is the collection *Für Bondys unbekannte Geliebte aneb Nepřeberné bohatství* [For Bondy's Unknown Love; or, Inexhaustible Wealth] (1951), which to some extent restores the direct connection to the poetics used by surrealists at that time (e.g. applying Dali's paranoid-critical method and Hynek's 'graphic poetry' principle), as well as *Velká kniha* [Great Book] (1952), which was to be highly popular in the *underground*, particularly with its groundbreaking section *Ožralá Praha* [Hammered Prague], its barbaric-style antipoetisms, its nursery rhyme pseudo-primitivisms and of course its 'naive realist' testimonies of the absurdities of the era, which form a striking counterpoint e.g. to Kolář's contemporary 'eye-witness' poetics. The long poem *Zbytky eposu* [Remnants of an Epic] (1955), is outstanding for several of its highly de-tabooing passages, which show inadvertent parallels between Bondy's early poetical works and several elements in those of the American beatniks, as well as being a splendid display of surrealist poetics linking the unlinkable and ultimately testimony of Bondy's return to some sources of Czech literary modernism (Erben, Mácha and Havlíček Borovský).

In his Půlnoc texts, Ivo Vodseďálek is far more consistent in adhering to the poetics of 'embarrassment', disrupting the traditional punchline and of course the imagery of the poetical text (e.g. in the collection *Cesta na Rivieru* [Trip to the Riviera], 1951, *Smrt vtipu* [Death of the Joke], 1951, *Pilot a oráč* [Pilot and Ploughman], 1951, *Americké básně* [American Poems], 1953) poetics, which in a reevaluation of the surrealist 'objet trouvé' and in contrast to Bondy's poetic work anticipates all the pathos-free poetics of American pop-art and hyperrealism. On ther other hand, he also revives the beauty of surrealist spectrality and chimerality in novel contexts (in the collection *Krajina a mravnost* [Landscape and Morality], 1953, and the prose work *Kalvarie* [Calvary], 1954), while generally in a number of his texts he uncovers the appeal of 'Soviet mythology' (e.g. in the collection *Kvetoucí Ukrajina* [Blooming Ukraine], 1950, 1953), while admitting to his defencelessness in the face of the myth accepted by the masses and the futility of any resistance, which he nevertheless does offer, even though he is aware of the absurdity of such conduct, thus again presciently anticipating the ideas of some of his underground successors. (However, Vodseďálek's work was unknown to the underground circle surrounding the Plastic People.)

In hindsight it is clearly quite tempting to see this grouping as a more or less monolithic school of poetry, if not actually as some kind of latent resistance cell, even though circumstances around the late forties and early fifties, i.e. the political reality of the times and the personal situations of the majority of members of that group, who were mostly around twenty years of age, largely rules out anything of that nature. Zand[9] calls them a 'poetic circle' in an attempt

9 ZANDOVÁ, Gertraude. *Totální realismus a trapná poezie. Česká neoficiální literatura 1948-1953* [Total Realism and Embarrassing Poetry. Unofficial Czech

to indicate the low degree of homogeneity within the group. The fact is that both initiators of the Půlnoc series – Bondy and Vodseďálek – were classmates at the Ječná Street grammar school in Prague, and they were brought together mainly by their interest in modern art in general and surrealism in particular, as well as ultimately to attempt a joint debut, which unfortunately took place during the period immediately following February 1948. These two artists, whose early works (i.e. at least until 1952) still bore many of the signs of juvenilia (e.g. experimenting and seeking out new forms, attempting a wide variety of genres, much 'finding oneself' as it were, and almost desperate attempts to come up with something novel, independent and non-epigonic), had the good fortune to find a couple of congenial writers and artists among their contemporaries (poet and collagist Pavel Svoboda, 1930–2014, Jana Krejcarová-Fischlová-Černá-Ladmanová, 1928–1981, sculptor and poet Karel Žák, 1929–2015, and later book graphic artist and photographer Jaromír Valoušek, 1928–1993, in the early 1950s chemistry student and for a short time Vodseďálek's wife Dana 'Dagmara' Prchlíková, 1931–2006, at that time the 'suprasexdadaists' Adolf Born, 1930–2016, and Oldřich Jelínek, *1930, later psychologist Miloš Černý, *1931, poet Emil Hokeš, 1931–2000 and perhaps a couple of others), who showed appreciation for their creative ambitions and who at least to some extent responded to them by showing them their own works. Another who was close to this group, or at least to some of its members, during the first half of the 1950s (typically, not all the aforementioned personally knew all those named below!) was a quite unknown secondary graphic art school graduate, Vladimír Boudník (1924–1968)[10] whom Zbyněk Fišer got

---

Literature 1948-1953]. Brno: Host, 2002; ZANDOVÁ, 'Básník - svědek - aktivista' - see Footnote 1.

10   Regarding his work see BOUDNÍK, Vladimír. *Z literární pozůstalosti* - see footnote No. 1; BOUDNÍK, Vladimír. *Z korespondence* [From the Correspondence] *I (1949-1956), II (1957-1968)*. Praha: Pražská imaginace, 1994; MERHAUT, Vladislav. *Zápisky o Vladimíru Boudníkovi* [Notes on Vladimír Boudník]. Praha: Revolver Revue, 1997.

to know as early as in 1948, as well as Mikuláš Medek (1926–1974), Emila Medková (1928–1985), Jaroslav Dočekal (1926–1975), Karel Hynek (1925–1953), Zbyněk Sekal (1923–1998) and Jan 'Hanes' Reegen (1922–1952)[11] to name at least those whose familiarity with illegal publishing activities at Půlnoc can be verified in some way.[12] (The Medeks and Hynek formed a connection for some time at least between Bondy's and Vodseďálek's circle and Effernberger's surrealist group, to whom it seems otherwise Bondy had a rather ambivalent relationship). The late avant-gardiste Bohumil Hrabal (1914–1997), who was

---

11   The literary work of Mikuláš Medek, in which connections can be found with the Půlnoc creators, was published in the volume: MEDEK, Mikuláš. *Texty* [Texts]. Praha: Torst, 1995. Of great informative value with regard to Medek and Boudník's relationship to Bondy and his circle is the correspondence between Medek and Boudník: A. HARTMANN - B. MRÁZ (eds.). 'Boudník a Medek, korespondence' [Boudník and Medek, Correspondence], *Umění / Art*, No. 3/4, 1997, Vol. XVL; A. HARTMANN - B. MRÁZ (eds.). 'Boudník a Medek, dodatek ke korespondenci a další 'texty pro Mikuláše Medka'' [Boudník and Medek, Additions to Correspondence and Other 'Texts for Mikuláš Medek'], *Umění / Art*, No. 5, 1997, Vol. XVL. The work of the artist and writer Jaroslav Dočekal has not yet been successfully collected in its entirety, nor has it been appropriately examined. For samples of his work see: DOČEKAL, Jaroslav. 'Smršťovače - hořké dávky' [Shrinkers - Bitter Doses] [letters to Jaroslav Rotbauer], *Revolver Revue*, No. 29, 1995. See also *Dopisy Jaroslava Dočekala Vladimíru Boudníkovi I.-II.* [Letters of Jaroslav Dočekal to Vladimír Boudník I-II], Praha: Jan Placák - Ztichlá klika, 2017. HYNEK, Karel. *S vyloučením veřejnosti* [With the Exclusion of the Public]. Praha: Torst, 1998. Regarding Jan Reegen see the samizdat volume: REEGEN, Jan. *LISTY PŘÍTELI. Dopisy Vladimíru Boudníkovi (1949-1952)* [Letters to a Friend. Letters to Vladimír Boudník 1949-1952], published by Václav Kadlec as the 56th publication in his samizdat Pražská imaginace series in 1989 (Knihy 4. proudu, Volume 8), here on p. 3 of the photo attachment there is an imaginary portrait of Fišer-Bondy by Reegen. Bondy provides a testimony of his friendship with Reegen in his memoirs: BONDY, *Prvních deset let* - see Footnote 1.

12   In his memoirs *Prvních deset let* (see above) for the 1949-1955 period Bondy also refers to contacts with e.g. Alexej Kusák, Miroslav Lamač, Jaroslav Puchmertl, František Jůzek, Blanka Sochorová, Josef Lehoučka, Konstantin Sochor, German studies expert Gottlieb, František Drtikol, psychiatrist Václav Pinkava, who subsequently became the author Jan Křesadlo, and Andrej Bělocvětov. At the Charles University Faculty of Arts, where Ivo Vodseďálek studied aesthetics part-time, he got to know Milan Kundera amongst others, and even though he maintained occasional contact with him throughout the 1950s, he allegedly never told him about his literary ambitions.

quite isolated in the late 1940s and early 1950s, did not get to know Bondy until the end of 1951 (according to the latter's information), although the dating and content of Boudník's short story *Noc* [Night] – 10th October 1951 – indicate that they actually got to know each other somewhat earlier. Bondy recalls that (evidently from 1951 or 1952) he met not only Boudník at Hrabal's, but also Karel Marysko.[13]

Surprisingly, however, the authors of the 'Midnight circle' did not have any demonstrable contacts with some of the other prominent artistes who at least for some time and in some respects 'went underground', and who were in frequent contact during the 1950s with Hrabal and particularly with Jan Zábrana, Jiří Kolář (whose work they knew at least to some extent according to various testimonies), and Kolář's artistic and human double Josef Hiršal, who stated himself that e.g. he got to know Bondy's translations of Morgenstern at Hrabal's maybe in 1952, but perhaps as late as 1955, i.e. at a time when contacts between Bondy and Hrabal were again very limited.[14] Out of all the Půlnoc authors, Jana Krejcarová was the one who always led the most gregarious life, and she evidently had most contacts with people outside the isolated circles of post-avant-gardistes, even though she evidently came across for the most part as the rather extravagant albeit charmingly eloquent and forthright daughter of Milena Jesenská and Jaromír Krejcar, not as an 'underground' writer, which is indirectly indicated by her alleged apprehension following the 'publication' of her prose work *Clarissa* in 1951.[15] A more remote awareness of

---

13 The conspicuous similarity between some of Karel Marysko's poetic work and some of Egon Bondy's is pointed out in a study by MACHOVEC, Martin. 'Literární dílo Karla Maryska' [The Literary Work of Karel Marysko], *Revolver Revue*, No. 34, 1997. Egon Bondy confirmed to the author of this study in a personal conversation that he met Marysko at Hrabal's home in Libeň.

14 HIRŠAL in MORGENSTERN, Christian. *Bim bam bum.* Praha: Československý spisovatel, 1971 and in MORGENSTERN, Christian. *Morgenstern v Čechách. 21 proslulých básní ve 179 českých překladech 36 autorů* [Morgenstern in Bohemia. 21 famous poems in 179 Czech translations of 36 authors]. Praha: Vida vida, 1996; HIRŠAL, Josef - GRÖGEROVÁ, Bohumila. *Let let* [Flight of Years]. Praha: Rozmluvy, 1993.

15 VODSEĎÁLEK in KREJCAROVÁ, *Clarissa a jiné texty* - see Footnote 2.

the Půlnoc authors' activities can be attributed to several more quite prominent writers who found themselves to be in more or less similar straitened circumstances in the early 1950s, e.g. Oldřich Wenzl, Zbyněk Havlíček, Ludvík Kundera (as testified e.g. by correspondence between Kundera and Zdeněk Wagner[16]), Vratislav Effenberger, Jaroslav Rotbauer[17], Jan Bouše and Libor Fára. Until their premature deaths, Záviš Kalandra and Karel Teige were also allegedly in contact with Bondy at least, although hard evidence is thin on the ground, and for the most part we can only rely on memories and indirect testimonies.[18] Clearly, as soon as the Půlnoc series was established, i.e. late 1950 / early 1951, its creators kept their activities hidden for obvious reasons, even from some of their former friends, from whom they had in any case gradually become artistically estranged one way or another.

The Půlnoc series is primarily the offspring of its two initiators, so that again in retrospect it is possible to gain the somewhat erroneous

---

16 Extracts from the correspondence of Zdeněk Wagner (1923-1991), a former participant in the *Židovská jména* anthology who became a veterinarian, were printed in TYPLT, J. Filip. 'Fascinantně divý muž Zdeněk Wagner' [The Fascinatingly Wild Man Zdeněk Wagner], *Host*, No. 5, 2000. An extract from a letter dated 3rd January 1949, entitled 'Slovo o pluku Fišerově' [A Word on Fišer's Regiment], testifies to the fact that at that time Fišer (E. Bondy) made a considerable impression upon Wagner (even if evidently a somewhat ambiguous one); though what is also rather conspicuous is that Wagner does not make the slightest mention of the *Židovská jména* project, which was to come to a head just as this letter was being written. Wagner's complete work (including quoted correspondence) was published in book form: WAGNER, Zdeněk. *Virgule*. Praha: Cherm, 2007.

17 EFFENBERGER, Vratislav. *Moderní kultura v socialistické revoluci* [Modern Culture in a Socialist Revolution] (manuscript from 1965, whose existence is testified in TYPLT, 'Dvě svědectví o Židovských jménech'- see footnote No. 1). To J. Rotbauer, see also DOČEKAL, 'Smršťovače - hořké dávky' - footnote No. 11.

18 See BONDY, *Prvních deset let* - footnote No. 1; [HERDA, Milan]. *Protokolární výpověď o trockistech* [Protocol testimony on Trotskyites]. (Czech Interior Ministry Archive, shelf No. 305-738-1 - Trotskyite surrealists. Testimonies to the police and Gestapo on Trotskyites. Trotskyite leaflets), section in *Jarmark umění (Bulletin Společnosti Karla Teiga)*, No. 11/12, 1996; [HERDA, Milan]. 'Protokolární výpověď M. H.' [M. H. Protocol testimony], in *Alternativní kultura. Příběh české společnosti 1945-1989* [Alternative Culture. The Story of Czech Society 1945-1989], J. ALAN (ed.). Praha: NLN, 2001, p. 523.

impression that its primary contents were mainly meant to be Bondy's and Vodseďálek's 'totally realistic', 'embarrassing', 'anti-poetic', 'de-tabooing', 'neo-Dadaist', often specifically political, or 'witness' reactions to some surrealist practices, which as has become evident with the passage of time, already had its precedent in the somewhat similar reactions of some members of Group 42 and the Ra Group (in any case Bondy undoubtedly found an affinity with Hrabal and Boudník due to this similarity). What is more likely is that this (partly illustrated) typescript series was originally meant to serve more as a platform for **creative dialogue** with parallel unofficial artistic trends, and even more probably as a platform for attempts to continue this dialogue even under the extraordinary and absurd conditions of the day. Evidence of these efforts includes the 'guest' appearances made by Hrabal, Boudník, Born and Jelínek. In 1950 it was still undoubtedly unclear where the artistic paths of these two – Bondy and Vodseďálek – were taking them and which of the other Půlnoc authors would produce works of lasting value that might compete with them one way or another, and in particular, in which political and social circumstances the work of all those involved might develop further. Back then in 1950 everything was bogged down by doubts and uncertainties that were surely much greater than those which twenty years later dogged Bondy and Vodseďálek's 'underground' successors, who were thrust into a situation that was otherwise quite similar. The fact that the creators of the series saw the early 1950s as some kind of stop-gap situation whose duration could only be guessed at is confirmed by Vodseďálek's statement[19] that the usual Půlnoc edition, represented generally by four typed copies (1 + 3), was primarily intended to **conserve** the texts that had been written, i.e. to preserve them until they could be published, which of course was ultimately to be four decades later, and the question arises as to whether just an intimation of this fact would not have entirely undermined the creativity

---

19 VODSEĎÁLEK – MAZAL, 'S Ivo Vodseďálkem o letech radostného budování 49-53'– see Footnote 1.

of writers who were around twenty years of age. The similarities between the early 1950s and the early 1970s were considerable for debuting artists and writers, e.g. the loss of the option to publish freely and the imposition of political repression, which had its precedent in the 1970s, when it was possible to look back and seek examples.

Hence while **in retrospect** it is evident (from an art history or literary history standpoint) that the most prominent 'core' authors in the 'Midnight circle' were Bondy and Vodseďálek, while Hrabal and Boudník remained on its 'periphery', this did not yet necessarily appear to be the case around 1950. There is no doubt that much was expected from Jana Krejcarová, whose literary work has only come down to us in fragments, though the reputation of her output is enhanced by the legend of her life.[20]

What might the **objective** of the Půlnoc series creators have been? Probably first and foremost to continue to address other non-conformists and modernists (hence in 1950 this could only take place 'underground') and to enter into debate with them. They undoubtedly wished to create a fitting and a true reflection of the times in which they lived, and not to succumb to the enormous pressure of mass psychosis and the general mythologization of reality, but rather to unmask the imposed myths with particular mockery, and thus somehow to actually 'disarm' them. They also wanted to maintain the continuity of modern art and modern literature (to be specific, at the time this meant the continuity of artistic work, which was still understood as avant-garde, i.e. inventive, pioneering and innovative). They

---

20   This is borne out not only by the Austrian documentary film by director Nadja Seelich made in 1992 *Sie sass im Glashaus und warf mit Steinen* [She was sitting in a glasshouse throwing stones], on Krejcarová's life, but also by a monograph which Krejcarová (Černá) herself wrote on her own mother: Černá, Jana. *Adresát Milena Jesenská* [Addressee Milena Jesenská]. Praha: Klub Mladé poezie, 1969 (1st edition); Praha: Concordia, 1991 (2nd edition); Praha: Torst, 2014 (3rd edition). There are also numerous testimonies stating that the poet also used this text to project her own twists and turns in life onto her mother's fate (e.g. Vodseďálek, *Felixír života* – footnote No. 1). Also see Bondy, *Prvních deset let* – Footnote 1.

might have also wanted a confrontation in which they could stand up for their particular articulated artistic credo and their own distinctive standpoint, but these efforts only succeeded to some degree: echoes of Bondy's work (but almost to no extent that of Vodseďálek) can be found in many works by Hrabal, to some extent Boudník, as well as to a limited extent e.g. in Medek, Hynek and Marysko. Only Bondy's poetic work, and of course his later prose and philosophical work, exercised a profound influence on the younger generations of underground authors some twenty years later, even though this was all rather spontaneous and had little to do with the Půlnoc authors' original aspirations. Hence Bondy's and Vodseďálek's attempt of some kind in the early 1950s to make their texts at least part of a substitute literary scene can be said for the most part to have been unsuccessful, as such a 'practice' only emerged to a very limited extent even within the Půlnoc series itself, and today it is clear that some of their publication activities between 1950 and 1955 were primarily rather **individual matters** of a 'piratical' nature which the other Půlnoc authors did not necessarily know about (as was the case for the compilation of the *Židovská jména* collection around 1948/1949: Not all of these authors were informed about being involved in this 'business'). Hence fear of prosecution clearly played a greater role here than the organizers cared to admit.

In the given circumstances, they could rule out any idea of accomplishing Bondy's subsequent objective, as testified by Vodseďálek[21], of making the Půlnoc authors into an artistic group which (doubtless on the model of the various surrealist groups!) would be highly homogeneous and would strive (as in the case, at least for some time, of André Breton's group) not only to achieve a 'revolutionary change in human consciousness', but also for a material 'revolutionary change throughout the world'. However, it is also evident that the mere declaration and articulation of such an immodest ambition could have been conceived by Bondy in the early 1950s as an inspiring and

---

21   See Vodseďálek, *Felixír života.* (op. cit.).

stimulating necessity. In any case a number of other 'immodest' aims and ambitions showed up in his subsequent life and work.

The **reactions at the time** of the Půlnoc authors' artistic fellow travellers were generally speaking, insofar as they can be followed at all, rather restrained.[22] We might well include those of Boudník, who indeed maintained an aesthetic distance from Bondy and Vodseďálek – more in the graphic arts than in literature – but less with regard to 'world view': his explosionism did not in the least lag behind Bondy's maximalist postulates in its radicalism, and his artistic work and lifestyle were viewed even by those artistically close to him with some distrust if not disdain. The most prominent **fellow-traveller** of the Půlnoc authors was undoubtedly Bohumil Hrabal, who was also the only one to always have a full understanding of, and high appreciation for, Bondy's work. However, he was certainly not one of them, as his age, education and life experience alone inspired respect and kept him at a certain distance. It is doubtless little exaggeration to conclude that artists like Medek, Fára, Havlíček, Wenzl, Effenberger (and ultimately, Born and Jelínek too, who were still Applied Arts College students in the early 1950s) were above all apprehensive about Bondy's political explicitness and so rather sought to distance themselves from the Půlnoc 'core'. This might also have been caused by nothing more than a simple distaste for Bondy's and Krejcarová's (not to mention Boudník's) extravagant, eccentric behaviour and minimum social adjustment, which could appear quite dangerous in the early 1950s.[23] Bondy's ostentatious leftish and 'revolutionary' tendencies[24] could also have been off-putting, while for many Bondy's

---

22 HAVLÍČEK, Zbyněk - PRUSÍKOVÁ, Eva. *Dopisy Evě / Dopisy Zbyňkovi* [Letters to Eve / Letters to Zbyněk]. Praha: Torst - Levret, 2003. See also MEDEK, *Texty* and DOČEKAL, 'Smršťovače - hořké dávky' - Footnote 11 and EFFENBERGER in TYPLT, 'Dvě svědectví o Židovských jménech'- Footnote 1.

23 [HERDA], Protokolární výpověď M. H., 2001 - Footnote 18.

24 For example, the graphic artist Vladimír Šmerda, who associated with the young Zbyněk Fišer 1947-1948 recalls how at that time Z. F. repeatedly assured a number of friends that after the victorious socialist revolution they would 'hang them in their own interest': whether he was serious, half-serious or only joking

and Vodseďálek's 'desertion' of 'high' art was incomprehensible. The question remains as to whether the primary objections and aversions involved in their disassociation with them were of a purely personal nature (and this applies not just to Bondy, but above all to Krejcarová, whose 'spontaneous animalism' simply frightened many of her contemporaries and friends, as a number of testimonies bear witness), or mainly aesthetic, artistic or relating to their world-view. Here we are compelled to remain in the realm of speculation, as we cannot ascertain to what extent the later testimonies of the participants are influenced by their view of that period through the prism of later events. In any case the Půlnoc group had fallen apart by 1955,[25] and communications between its former participants were irregular and occasional in the following years, as they all went their separate ways.

It is no exaggeration to say that the Půlnoc series and the literary works published in it have become a tale, a pseudo-fiction and a legend, which is occasionally perpetuated, no doubt deliberately and consciously, by Bohumil Hrabal in his works published during the 1960s, but whose original creator is no doubt Egon Bondy: let us recall his cycle *Legendy* [Legends] from the collection *Für Bondys unbekannte Geliebte*.[26] Several contemporaries testify to his numerous statements from the 1960s in 'as the poet Bondy spake' mode. (Bondy's 'split' into 'I' and 'he', which is well-represented as an autostylization throughout his lifelong work, was repossessed in masterly fashion by Hrabal in his *Něžný barbar*, 1973[27], which is actually a kind of legend of a legend.)

---

it was clear that such arguments were not necessarily to everybody's taste (from a personal conversation between the author and V. Š. in spring 2000).

25   BONDY, *Prvních deset let* - footnote No. 1; VODSEĎÁLEK – MAZAL, 'S Ivo Vodseďálkem o letech radostného budování 49-53' - Footnote 1.

26   BONDY, Egon. *Básnické spisy I.* [Collected Poetic Works I], Praha: Argo, 2014.

27   It is to come out in English under the title *The Tender Barbarian* by Archipelago Books - see their website https://archipelagobooks.org/book/the-tender-barbarian/ , visited 26th January 2017. (Edit. note)

As regards the State Security's familiarity with Bondy's and Vodseďálek's activities, the only material that is so far publicly available at the Interior Ministry archive relates mostly to the 1948–1949 period, i.e. **before** the Půlnoc series was launched. There is an undated testimony from Milan Herda, imprisoned in the 1950s, evidently from the period between 1952 and 1954, which indicates two things: although the testifier attempted to rather trivialize the artistic (and indeed the political) activities of Bondy (always called Fišer in the report), Vodseďálek and Krejcarová (Fischlová), to portray them as grandiose mystifications, or as ordinary economic crime (especially in comparison with the 'seriousness' of the activities of Karel Teige, to whom the entire testimony relates), although he provides facts which could definitely have been of some use to State Security.[28] (For example, he mentions the plan – subsequently accomplished – to smuggle Czech glass to Vienna.) Hence it can be assumed that if the State Security had wanted, they could have monitored the Půlnoc organizers' activities from an early stage.[29]

Public reactions to the activities of one of the first and most original *underground* artistic groupings were in general practically zero until the late 1960s: the Půlnoc works from the 1950s were not published and the activities of the initiators are only a 'legend'. (One exception is Boudník's **artistic** work, but that is only rather indirectly related to the Půlnoc authors' literary activities, running in parallel to them.)

So again it is only some exaggeration to say that if **Bondy's** poetic work had not been discovered in the late 1960s by director Radim

---

28 [HERDA], Protokolární výpověď o trockistech – footnote No. 18. Another part of this testimony, this time dealing directly with the Fišer-Bondy circle and friends, was printed in the Documentation section in ALAN, *Alternativní kultura* op. cit, pp. 523-527. See also BONDY, *Prvních deset let*.
29 Research over the last few years has confirmed that throughout the 1950s State Security monitored the activities of people connected to Půlnoc, not just because of their literary work, but also due to their political, i.e. anti-Soviet attitudes, which were considered 'Trotskyist'. See the 'Surrealists' file No. 11135 from the Czech Security Services Archive.

Vašinka,[30] literary critic Jan Lopatka and in the early 1970s art historian Ivan Martin Jirous, the 'Půlnoc underground' would only have
lived on as Bondyian and Hrabalian legend until 1989, if not to this
day. It is only the fact that the *underground* artists enthusiastically
seized upon Bondy's poetry and began to put it to music and so to
spread it among a public that was of a very different character, education and social origin that allows the *underground* Půlnoc circle to be
understood in retrospect as a kind of prelude to the greatly differentiated 'underground activities' of the 1970s and 1980s. Without this
capitalization the Půlnoc circle would have remained a mere episode
in the history of the Czech unofficial cultural scene, as was unfortunately the case with so many small groups and individuals, e.g. the
'Libeň psychics' and the various regional activities. The public (albeit
narrow and limited) only started to be aware of the importance of
the Půlnoc authors' artistic and literary activities, indeed only those
of Egon Bondy and perhaps also of Jana Krejcarová, in the late sixties
and the early seventies, i.e. only many years later as the importance of
the role played by this little group in the creation of the later Czech
underground movement became evident.

The circle around the Půlnoc series can in any case be considered
to be one of the most prominent examples of underground artistic
activities in the 1950s. The main reason is that the group did not carry
on its previous **public** activities underground, as in the case of the
great majority of other unofficial activities performed by individual
artists, who after February 1948 were merely trying to **continue** il-
legally, i.e. underground, what they had been able to do legally up
until that time, but they were now actually 'making their debut' in
the underground. Hence for the public it was now 'dead', 'inexistent' and indeed 'underground' in the true sense. Moreover the Půlnoc initiators made their underground debut with artistic works that

---

30 VAŠINKA, Radim. 'Vydolováno z nepaměti I.-V.' [Retrieved from Time Out
of Mind I-V], *Divadelní noviny*, No. 5-9, 2001, Vol. X.; VAŠINKA, Radim. 'Bondy
a Orfeus' [Bondy and Orpheus], in *Bouda Bondy. Projekt Bouda IV.* [Czech
National Theatre Summer Stage]. Praha: Národní divadlo, 2007.

were for the most part so innovative that it would be difficult to find anything similar even in published literature before February 1948 (hence they were not weighed down by any concerns at all regarding censorship or the 'acceptability of the work', which any **publishing** author would have had to deal with to a greater or lesser extent). These were works which often very specifically, drastically, veristically and realistically portrayed the times in which they were written, i.e. the Stalinist pandemonium of the early 1950s in Czechoslovakia: ergo **they could not have been written in any other way outside the underground**, in a form which a couple of decades later was first called **samizdat** on the Anti-Soviet model.

Sixty-Eight Publishers in Contact with Domestic Samizdat and Competition in Exile

Alena Přibáňová – Michal Přibáň

It has become customary to say that at least in the seventies and eighties Czech literature developed along three lines: 'official', samizdat and exile. Although the use of these three terms might well help some to clarify the situation, it is generally well known that things were not as simple as that, and all three streams came together and permeated one another in various ways. As regards samizdat and exile publication, although they were never directly linked organizationally, there were undoubtedly dozens of cases where work by a domestic author came out in exile or transcriptions of books by authors in exile were distributed in samizdat form. We accept this fact these days as a matter of course.

In the following notes, however, we would like to point out that the paths which led to what we now take for granted as history were actually very complicated. Although Czech publishers in exile had appeared from the very end of the 1940s, collaboration with domestic authors did not take place until the mid-1970s. During the 1950s, a period of long prison sentences and capital punishment, only anonymous and pseudonymous poetry found its way into exile: a collection of anonymous prison poetry entitled *Přadénko z drátů* [Skein of

Wires], and a work of poetry by Antonín Bartušek entitled *Atomový věk* [Atom Age], which was published in magazines and just recently as a book in exile, naturally under a pseudonym, are not only the most famous, but in practice also the only cases when a work by an author living at home was published at the time in exile with his knowledge.[1]

Twenty years later the situation was different. Husák's normalization did not just exclude individuals from literature, but dozens of authors who had been the face of Czech literature in the 1960s. Most of them were at the peak of their creative powers, and many of them, we now know, still had their best work ahead of them. A substantial part of the artistic elite at that time remained captive behind the Iron Curtain in Czechoslovakia, dependent upon slow-motion samizdat circulation, which was truly 'small-scale' despite the dedication of those involved, the task being willingly taken on by the publishers in exile to help readers acquire this suppressed literature. Although financial gain was not usually the primary objective of their activities, it cannot be denied that even in the case of non-profit organizations some economic benefit was an essential condition for development, or even just for bare survival. Hence it comes as no surprise that competitive disputes arose among publishers in exile from time to time, mostly involving the publication of books by authors living in Czechoslovakia.

Both of the most important publishers in exile during the 1970s, i.e. Adolf Müller's and Bedřich Utitz's Index, which was launched in autumn 1971, and Sixty-Eight Publishers run by Zdena Salivarová and Josef Škvorecký, who were preparing their first book at the same time, made great efforts to establish, maintain and develop contacts with them, while both enterprises were able to reassume their contacts from the recent past: the Index founders had a number of friends among historians, politologists and journalists living in Czechoslovakia (many leads were opened up by collaboration with Jiří Pelikán, the

---

1 K. VOLKOVÁ (ed.). *Přadénko z drátů*. Praha: Libri prohibiti - Gallery, 2010; A. D. MARTIN [=BARTUŠEK, Antonín]. *Atomový věk*. Stockholm: Česká kulturní rada v zahraničí, 1956.

publisher of the *Listy* magazine in Rome, who successfully built up a network of Prague correspondents), while the Škvoreckýs were able to depend from the outset on their long-term personal friendship with popular novelists. However, things were not that simple.

For example, Škvorecký's closest friend, writer and translator Jan Zábrana, who remained in Prague after 1968, was explicitly enthusiastic about the idea of a free publisher in exile, but he considered the invitation to supply manuscripts from home, which was passed on to him by Romance specialist Jitka Křesálková, legally active in Italy, as almost insane:

> '*Your request has not yet come up for consideration, maybe later. Now I have decided (…) to carry on living here, I have to keep playing it the way we have played it together these last fifteen years we have known each other, otherwise it just will not work.*'

Zábrana wrote to Škvorecký in a letter dated 7th October 1971.

> '*Showing my cards now will mean ending up like thousands of others building the Metro or the Prague sewerage system, my wife will lose her job and my child will not get into school when the time comes. You know all that very well – you lived in all that for years. I understand very well that the ozone de la liberté is very heady and that you can cast off all your needless and truly senseless worries, but so far nothing can be done (…). Thank you for the offer. Just thinking about the possibility is so marvellous that my head spins, but currently it is just not on. (…) Here the situation is developing in quite a different way to that of the 1950s. Only a couple of people have been locked up and not for any long stretches, but then in all other respects it is far more hopeless, insomuch as it is total, slow, deliberate strangulation and suffocation, like a python squeezing you, tighter and tighter until you breathe your last.*'[2]

---

2 ŠKVORECKÝ, Josef – ZÁBRANA, Jan. *Jak je ve větě člověk. Dopisy Josefa Škvoreckého a Jana Zábrany* [How One Is in the Sentence. Letters of J. Škvorecký and J. Zábrana]. Vol. 39, Correspondence, Part 3. Praha: Books and Cards, 2010, pp. 146–147.

In response to Zábrana's letter, Škvorecký sent word that he was not compelling anybody and that he just wanted it to be known at home that the option of publishing freely was open even to domestic authors.[3] In actual fact, however, he had a very detailed knowledge of which manuscripts could be available at the time. He knew of new prose works by Ivan Klíma and Alexandr Kliment, he knew that the entire print-run of Hrabal's *Poupata* [Burgeons] had been destroyed, he knew of the manuscript of the novel *Kuře na rožni* [Chicken[4] on Roaster] by Jiří Šotola (which was then published by Petlice series and soon after, surprisingly, by the official Československý spisovatel publishers), he knew of Zábrana's translation of Pasternak's *Doctor Zhivago* (which practically everybody in Prague also knew about, so that not even a pseudonymous publication came into consideration).[5] The manuscript of Vaculík's *Morčata* [The Guinea Pigs, 1974] actually found its way to Toronto before Sixty-Eight Publishers was established. In a letter to Jitka Křesálková, Škvorecký noted with regard to this work:

> 'We have the manuscript of Vaculík's Morčata here, but Utitz in Cologne says that Vaculík promised it to them (they had established the Index series). It strikes me as embarrassing to argue over manuscripts by an author who is taking an awful risk if he gives any permission at all. But if you know Vaculík at all then do please tell him about our enterprise and of course I would be happy if he chose us.'[6]

Hence the actual preparations for the establishment of Index and Sixty-Eight Publishers did not pass off without minor disputes and misunderstandings, and not just involving Vaculík's prose works. The Index founders, evidently not guessing the Škvoreckýs' plans,

---

3 Ibid, p. 155.
4 Kuře (Chicken) is the name of the main character.
5 HRABAL, Bohumil. *Poupata*. Praha: Mladá fronta, 1970 – almost the entire print-run was destroyed. ŠOTOLA, Jiří. *Kuře na rožni*, Praha: Československý spisovatel, 1976. PASTERNAK, Boris. *Doktor Živago*. Praha: Lidové nakladatelství, 1990.
6 See ŠKVORECKÝ – ZÁBRANA, *Jak je ve větě člověk*, op. cit., p. 145.

paradoxically wanted their series to start off with Škvorecký's novel *Tankový prapor* [The Republic of Whores, 1994], which was also being prepared at the same time by the Toronto publisher as his first volume. Apparently with the best intentions in mind they even sent the author in Toronto a finished cover design without any prior agreement! At the same time the Škvoreckýs clarified Index's legal form, the anticipated method to be used for distributing the publications and in particular the ways to build up reliable financial support.[7] This was not meant to merely involve the results of publishing activity, but also subsidies from the funds of hitherto unnamed sponsors and foundations. Here we need to understand one of the reasons why the Škvoreckýs rejected the offer of close collaboration or even a merger of the two enterprises. If it was not clear who was sponsoring the activity then there was no guarantee of absolute independence, which was Škvorecký's primary concern. They had no reason to delegate their business idea to anybody else. The Index plans anticipated that the two spouses would make their own decisions over the new series, i.e. just the two of them out of many. Perhaps the only cogent reason to merge the two companies might have been their fears of the consequences of dissipating their energies. Whereas the Index founders' conception of publishing activity was based on the unwritten motto 'strength in unity in exile' (and the experience of writers from the 1948 emigration wave seemed to prove them right), the Škvoreckýs preached that strength came from variety. Moreover, Škvorecký was not familiar with the idea that the programme of a single publisher in exile was to be entrusted to former members of the Communist Party. In an interview for the Edmonton *Telegram*, Adolf Müller and Bedřich Utitz subsequently admitted that *'in one sense it might even be a good thing that there is more than one publisher, even though it wastes effort*

---

7 V. Prečan (ed.). 'Ke spolupráci dvou posrpnových exilových nakladatelství. Korespondence z let 1971–1987 s dodatky z roku 1996' [On Collaboration between the Two Post-1968 Publishers in Exile. Correspondence from 1971–1987 with Appendixes from 1996], in *Ročenka Československého dokumentačního střediska 2003*. Praha: Československé dokumentační středisko, 2004, pp. 66–70.

and complicates marketing,[8] while at the same time they asked for the individual enterprises to differentiate themselves in a more obvious and original way. This should come as no surprise, as original Czech prose work, primarily written in exile from the outset was the most attractive element in the publishing schedule of both Index and Sixty-Eight Publishers. And although both publishers eventually did distinguish themselves sufficiently, with Index focusing more on politological literature and Sixty-Eight Publishers more on memoir literature, their publishing plans stayed based on new Czech prose works. At the same time it should be pointed out that no other publishers in exile came to any prominence in this field until the establishment of Rozmluvy in London in 1982.

Vaculík's *Morčata* did eventually come out in Toronto and not in Cologne, but this did not happen until August 1977, i.e. a full six years after Josef Škvorecký mentioned that he had the manuscript available in the letter quoted above, as the publication of authors living in Czechoslovakia involved political and legal risks to which the émigré publishers did not want to expose themselves or their authors. People at the time just could not yet imagine the ways in which the Communist regime was able to punish them. And even if they possibly could – the very first title at Index was the book *Jelení brod* [Deer Ford] by a journalist living in Czechoslovakia called Jiří Hochman. Shortly after its publication the author was arrested and held in custody for six months from 31st January 1972. Although the publication of *Jelení brod* was not the immediate reason, one of several justifications was Hochman's participation in the group that was sending articles to Pelikán's journal *Listy*.[9] The next book by a domestic author – a study by František Šamalík *Československý problém* [Czechoslovak Problem] – came

---

8   MÜLLER, Adolf – UTITZ, Bedřich (Prepared by K. NEŠVERA). 'Hovoří Index' [Index Speaks], *Telegram*, No. 2, 1973.

9   CUHRA, Jaroslav. *Trestní represe odpůrců režimu v letech 1969–1972* [Penal Repression of the Regime's Opponents, 1969–1972]. Praha: Ústav pro soudobé dějiny AV ČR, 1997, p. 64.

out in Index under a pseudonym.[10] With due circumspection, Škvorecký announced in his first catalogue of offers: '*a novel by a well-known Czech writer from Prague (…)*', who '*has not yet decided whether to risk it*'[11] (this was probably the aforementioned *Morčata*), and the forthcoming publication of Pecka's *Štěpení* [Cleavage] was announced in 1974 without any mention of the author's name, under an invented title, with a deliberately incorrect author's residence and even a rather fanciful résumé of the novel's plot.[12] However, Karel Pecka found the courage and became the first of the Toronto publisher's authors to add his work to the samizdat and exile mainstreams of Czech literature.[13] He was followed by Václav Černý, Jaromír Hořec, Ludvík Vaculík, Václav Havel and others, while Index published novels by Mojmír Klánský, Eva Kantůrková and several collections of feuilletons. Interestingly, the Toronto and Cologne publishers first brought together the work of domestic authors in special series (in Toronto the 'open Padlock series', and 'Stories from the Drawers' in Index), but soon this came to be an automatic part of their output, and so it was pointless to distinguish it from the other titles.[14]

However, other authors were very slow to make up their minds to take the bold step taken by Karel Pecka and a few others. And because open communication across the western Czechoslovak border was by no means easy there were frequent misunderstandings. One of these involved *Morový sloup* [The Plague Column, 1979], a collection by Jaroslav Seifert, the first samizdat transcriptions of which were distributed from 1972. Index published it in 1977 to the great dissatisfaction of

---

10   Antonín OSTRÝ [=ŠAMALÍK, František]. *Československý problém* [Czechoslovak Problem]. Köln: Index, 1972.

11   [Z. SALIVAROVÁ – J. ŠKVORECKÝ] (eds.). *Nakladatelství 68 Toronto*. [Toronto, Sixty-Eight Publishers. Publication catalogue]. Toronto: Sixty-Eight Publishers [1971], p. 20.

12   [SALIVAROVÁ, Zdena – ŠKVORECKÝ, Josef]. 'Milí čtenáři…' [Dear readers…], in *Jak to bylo*, L. PACHMAN (ed.). Toronto: Sixty-Eight Publishers, 1974, p. 388.

13   PECKA, Karel. *Štěpení*. Toronto: Sixty-Eight Publishers, September 1974.

14   Cf. ZACH, Aleš. *Kniha a český exil 1949-1990* [Book and Czech Exile 1949-1990]. Praha: Torst, 1995.

Josef Škvorecký, who also had access to the manuscript, as well as the author's consent to publication, albeit posthumous (as Škvorecký was informed from Prague that Seifert did not yet wish for publication in exile due to fears that he and his family would be persecuted).[15] However, unlike the manuscript, this message did not reach Index, so that when later new books by Pavel Kohout (who still lived in Czechoslovakia at that time) and Ivan Klíma were under consideration by Index, Josef Škvorecký basically objected on legal grounds.

Why legal grounds? Publishing works in exile by authors still living at home without their consent and awareness was more or less common in magazine publications. In book publications, however, international copyright conventions might be breached and publishers in exile were afraid they might face legitimate lawsuits. Moreover, by exerting various forms of pressure the Czechoslovak authorities were able to make the authors of the published manuscripts themselves file lawsuits against publishers in exile, so there was a need to find ways to eliminate this danger. From the outset Škvorecký wanted to deal directly with the official Dilia agency, which held a monopoly at the time over representation of Czech writers, although his argument that '*after all we are a properly registered Canadian company*' did not cut any ice with the normalization regime. However, in the aforementioned letter to Jitka Křesálková, Škvorecký also wrote: '*It would be best if the authors sold the rights to a Western publisher, who could then sell them on to us.*'[16]

And this way forward proved feasible almost immediately. The first to take on the role of mediator was Jürgen Braunschweiger at the Swiss Bucher publishers, who as Ivan Klíma recalls, was recruited to the cause by Pavel Kohout.[17]

The first contracts that Braunschweiger signed with several authors were paradoxically actually mediated by Dilia as their official

---

15 Seifert's collection *Morový sloup* was also published soon afterwards in Prague (by Československý spisovatel, 1981).

16 See ŠKVORECKÝ – ZÁBRANA, *Jak je ve větě člověk*, op. cit., p. 145.

17 KLÍMA, Ivan. *Moje šílené století II*. [My Crazy Century II]. Praha: Academia, 2010, pp. 125–126.

representative. However, for subsequent books the role of literary agent was de facto taken over by Braunschweiger himself, whose employee then granted Czech-language publishing rights e.g. to the Toronto publishers. The same role was later played by other publishers and editors, who published translations of other works by authors living in Czechoslovakia.

However, this was just one of the possible methods involved. Another was the direct agreement of the author, although few were willing to provide it. Hence publishers had to place their trust in various communications, whose reliability and durability were often in doubt.

The conditions were basically quite unnatural and a number of books were brought out by émigré publishers that were indeed to a large extent 'without the awareness and the agreement of the author'. Hence readers in exile, but no longer those at home, who came into possession of exile books in roundabout ways were certainly not upset at the publishers. Besides, it is very likely that in more than one case the samizdat authors themselves gave several publishers their consent to publication from a distance, because it was all the same to them whether their work was published in Canada or Western Germany, and they did not understand the relations between émigré publishers. A very telling example of this is a letter sent by Pavel Kohout to Josef Škvorecký on 7th November 1978, i.e. at a time when he was legally living abroad (before the Czechoslovak authorities stopped him from going back home):

'...we really do not understand what seems to us from a distance to be a competitive struggle that belongs to a different age. Even friends ask me why we do not come to an agreement between ourselves and above all, why the two groups don't join forces for advertising and trade, why they don't advertise for each other or even make attractive titles into a prestige-quality co-production series.'[18]

---

18   See PREČAN, 'Ke spolupráci dvou posrpnových exilových nakladatelství', op. cit., pp. 93-94.

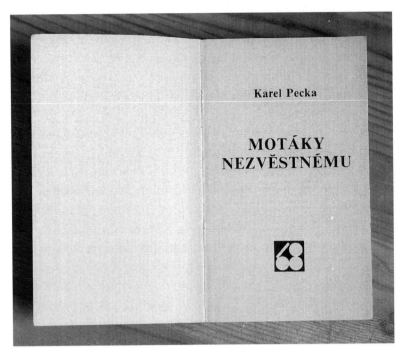

Karel Pecka

MOTÁKY
NEZVĚSTNÉMU

Front-page of Sixty-Eight Publishers' book by Karel Pecka

Škvorecký replied to Kohout and so in a roundabout way to his Prague colleagues with a detailed exposition of all previous competitive disputes. Kohout responded as expected: he had his next novel – *Katyně* [Executrix] – published by Index, and the one after that – *Nápady svaté Kláry* [The Ideas of St. Clara] – by the Škvoreckýs. And a co-production did happen: in 1981 Index and Sixty-Eight jointly published Seifert's memoirs *Všecky krásy světa* [All the Beauties of the World].

Likewise Toronto and Cologne eventually shared Bohumil Hrabal's work, even though his first samizdat titles were published exclusively by Index without any publishing details. In this unusual way he made it easier to smuggle books by a partially tolerated author to Czechoslovakia, while avoiding certain legal difficulties. The fact that Hrabal was missing from among the Toronto publisher's authors was not taken well by Škvorecký. However, the Index head office was geographically more convenient, as it was basically easier to get to from Prague, so Hrabal was published in Cologne, even though his rights were negotiated in the West by translator Susanne Roth, who was willing to assign them to Škvorecký, but not to Index.[19] However, Sixty-Eight Publishers did not take advantage of this until 1987 in connection with Hrabal's book of memoirs *Proluky* [Gaps, 2011] – and as it turned out the book was brought out at the same time both by Index (without publishing details) and in Toronto (with publishing details).

Although there were many partial and total misunderstandings between those at home and in exile, it cannot be said that either side failed to make an effort to understand the other. This is demonstrated by the circumstances behind one of the unrealized plans of the Škvoreckýs' publishing house in the late 1980s. After Jan Zábrana died in September 1984, Sixty-Eight Publishers showed interest in publishing any of his works, even though they knew well that in Czechoslovakia Zábrana was only a partly tolerated author, so they even adapted their publishing plans to those of the official Prague publishers. Regarding the possible publication of Zábrana's poetry collection *Stránky z deníku* [Pages of the Diary], Škvorecký wrote a letter to Lubomír Dorůžka in Prague in September 1988:

'...I would be very pleased to publish this book. But if they are going to publish Jan's collection of translations in Prague then there is a chance they would also publish Stránky z deníku. No way would I want to spoil that by publishing it ourselves.'[20]

In order to be able to analyse in detail the relations between authors at home and publishers in exile, we should not limit ourselves to just

19   Ibid. p 115.
20   ŠKVORECKÝ, Josef - DORŮŽKA, Lubomír. *Na shledanou v lepších časech. Dopisy Josefa Škvoreckého a Lubomíra Dorůžky z doby marnosti* [Letters of J. Škvorecký and L. Dorůžka from Times of Vanity]. Praha: Books and Cards, 2011.

these publishers and so few problematic titles, and in addition to the questions raised so far, we should also deal with other no less interesting ones (e.g. the question of textual faithfulness and the textological standard of books whose authors could not take part in editing for publication). However, for now we have only wanted to at least outline the issue, which is still paid so little attention even more than twenty years after the Velvet Revolution.

Parallel Circulation as a Consequence of Censorship

Petr Šámal

The almost total exclusion of many active writers from official (i.e. from the standpoint of regulations then in effect, legal) literary communication in Czechoslovakia, which was usually accompanied by persecution in the workplace, had a powerful impact on all literary activity. The traditional media of modern book culture, which had been continuously developing over many decades, were now completely closed off over a short period of time, not just to individuals, but to hundreds of active authors; the samizdat-compiled *Slovník českých spisovatelů* [Dictionary of Czech Writers] included entries for around four hundred authors affected to varying degrees by prohibitions.[1]

BOOKS IN A PARALLEL SPACE

Works duplicated and distributed in parallel literary circulation moved around beyond all the 'dispersed censorship system'[2]

---

1 Cf. BRABEC, Jiří – GRUŠA, Jiří – HÁJEK, Igor – KABEŠ, Petr – LOPATKA, Jan. *Slovník českých spisovatelů. Pokus o rekonstrukci dějin české literatury 1948-1979* [Dictionary of Czech Writers: An Attempt to Reconstruct the History of Czech Literature, 1948-1979]. Toronto: Sixty-Eight Publishers, 1982; first official publication in Czechoslovakia under the name *Slovník zakázaných autorů 1948-1980* [Dictionary of Prohibited Authors, 1948-1980]. Praha: Státní pedagogické nakladatelství, 1991.
2 We use the term 'dispersed censorship system' to describe the complex system of supervision over literary communication that existed in Czechoslovakia

channels, while personal contacts and social networks again increased in importance, even though compared with the 1950s substantially more people took part in the exchange of secretly duplicated and distributed texts.

The pattern for Czech literary samizdat was set by Ivan Klíma's readings that took place at his apartment from autumn 1970. Jiří Gruša described the meetings, attended by at least thirty odd people, as a return to the tradition of the literary salon.[3] Those taking part in the readings, centring around former high-profile figures at *Literární noviny*, whose manuscripts had been repeatedly sent back by publishers since 1969, came up with the idea of transcribing the texts and distributing them in several copies. In 1973, the first volume was brought out by the largest samizdat 'publisher', later called Edice Petlice (the Padlock series – the name alluded to the Klíč [Key] series brought out by the Československý spisovatel publishers), a novella by Ludvík Vaculík entitled *Morčata* [Guinea Pigs, 1974]. This was not the first ever samizdat project, which is normally presumed to be the Texty přátel [Friends' Texts series] from Olomouc, but it is the Petlice model of samizdat that is most frequently followed. In subsequent

---

throughout the existence of the Communist dictatorship. The main features of this censorship system were both its multilevel nature and the constant interconnection of its planning, management and control processes. This supervision system comprised approval at party level (Communist Party Central Committee), government level (Ministry of Culture) and company level (individual publishers). As for the publication of fiction, the decisions of a selective professional organization, e.g. the Union of Czechoslovak Writers, were sometimes influential. Between 1953 and 1968 there was also an office specializing in preliminary censorship (*Hlavní správa tiskového dohledu* – Central Press Supervision Office); its function was basically that of monitoring, i.e. checking to prevent the potential failure of other elements within the dispersed censorship system.

3 GRUŠA, Jiří. *Umění stárnout. Rozhovor s Daliborem Dobiášem* [The Art of Growing Old. Interview with D. Dobiáš]. Praha – Litomyšl: Paseka, 2004, p. 152, this practice is summarized by Jonathan BOLTON in *Worlds of Dissent. Charter 77, The Plastic People of the Universe and Czech Culture under Communism.* Cambridge (MA) – London: Harvard University Press, 2012, pp. 72–114.

years, other intellectuals who had been deprived of the opportunity to officially publish proceeded in a similar manner.[4]

Apart from transcribing works on a typewriter, it was difficult at that time to find any other ways to duplicate works, as in the early 1970s state authorities undertook several measures aimed at restoring supervision of duplication equipment. On 14th July 1971 the Czech Industry Minister brought out a regulation on the establishment of printing and duplicating centres and the compulsory recording of printing machines (Act 67/1971 Coll.), under which all printing and duplicating centres had to re-acquire approval for subsequent operation while having to also maintain systematic records of orders and designate all their output.[5] Likewise, State Security attempted to maintain supervision of where samizdat copies originated. As a central register of typewriters was not feasible in view of their widespread distribution, they at least tried to compile records of confiscated samizdat documents based on the typewriters on which they were written.[6] As time went by, supervision of duplication machines relaxed. For example, although mimeograph stencils were recorded

---

4   The nature of samizdat literary output is summarized in articles by Tomáš VRBA and Jiří GRUNTORÁD in *Alternativní kultura. Příběh české společnosti 1945-1989* [Alternative Culture: The Story of Czech Society 1945-1989], J. ALAN (ed.). Praha: NLN, 2001, pp. 265-305, 493-507. (Both edited texts make up part of this publication.) A more recent attempt to categorize samizdat publications, taking account of their motivation and forms of distribution is offered by Martin MACHOVEC: 'The Types and Functions of Samizdat Publications in Czechoslovakia, 1948-1989', *Poetics Today*, No. 1, Spring 2009, Vol. XXX, pp. 1-26. There is also a summary of the key literature on the subject. The risks involved in samizdat activities are described in detail by Gabriela ROMANOVÁ, based on the example of a single project: *Příběh Edice Expedice* [The Story of Expedice Series]. Praha: Knihovna Václava Havla, 2014.

5   Regulation of the Minister of Industry of the Czech Socialist Republic on the establishment of printing and duplicating centres and compulsory records for printing machines <http://www.epravo.cz/vyhledavani-aspi/?Id=31923&Section=1&IdPara=1&ParaC=2>, accessed 17th September 2014. This regulation superseded older regulations from 1958.

6   Cf. PLACÁK, Petr. 'StB a 'protizákonné písemnosti' v osmdesátých letech' [State Security and 'Illegal Literature' in the 1980s], *Securitas imperii*, No. 1, 1994, pp. 32-59; also more recently ROMANOVÁ, *Příběh Edice Expedice*, op. cit., p. 50.

at companies that owned mimeographs (known as cyclostyles), they were freely on sale in shops.[7] A different situation arose in the mid-1980s, when some samizdat operators even had modern copying machines as their disposal, either secretly brought in from abroad or available to them at one of the state enterprises (e.g. the xerox at the Czechoslovak State Bank), or even the first personal computers.[8]

While officially published books circulated in print runs of tens or hundreds of thousands of copies, the circulation of publications brought out beyond the supervision of the censorship systems was very varied and ranged between several dozen and several thousand readers, depending on the type of publication. Readership availability of samizdat publications substantially varied over time and in connection with the type and size of the community whose members were determined by the individual titles. For example, Tomáš Vrba distinguishes the extent of readership on the basis of various distribution networks – Charter 77, underground, Musicians Union Jazz Section, Eurocommunists, various religious communities and the like.[9] Whereas in the early 1970s dozens or occasionally hundreds of recipients had access to samizdat, during the 1980s as the technical means for publishing activities developed, several thousand readers are presumed in the case of a few publications, and tens of thousands are referred to in the case of the xeroxed *Lidové noviny* [The People's Newspaper].[10] The state publication monopoly was also disturbed by

---

7   Cf. the explanatory note in Švestka, Jaroslav. *Orwellův rok* [Orwell's Year], K. Volková - J. Gruntorád -D. Havránek (eds.). Praha: Libri prohibiti, 2013, p. 6.
8   Cf. Suk, Jiří. 'Podrobná zpráva o paralelní polis. Nad korespondencí Václava Havla a Františka Janoucha' [A Detailed Report on the Parallel Polis. On the Correspondence between Václav Havel and František Janouch], in Havel, Václav - Janouch, František. *Korespondence 1978-2001.* Praha: Akropolis, 2007, pp. 9-29.
9   Vrba, Tomáš. 'Nezávislé písemnictví a svobodné myšlení v letech 1970-1989' [Independent Literature and Freedom of Thought, 1970-1989], in Alan, *Alternativní kultura*, op. cit. pp. 295-297. The edited text makes up part of this publication.
10   Jiří Gruša estimates the approximate number of samizdat title readers (taking transcriptions into account) at several hundred - Gruša, Jiří. *Cenzura*

the presence of Czech books smuggled in from abroad; the usual print run at the 'large' publishers in exile, Sixty-Eight Publishers and Index, ranged around one to two thousand copies (usually fewer for poetry).

Participants in samizdat activities created parallel literary institutions, and sometimes even attempted to uphold the quality and formal standards of book culture. Within the context of literary samizdat, the Petlice series played a similar role to that of the state publishers Československý spisovatel, the main publisher of Czech (and Slovak) fiction. Ludvík Vaculík endeavoured to make sure that all the 'prominent authors' who could not do so officially elsewhere published there; he stated that the aim of Petlice was to escape the negative effects of literary censorship, to smash through the silence, *to preserve manuscripts and secure or duplicate their existence*.[11] A parallel communication space was created during the mid-1970s for a particular circle of writers who were of importance to Czech literature as a whole. This space operated so comprehensively that it provided authors with important feedback.

The endeavours of some samizdat publishers to operate like standard publishers reflected growing demands for manuscripts to be edited. Some series even offered a particular form of readership procedure and an editorial board that took part in selecting manuscripts (Expedice operated in this way after Daňa Horáková went into exile)[12], Ludvík Vaculík mentions that it was his ambition for publication of any particular manuscript to be supported by two or three people; a prominent example of the aesthetically induced

a literární život mimo masmédia [Censorship and Literary Life beyond the Mass Media]. Praha - Scheinfeld-Schwarzenberg: Ústav pro soudobé dějiny ČSAV – Československé dokumentační středisko nez. literatury, 1992, pp. 23-24. The edited text makes up part of this publication. In the case of bestsellers (e.g. texts by Bohumil Hrabal) the estimates range around several thousand readers.

11   ČERVENKA, Miroslav. 'Dvě poznámky k samizdatu' [Two Notes on Samizdat], *Kritický sborník*, No. 4, 1985, Vol. V, pp. 1-12, reprinted in *Kritický sborník 1981-1989. Výbor ze samizdatových ročníků* [Critical Review. Samizdat Anthology Selection], K. PALEK (ed.). Praha: Triáda, 2009, pp. 21-29. The edited text makes up part of this publication.

12   See ROMANOVÁ, *Příběh Edice Expedice*, op. cit., pp. 23-30.

rejection of a work can be found in the fortunes of *Medvědí román /
Urmedvěd* [A Bear's Novel / Ur-Bear] by Jiří Kratochvil.

[...]

If along with Tomáš Glanc and other authors[13] we look at samizdat as
a specific medium through which a new pre-Gutenberg culture had
broken into the communication sphere, then other effects of literary
communication within a parallel space also emerge.[14] This change of
medium is inseparably associated with the fact that the various forms
of contact with the world of samizdat (authorship, duplication, distribution and ownership) were linked to a risk of criminalization. This
state of permanent threat increased the symbolic value of participation in parallel communication circulation and at the same time (at
least in some circles) it increased the cogency of ethical criteria: '*one
key value that acquired the form of an ethical commitment was a feeling of inner
justification, and responsibility towards oneself as a creator and towards one's
work (...). Ethics was transferred to the ground of aesthetics, and aesthetics
came to be the ground for ethical positions.*'[15] Hence the censorship situation ascribed a particular type of significance to texts; the following
recollection makes this clear:

> '*One of the few advantages of samizdat literature consisted in the fact that
> the reader and publisher in one person acquired what was literally a physical
> relationship to the book. Hence George Orwell's* 1984 *will always be associ-
> ated with the Consul typewriter on which my then girlfriend and subsequent
> wife transcribed the text in the 1980s and the woody smell of the cheap paper
> and blotches from the poor-quality copying ink. In these days of iPads and*

---

13 SKILLING, H. Gordon. 'Samizdat: A Return to the Pre-Gutenberg Era?', *Cross
Currents*, No.1, 1982, pp. 64–80, especially pp. 69–70.
14 GLANC, Tomáš. 'Samizdat jako médium' [Samizdat as a Medium], *Souvislosti*,
No. 3, 2013, Vol. XXIV, pp. 183–193. The edited text makes up part of this
publication.
15 ALAN, *Alternativní kultura*, op. cit., p.45.

instant online connection, with omnipotent information, books and other artefacts hung up in "clouds", all this looks like technological prehistory.'[16]

On the other hand, works that had been through the approval procedures at official institutions might be perceived negatively by readers: *'In a state like the one that we live in, the very fact that books have been through censorship and can then be published is sufficient for people not to be tempted to take an interest in them, and the very fact that films have been through censorship and can be made is enough to totally reassure people that they can't be any good.'*[17]

Some of the parallel cultural activities, particularly on the underground circuit, refused any collaboration with official cultural institutions on principle; Ivan M. Jirous formulated it clearly in his keynote text: *'the first culture does not want us, and we do not want to have anything to do with the first culture.'*[18] Moves away from parallel circulation towards official institutions were often attacked, as can be seen in some of the reactions to Jiří Šotola's and Miroslav Holub's self-criticisms.[19] Their return to publication was perceived as an attempt made by the state authorities to disrupt the internal cohesion of the community of prohibited authors. The most contradictory response was evoked by Bohumil Hrabal's interview in the *Tvorba* [Creation] magazine,[20] after which he was permitted to publish some of his work in censored

---

16 PŘIBÁŇ, Jiří. 'Meze politiky. Jak a proč číst George Orwella po samizdatu' [The Boundaries of Politics: Reading George Orwell after Samizdat – How and Why], *Právo* 12th February 2015, *Salon* supplement, pp. 3, 5.

17 ZÁBRANA, Jan. *Celý život 1.* [Throughout Life]. Praha: Torst, 1992, p. 287, the entry is dated 6th January – 17th February 1974.

18 JIROUS, Ivan M. 'Zpráva o třetím českém hudebním obrození' [Report on the Third Czech Musical Revival], in *Magorův zápisník* [Magor's Notebook], M. ŠPIRIT (ed.). Praha: Torst, 1997, pp. 171-202.

19 Cf. Selected responses in these books of interviews: LEDERER, Jiří. *České rozhovory* [Czech Interviews]. Köln: Index, 1979; HVÍŽĎALA, Karel. *České rozhovory ve světě* [Czech Interviews Worldwide]. Köln: Index, 1981.

20 'Rozhovor s Bohumilem Hrabalem' [Interview with Bohumil Hrabal], *Tvorba*, No. 2, 1975, *Literatura – umění – kritika* supplement, No. 1, p. viii; this interview came out in an unauthorized editorial form.

form. The underground circuit rejected the widely recognized author, and the public burning of several of his books came to symbolically express this decision. The short prose work in which Ivan M. Jirous described this event testifies to the aforementioned symbolic value of participation in the parallel space, enhancing the literary value of work that was created there:

[...]

'*Eugen Brikcius and I had decided on the burning five days previously. There was nothing else for it after Hrabal's interview in* Tvorba. *If he were some insignificant prick it would never have occurred to us. (...) What Hrabal did was totally unforgivable. He had shat himself in his dotage just as people were starting to transcribe and lend out his books themselves. Had he not understood that secret fame is the highest fame? That a book transcribed on crummy carbon paper is of greater importance than his two turds in ornate covers that had been published in print since then? Hrabal paid a bloody price for that.*'[21]

The act of book-burning, harking back deliberately to the inquisitorial tradition and church censorship, can also be understood as a specific response to the situation of exclusion: as a defence against repression the group isolates itself from those around it and makes sure that the (unwritten) rules confirming its identity are respected.

[...]

PUBLICATION CONDITIONS ABROAD

Publishing a book in Czech or translated into a foreign language at one of the publishers in exile was practically the only way for banned

---

21 Jirous, Ivan M. 'Autodafé', manuscript anthology *Ladislavu Dvořákovi k 1. prosinci 1980* [To Ladislav Dvořák on 1st December 1980], reprinted in *Revolver Revue*, No. 41, 1999, Vol. XV, pp. 223-225.

authors living in the Czechoslovak Socialist Republic to see their work in the form of a standard book, i.e. in a medium that had been taken for granted by them up until that time. For established writers a ban on publication was also a substantial existential threat, as literary or journalistic activities were often their chief source of income. In these circumstances it was natural for publication opportunities abroad to increase in importance.

From the early 1970s Czechoslovak state authorities had attempted to restrict contacts between writers and foreign publishers located beyond the reach of the dispersed censorship system. They took advantage of the fact that under Section 20 of the Copyright Act of 1965, foreign publishing agreements had to be mediated for Czechoslovak citizens by the Dilia Theatre and Literary Agency. The fact that its Director from mid-1971 was Karel Boušek, who was largely responsible for the reintroduction of the dispersed censorship system (running the important Book Culture Department at the Ministry of Culture in 1970 and 1971), shows that the control and regulation of the publication of Czech authors abroad was ascribed great importance. After he was made the head of Dilia, Boušek ordered that contacts with those Western publishers that were bringing out politically undesirable works by Czechoslovak authors should be curtailed, and he temporarily suspended the payment of foreign royalties for 'typical right-wing representatives' (e.g. Pavel Kohout, Ludvík Vaculík, Ivan Klíma and others).[22]

During 1972 the state authorities sought other ways to penalize authors and cut them off from the foreign income that gave them partial or total financial independence from the state. Hence at the urging of the Dilia agency, the Ministry of Finance adopted a secret regulation introducing basic tax penalties on the payment of royalties for

---

22   Letter dated 27th December 1971 quoted from R. SCHOVÁNEK (ed.).
Svazek Dialog. StB versus Pavel Kohout. Dokumenty StB z operativních svazků Dialog a Kopa [Dialogue file: State Security versus Pavel Kohout. State Security Documents from the *Dialog* and *Kopa* Operational Files]. Praha - Litomyšl: Paseka, 2006, p. 15.

works which the state authorities deemed to have *'anti-state or anti-socialist content, and for works by authors whose distribution has been halted in Czechoslovakia.'*[23] Out of all the writers who were targeted by the regulation, it was primarily Pavel Kohout, whose plays were regularly produced abroad and who had a valid (i.e. confirmed by the previous Dilia administration) contract with the Swiss publisher Bucher to be represented abroad, who took an active role. In 1973 and 1974 Kohout took Dilia to court over the discriminatory nature of the new tax regulations, as the deductions from royalties in 1973 increased by 40%, although the Ministry of Culture issued a private 'inside report' ['intimát'] granting an exclusion from payment of this tax for all (!) writers except the aforementioned category, i.e. those whose works had been banned from distribution in Czechoslovakia. Although the dramatist's litigation did not succeed, the state authorities had to deem his income legal, thanks to the aforementioned contract on representation abroad. Jürgen Braunschweiger, a Bucher publishing house staff member and a great supporter of persecuted Czech writers, whose accommodating approach played a considerable role in the conclusion of the contract, also managed to sign contracts with six other authors (Jiří Gruša, Alexandr Kliment, Eda Kriseová, Jiří Šotola, Ludvík Vaculík and Ivan Klíma) before the change of administration at Dilia,[24] thanks to which they at least became economically independent to some extent from the Czechoslovak state, and it was in this circle of authors that one of the key institutions of literary samizdat was born – the aforementioned Petlice series. To enable the authors who did not collaborate with Dilia (a circle that expanded over time) to avoid discriminatory rules, royalties were paid for works brought out without Dilia mediation in cash that was smuggled into Czechoslovakia either by the publishers themselves, or by their trusted intermediaries (in cases where the publisher himself was barred from entering Czechoslovakia,

---

23   Cf. ibid, p. 17.
24   KLÍMA, Ivan. *Moje šílené století II.* [My Crazy Century]. Praha: Academia, 2010, p. 125.

e.g. Eric Spiess, who is very much to be credited for productions of dramas by Czech authors abroad).[25]

Hence prohibited authors were not entirely deprived of opportunities to publish translations of their work abroad, but the limited contacts prevented them from communicating more intensively with their publishers or translators. Ivan Klíma recalled that when the German translation of his novella *Malomocní* [Lepers] and three of his other stories were being published by the Swiss publishers Reich, without his knowledge four prose works were combined, the chief protagonists were given the same name – Matthias Leopold – and the entire book came out under a title and a genre subtitle that explicitly emphasized it was a single work: *Machtspiele: Roman* [Power Plays: A Novel].[26] In this case the alterations were brought about by the publishers' endeavour to accommodate Western readers' demand for 'novels'. Readers' interest in more extensive prose works, which Jürgen Braunschweiger repeatedly pointed out to Klíma, was increased by hopes of filming the novels and the subsequent profits. This standpoint involving the specific expectations of the public abroad did actually have an influence on Klíma's decision to attempt a truly extensive prose work – he began work on a large novel *Soudce z milosti* [Judge on Trial], original title *Stojí, stojí šibenička* [There Stands a Little Gallows]. However, not even this testimony of a generation avoided unauthorized interference by the publishers. After the completed typescript was smuggled across the border, the author received a request to '*shorten it by at least a third and ideally by a half (...), they do want novels but not big fat sagas like that*'.[27] So eventually Klíma reduced the text by a hundred pages, and at the next stage the publisher did likewise without the author's knowledge as in the previous case.[28]

---

25   Ibid, p. 126.
26   Ibid. p. 130; KLÍMA, Ivan. *Machtspiele: Roman*, translated by Alexandra and Gerhard BAUMRUCKER, Luzern: Reich, 1977.
27   KLÍMA, *Moje šílené století II.*, op. cit., pp. 207-208.
28   KLÍMA, Ivan - ČERMÁK, Miloš. *Lásky a řemesla Ivana Klímy* [The Loves and Trades of Ivan Klíma]. Praha: Academia, 1995, p. 90; KLÍMA, Ivan. *Der Gnadenrichter*,

These shifts were brought about by the endeavour to adapt work not only to anticipated good taste, but also to the experience of the new public and the differing cultural and literary traditions, which the publishers would sometimes attempt to reflect, along with current political events. Some Czech authors perceived such behaviour as a manifestation of censorship not dissimilar to that which they came up against when publishing their works in Czechoslovakia. Back in 1969 Milan Kundera published an open letter in the *Times Literary Supplement*, taking exception to extensive omissions in, as well as the abridgement and rewriting of, reflective passages in the English translation of *Žert* [The Joke], where the publishers changed around the order of individual chapters and even left out one of the subchapters.[29] Kundera's text drew parallels between the mentalities of a '*London bookseller*' and Soviet art overseers: '*The depth of their contempt for art is just as incomprehensible.*'[30] This topic of (alienated) authorship later came to be a leitmotiv running through Kundera's novels and his thought, as the writer himself expended considerable effort reviewing books just published in translation. These commercial and in particular ideological standpoints may have affected foreign productions and stagings of dramas by Czech authors, which in some cases clashed with the explicit instructions that they had given.

Legal regulations on the publication of translations were also applied to other 'foreign' institutions of fundamental importance to Czech literature during the normalization period, namely periodicals and publishers in exile. Secret communication channels operated practically throughout the 1970s and 1980s, through which information and books moved back and forth between Czechoslovakia and

translated by Alexandra and Gerhard BAUMRUCKER. Luzern – Hamburg: Hoffmann und Campe, 1979.

29 KUNDERA, Milan. *The Joke*, translated by David HAMBLYN and Oliver STALLYBRASS. London: Macdonald, 1969.

30 KUNDERA, Milan. 'The Joke', *Times Literary Supplement*, No. 3531, 30th October 1969, p. 1259.

the outside world.[31] Here the ordinary postal services could not be relied upon, as a substantial number of consignments dispatched to the West were vetted by the Security Services[32] (and in any case, the internal correspondence of those individuals selected for the attentions of the secret police was subject to inspection).[33] The letter writers anticipated potential breaches of their mail privacy, so they often encoded the communications in their ordinary mail, and often assumed false identities or asked third parties to mediate.[34]

Secret communication channels were not used exclusively for the transfer of literary works abroad, but fiction made up a significant proportion of smuggled texts. The links that were in operation from around 1970 have been described in particular detail. On the Czech side a key role was played from the outset by historian Petr Pithart; he collected texts reflecting current political circumstances and arranged for them to be transferred to partners in exile, specifically Jan Kavan and Ivan Hartl, who had established the Palach Press news agency. They subsequently conveyed news and, for example, samizdat publications and manuscripts to publishers and periodicals in exile, or they arranged for their translation and printing in Western media. The other mediators primarily included Jiří Pelikán and Pavel Tigrid, and after he left Czechoslovakia in 1976 Vilém Prečan, who systematically built up an archive of Czech samizdat literature in West

---

31 A summary of unofficial links is given by Roman TUREČEK: *Neoficiální informační kanály mezi Československem a Západem v období 1969-1989 se zaměřením na tzv. kurýrní cestu* [Unofficial Information Channels between Czechoslovakia and the West between 1969 and 1989, with the Focus on the Courier Route], thesis. Brno: Masarykova Univerzita, Philosophical Faculty, 2010.
32 Regarding the vetting of correspondence cf. POVOLNÝ, Daniel. *Operativní technika v rukou StB* [Operative Technology in the Hands of State Security]. Praha: Úřad dokumentace a vyšetřování zločinů komunismu [Office for the Documentation and Investigation of the Crimes of Communism], PČR [Czech Police], 2001.
33 Cf. SCHOVÁNEK, *Svazek Dialog*, pp. 44-75 - see footnote No. 22.
34 For numerous proofs cf. ŠKVORECKÝ, Josef - ZÁBRANA, Jan. *Jak je ve větě člověk. Dopisy Josefa Škvoreckého a Jana Zábrany* [How One Is in the Sentence. Letters of J. Škvorecký and J. Zábrana]. Praha: Books and Cards, 2010 Writings of Josef Škvorecký, Vol. 39, Correspondence, Part 3, p. 146.

Germany; his efforts resulted in the creation of the Czechoslovak Documentation Centre in 1986.

Literary works were also often exported across the borders by staff at the embassies (collaboration with Wolfgang Scheuer, a German embassy staff member, was of particular importance).[35] Sizeable manuscripts were smuggled out particularly on car trips abroad. Petr Pithart was followed by Jiřina Šiklová as the chief coordinator of this important link-up with those in exile; in addition to the regular movement of hundreds of kilograms of printed émigré work every month, equipment for their duplication was also being imported.[36]

The attitude of the state authorities towards collaboration with institutions in exile differed substantially under normalization from the situation in the period prior to that. When prose writer Jan Beneš published his short stories and journalism in *Svědectví* [Testimony] in the mid-1960s under a pseudonym, he was accused of state subversion and sentenced to five years in prison. At the beginning of the 1970s authors living in Czechoslovakia hid behind pseudonyms in émigré publications; in later years their contributions came out with the 'immunizing' note that the text was published without the knowledge and consent of the author. For example, Oldřich Mikulášek's poetry published in *Svědectví* in 1974 came along with the following note: *'The first part entitled "Metaphors", has the same name as the collection of poems that is currently circulating in Czechoslovakia as a samizdat. It is published here without the knowledge and consent of the author.'*[37]

Émigré books were understandably overshadowed by fears of suppression. When Josef Škvorecký and Zdena Salivarová set up their

---

35   Cf. V. Prečan – M. Uhde (eds.). *Ve službách společné věci / Im Dienst der gemeinsamen Sache* [In Service to a Common Cause]. *Wolfgang Scheur und Prag 1981-1989*. Brno: Atlantis, 2001.

36   The links between domestic opposition initiatives and those in exile are described in detail by Petr Orság in his dissertation work *Média československého exilu v letech 1948-1989 jako součást alternativní veřejné sféry* [Czechoslovak Exile Media 1948-1989 as Part of the Alternative Public Sphere]. Olomouc: Palacký University, Faculty of Philosophy, 2011.

37   *Svědectví*, No. 47, 1974, Vol. XII, p. 499.

own company in 1971 and asked close friends to pass on manuscripts, they initially received a decidedly negative response from home: '*Your request does not yet come into consideration. Perhaps later. If I ever decide (…) to carry on living here, I will have to carry on playing it the way we have played it together the last fifteen years we have known each other, because there's no other way.*'[38] The first one to publish under his own name abroad was Jiří Hochman, a journalist living in Czechoslovakia. In 1971 the Index publishers brought out his satirical prose work *Jelení brod* [Deer Ford]. However, other authors did not immediately follow Hochman's example, perhaps because soon after its publication the author was imprisoned for several months (not just because of his publication abroad, but also because he was involved in providing the émigré journal *Listy* [Sheets] with texts).[39] This habit was not broken until Karel Pecka's decision to smuggle his novel *Štěpení* [Cleaxage], (published in 1974) to Škvorecký. Although the publishers suggested that he should conceal his authorship he refused this offer. When the State Security were later interrogating him, he defended himself by saying he did not know how the work found its way abroad.[40] Pecka's example was slowly followed by other authors, who as a rule entered into an agreement with the publishers through the literary agent who represented them in negotiations over the translation.

Exile did not mean that the published version of a work was not influenced by other forms of social control. Demonstrable interventions, which as a rule had been authorized by the authors, frequently stemmed from economic causes. The publishers were dependent on

---

38   Jan Zábrana to Josef Škvorecký 7th October 1971, in ŠKVORECKÝ – ZÁBRANA, *Jak je ve větě člověk*, op. cit. p. 146.

39   The gradual movement of authors living in Czechoslovakia towards publishers in exile was described by Michal PŘIBÁŇ and Alena PŘIBÁŇOVÁ: 'I rapporti di Sixty-Eight Publishers con il samizdat cecoslovacco e la concorrenza con le altre case editrici dell'emigrazione' [Sixty-Eight Publishers in Contact with Domestic Samizdat and Competition in Exile], in *Il samizdat tra memoria e utopia*. *eSamizdat* 2010-2011, Vol. VIII, pp. 233-238; The edited text makes up part of this publication.

40   LUKEŠ, Jan. *Hry doopravdy* [Games for Real]. Praha – Litomyšl: Paseka, 1998, pp. 193-198.

the community of readers and endeavoured to keep them for themselves. One example of this might be Iva Pekárková's novel *Péra a perutě* [Truck Stop Rainbows, 1992], which was brought out in 1989 by Sixty-Eight Publishers. In view of the conservative character of some of his publishing house subscribers, Josef Škvorecký suggested that the author should leave out a large part of one of the chapters in which the chief protagonist's lesbian girlfriend appeared, revealing the bisexual orientation of both girls. The author did not return to the original version until the 1998 edition.[41] At a more general level, Jan Vladislav, who lived in France from 1981, identified this new experience with the commercial aspects of literary work:

> '*There are real difficulties publishing Czech books abroad: the only solution is to publish them for yourself using a computer and a decent printer. That is the solution that I have decided on... I duplicate a few copies, distribute them to whomever I want and that's that. After all, remember books used to come out in our country in print runs of just a few hundred. It's not just a problem among authors in exile. Poets at home are also suffering as a result, and I believe **self-service** of this kind is clearly one way to resist the commercialization that **everywhere** threatens to suffocate everything that is even slightly distinctive and that does not come under the category of goods in demand. In a word, it's all the same wherever you look. The means and the obstacles only vary from place to place.*'[42]

41   PEKÁRKOVÁ, Iva. *Péra a perutě*. Praha: Maťa, 1998, pp. 107–126.
42   J. VLADISLAV (ed.). 'Dialog přes hranice 1985-1990. Z korespondence Jindřicha Chalupeckého s Janem Vladislavem' [Dialogue Across Borders 1985-1990, From Correspondence between Jindřich Chalupecký and Jan Vladislav], in *Ročenka Československého dokumentačního střediska 2003*. Praha: Československé dokumentační středisko, 2004, pp. 9–52.

Post-Gutenberg Revolution?

On the Polish 'Second Circulation' and Czech Samizdat

Weronika Parfianowicz-Vertun

The authorities do not even guess how very much they stand accused by every new poetry book or prose work transcribed on a typewriter five hundred years after the invention of typography!
Pavel Kohout

During the mid-1970s, Polish and Czech independent culture found itself in a paradoxical situation. At the end of the 'Gutenberg era' and the beginning of the technological and media revolution, Central Europe was going back to the most traditional ways of producing texts. An obvious analogy with the period before the 'typographical revolution' was used both by samizdat authors and by their western commentators, e.g. Gordon H. Skilling in *Samizdat. A return to the pre-Gutenberg era?*[1] – primarily as a convenient and suggestive metaphor. Bearing in mind that a change in the medium of the written word leads to a recreation of communication systems, social processes, common mentality and ways of gathering and presenting research information, we have to raise a question over the way in which a return to a practice characteristic of a handwritten

---

1 SKILLING, H. Gordon. 'Samizdat. A return to the pre-Gutenberg era?', in *Cross Currents: A Yearbook of Central European Culture*, No. 1, L. MATĚJKA – B. STOLZ (eds.), Ann Arbor: Michigan Slavic Publications, 1982.

culture and the initial stages of print culture affected independent Polish and Czech culture as a whole.

PHENOMENOLOGY OF THE TYPEWRITER

The restriction on literary and communicational circulation imposed by the Communist regime resulted in an unprecedented boom in independent publishing initiatives. Everybody could become a writer, or a transcriber, publisher and printer. The trade could be learnt from experienced polygraphers or from such books as *Mały konspirator. Poradnik dla dorosłych i młodzieży* [The Little Conspirator – A Guide for Youngsters and Adults] or *SAMI luštíme ZDATně křížovky* [We Make Out Crosswords Alone].[2] This meant a return to traditional ways of passing down the craft in a 'master-apprentice' relationship, thus transforming a craftsman ethos into an ethos for intellectuals, so that the skill of (re)producing texts could be said to have become a practical applied discipline.

Remarkably, and fascinatingly from the anthropologist's perspective, there were numerous methods and devices used to produce underground magazines and books. What is characteristic is the creative and innovative approach to everyday utilitarian objects, which were used both to create and to duplicate texts (children's printing presses, photographic paper, mimeograph stencils and washing machine wringers), and for the transportation of illegal materials (e.g. prams, sleighs and shopping bags). Publishing activity got into private life, recreating the household space and everyday lives of the publishers and their families, establishing new habits, affecting their language and even their bodies.

It is also worth considering the specific ways in which texts were produced, which came to be emblematic of the 'samizdat era', i.e.

---

2 *Mały konspirator. Poradnik dla dorosłych i młodzieży*. Lublin: Informator Regionu Środkowo-Wschodniego NSZZ Solidarność, 1983. See supplement to *Nový Brak* magazine (samizdat), issue No. 10/1987.

typescript, and the phenomenology of the typewriter itself. The typewriter opens up a hermetic world of progressive typographical culture, affording access to the world of print by a side entrance, without the mediation of other people and institutions. Typescript is something between a 'quasi-book' and a manuscript, combining the vagaries, capriciousness and fallibility of the human hand with the serious and official nature of a mechanically produced text. Typescript needs to be examined together with the 'physical' dimension of its creation – the sound of tapping, the smell of the ink, the craftsmanship of the paper, the physical effort of writing, the visual untidiness of the corrected mistakes – all this affects its character. The personal relationship towards the typewriter, nostalgic memories of particular brands and transcription details are an important motif in most samizdat authors' memoirs. Typewriters even played an important role as part of most independent publishers' activities, not because they actually facilitated text duplication (as they were only limited to ten to twelve copies), but more due to the creation of new practices on the part of both authors and readers. Text transcription came to be an indication of the reader's active approach, the very act of transcribing came to be a specific type of reading. The number of transcribed copies reflected the reader's interests and these primarily involved popular literature, which inspired a real popular transcribing initiative.[3]

READING AS A PHYSICAL ACCOMPLISHMENT

The handwritten culture – as highlighted by Walter J. Ong in his book *The Technologizing of the Word*[4] – was more geared towards the producer, while print culture is geared towards the reader. The 'samizdat era' meant these two roles were combined, with all due consequences.

---

3   See also the essay 'Independent Literature and Freedom of Thought' by T. Vrba in this book. (Edit. note)
4   Ong, Walter J. *Orality and Literacy. The Technologizing of the Word.* London: Methuen, 1982. (In Czech *Technologizace slova.* Praha: Karolinum, 2006.)

Ong noted that *'Print encourages a sense of closure, a sense that what is found in a text has been finalized, has reached a state of completion. (...) Print involves many persons besides the author in the production of a work – publishers, literary agents, publishers' readers, copy editors and others.'*[5] In a situation where printing workshops were making a comeback, this closure was disrupted. The chain of mediators between the author and the finished text, both people and institutions, is shortened. The arbitrary division of functions is suspended, the author becomes a printer and the printer becomes an author.

The increased activities of amateur printers and their technical imprecision also had other consequences. Although Ong wrote that *'typographic control typically impresses more by its tidiness and inevitability: the lines perfectly regular, all justified on the right side, everything coming out even visually, and without the aid of the guidelines or ruled borders that often occur in manuscripts,'*[6] this certainly does not apply to samizdat.

A large number of texts produced by independent publishers are barely legible or even illegible. The letters are too small, as is the line spacing, the pages lack light, the copies are barely visible and the paper is almost transparent. Reading samizdat texts is time-consuming, physically demanding and exhausting work. For example, the literary scholar Miroslav Červenka complained about the endless torment involved in reading most samizdat works in the fourth issue of *Kritický sborník* in 1985.[7]

During the 1980s printing technologies gradually developed and the quality of production improved. By the end of the decade we can practically refer to professional publishers, particularly in Poland. However, the issue of the content of independent publications remained unresolvable. Debates over the quality of independent output raged from the very beginnings of underground publishing. After the initial enthusiasm for all displays of independent social activity,

---

5   Ibid., pp. 129 and 120.
6   Ibid., p. 120.
7   Červenka, Miroslav. 'Dvě poznámky k samizdatu' [Two Notes on Samizdat], *Kritický sborník*, No. 4, 1985. The edited text makes up part of this publication.

opinions emerged that opposition circles might be shutting themselves off in a ghetto, where the fact that a text had been printed by an independent publisher was enough for it to be applauded.

GRAPHOMANIACS AND THE LANGUAGE OF PRINTERS

In Poland, where the boundary between official and unofficial culture was much more unstable, and where censorship was not as strict as in Czechoslovakia, the issue of what the 'second circulation' was meant to serve apart from political purposes was urgently dealt with from a certain time. Authors commented that it had come to be a refuge for graphomaniacs, who found in it limitless space for their work, while journalists complained about magazines lacking any real debate in which every critical voice involving the opposition was gagged. Moreover, the distributors complained that these publications were difficult to sell, as people were now tired of reports about persecutions in the Soviet Union and would rather read something other than politics. Despite the large number of high-standard titles published as part of this 'second circulation' (e.g. Leszek Kołakowski, Tadeusz Konwicki and a number of world-famous writers and philosophers), however, critics point out that no important literary debut was ever made this way.

An affinity to independent culture was established more by writing (or creating) the relevant books rather than by reading them, as transcription turned out to be a special form of reading. In any case it is in keeping with the main principle of alternative culture and with active participation in the creation of cultural values, as well as the disappearance of the boundaries between professional and amateur art.

The samizdat era was one of those times when printing revealed its internal mechanisms. Over the century, books had gradually turned into a commercial product, and the recipient found the process of their production to be opaque, unimportant or inaccessible. The crisis in cultural circulation necessitated reflection over the actual process of creation, reproduction and distribution of texts and cultural assets in general, transforming the entire economics behind this circulation and compelling its participants to adopt an active position towards all these mechanisms. The creators became aware of the advantages of unofficial publishers, who were dependent neither on the government, nor on free market mechanisms. At the same time they intuitively grasped that technical developments would change western literary culture and that their experience might be very helpful in this context. It was also one of the times when print culture practice was so closely tied in with everyday life that terminology associated with printing technology penetrated colloquial language and transformed the language of independent groups into polygraphic jargon, while the actual process of text production became an important subject of conversation and not just in professional contexts. Independent publishing activity should also be seen in the context of alternative culture as a whole, with its shared principle of dialogue and its stress on amateur production.

Samizdat as a Medium

Tomáš Glanc

Whereas the set of texts that circulated as samizdat is not infinite, they cannot be based on a common denominator either, such as content, authorship, aesthetics, politics or even technology. So what do they have in common?

If we are going to look at the text not so much as the bearer of meaning, but more as a medium[1] distinguished by its specific materials, then samizdat is a subset of text to be understood in this manner, i.e. an independent medium, even if the techniques and media used in samizdat were highly varied, and the ways in which samizdat was brought out also turned out to include a broad range of techniques from handwriting, classic typewriting and various duplication and photo-reproduction techniques to unauthorized typography (which was particularly popular in Poland, where it was described by the fitting expression '*drugi obieg wydawniczy*'[2]).

Hence when we attempt to define samizdat we come up with hypotheses which do not have any absolute applicability, but which comprehend samizdat as a particular type of output not related to the opinions and standpoints of the distributors, and independent of the semantics of the particular works duplicated, distributed and read in this manner. So which characteristics are involved here?

---

1 DUCHASTEL, Philippe. 'Textual Display Techniques', in *The Technology of Text: Principles for Structuring, Designing, and Displaying Text*, D. Jonassen (ed.). Englewood Cliffs (NJ): Educational Technology Publications, 1982, p. 170.

2 As in Czechoslovakia, 'drugi obieg' was distinctive for the structure of its 'shadow' publishers, which basically did not exist even in a great samizdat power like the Soviet Union. See Nowa, Krąg, Przedświt, CDN, Oficyna Literacka inter alia.

Samizdat publications were not recorded in bibliographies of state book output, although even here problems arise, mainly in Czechoslovakia from the mid-1980s,[3] when we take into account publications such as the National Theatre Archive's internal mimeographed bulletin, which indeed came out under the heading of a state institution, but whose content, officially designated as 'for internal requirements', was not subject to ordinary approval procedures and was not registered as a publication. The field of institutional mimeographs and bulletins of this kind, whose number and range in Czechoslovakia increased during the latter half of the 1980s, has not yet been sufficiently researched, and has its counterpart in other countries, including cases where a type of samizdat was initiated by the state institutions themselves, which at the same time were combating 'authentic' samizdat – it was in this way that texts marked 'DSP' (dlya sluzhebnogo pol'zovaniya [for working requirements]) were published secretly for the needs of members of the Soviet politburo[4] or for the official representatives of the Orthodox Church. Hence, for example, Anatoli Zhigalov, who was active on the unofficial artistic scene and one of the founders of

---

3 In the Soviet Union at this time samizdat was on the one hand expanding its sphere of influence beyond the capital and becoming increasingly differentiated, while on the other hand it was also on the wane, because it was becoming increasingly easy to publish texts legally, including magazines, almanacs and books. The situation was different in Poland, where 'drugi obieg' basically constituted an alternative book market, whose output did not necessarily differ in its technology from that of state production, the difference only being in the absence of permission from state authorities. A sizable proportion of the population took part in this (estimates vary from around a hundred thousand to a quarter of a million people). SIEKIERSKI, Stanisław. 'Drugi obieg. Uwagi o przyczynach powstania i społecznych funkcjach' [Second Circulation. Deliberations on the Causes behind the Movement and the Social Functions], in *Pismiennictwo, systemy kontroli, obiegi alternatywne (Z dziejów kultury czytelniczej w Polsce)*, J. KOSTECKI – A. BRODZKA (eds.). Warszawa: Biblioteka Narodowa, 1992, p. 285 et seq.

4 BLJUM, Arlen. *Zakat Glavlita. Kak razrushalas' sistema sov. tsenzury: dokument. chronika 1985-1991* [How the Soviet censorship system was subverted. Documentation 1985-1991]. Moskva: Terra, 1995, p. 179.

the underground artistic group Tot-art during the 1970s, translated works by Rudolf Otto and James Hastings for the requirements of the Soviet Moscow Patriarchate. Although he had strict orders to give all copies to the client, he also managed to arrange for carbon copies, which went into circulation among his friends instead of among the highest church dignitaries as 'samizdats'.[5] The production, distribution and reception of texts that were not approved by the state press authority is not just a 'democratic' answer to the 'totalitarian' administration of public affairs. Doyen of Soviet samizdat Nikolai Aleinikov writes that samizdat formed its own autocracy,[6] even though there are no power-based or repressive bodies behind it, in contrast to the state apparatus. Decision-making and implementation powers over samizdat were 'usurped' by the individual or a relatively small group of individuals not subject to ordinary control mechanisms or to other rules and standards than those they had set for themselves. Subsequently, as Aleinikov stresses, samizdat held a power over the participants in the processes involved.

In particular the end of the classic era of samizdat allowed us to feel nostalgia for the disappearance of a field of communication that was distinctive not only for all its unfavourable aspects (e.g. the possibility of prosecution, the arduous labour involved in production, the frequent illegibility, limited distribution options and the restricted commercial opportunities for publication activities), but also for its indisputable advantages, the most notable of which included the unique collective intimacy of participating in a common interest, which generated various activities involving communities of individuals who were closely interconnected even at the physical level through the texts (even though they did not actually have to know each other personally). Typically, the first samizdat series

---

5   See the letter from Anatoli ZHIGALOV dated 22nd April 2009. Archiv Forschungsstelle Osteuropa an der Universität Bremen, Fond 217.
6   V. PARISI, (ed.). *Samizdat. Between Practices and Representations. Lecture Series at Open Society Archives. Budapest, February–June 2013.* Budapest: Central European University, Institute for Advanced Study, 2015, p. 7.

in Czechoslovakia, published in Moravia, was called Texty přátel [Friends' Texts].

Samizdat material in countries where samizdat attained systemic parameters (obviously including the Soviet Union and Czechoslovakia), was printed or transcribed materially and typographically in a different way to state sanctioned publications. In samizdat polls this finding kept repeating like a cliché, though without being taken into account, the phenomenon itself was difficult to identify: this type of production brought with it a newly incentivized pre-Gutenberg culture which broke into the field of communication.[7]

This archaicization of communications was highly reminiscent of certain features of book culture before the introduction and expansion of typography: production basically served a closed community of users, and books were not just intended for one-off reading, but for repeated usage and circulation. At this point a striking difference becomes evident: whereas in the pre-Gutenberg era the community usage of books in monastery reading rooms was associated with the expensive and sophisticated standard of their material workmanship, which centred around their durability, as typified by parchment, the opposite is usually the case for samizdat. Here a return to older technologies does not mean a return to expensive durability: if paper has been more inexpensive since the late medieval period than parchment made from the skins of new-born animals in the case of 'pergamum abortivum', and perhaps even from unborn animals (lambs),[8]

---

7 Skilling, H. Gordon. 'Samizdat: A Return to the Pre-Gutenberg Era?', in Cross Currents. A Yearbook of Central European Culture, L. Matějka, B. Stolz (eds.). Ann Arbor: Michigan Slavic Publications, 1982, pp. 64–80; Wilson, Paul. 'Living Intellects: An Introduction', in M. Goetz-Stankiewicz (ed.). Good-bye, Samizdat: Twenty Years of Czechoslovak Underground Writing. Evanston: Northwestern University Press, 1992, pp. 138; Komaromi, Ann. 'Samizdat as Extra-Gutenberg Phenomenon', Poetics Today, No. 29, 2008, pp. 629–667.

8 Doubt has been cast by recent research on this theory passed down over centuries: methods evidently existed to soften the skin, which led to the belief that animals in the womb were involved, see Keys, David. 'Secrets of medieval Europe's large-scale publishing industry revealed: Continent's craftsmen

which has gradually replaced it, the replacement of socialist book printing by typewriters, copying and carbon paper or mimeograph stencils did not mean a return to the beauty of manuscripts, which were (justifiably) expected to last thousands of years, but in view of readers' convenience, ease of production and durability, it actually meant development towards transient, makeshift production that was even cheaper and of worse quality than mass paper production by the state.

This return to pre-Gutenberg production after five hundred years actually radicalized the Gutenberg revolution in the sense that it was a move towards easily available cheap media. In view of the genealogy of (Soviet) samizdat as published by pioneer Nikolai Glazkov, we might even consider the metaphor of samizdat text as precoded toilet paper – a medium whose primary purpose makes it extremely ephemeral and valueless. From that standpoint it involves texts with maximum value distributed on waste materials on a medium used originally to wipe off ordure and flush it away (if one had a flushing toilet) or throw it away in the cesspit (see below regarding the birth of samizdat from toilet paper).

The context of Central European scriptorium values in samizdat became relevant again in two respects: each samizdat copy had an exceptional symbolic value in view of the risks associated with its production and distribution and in view of the small number of copies, while the lack of availability increased the value of each copy. The second analogy consists in the fact that in contrast to mass produced copies for one-off usage, these books were meant to be circulated and repeatedly 'used', even though the quality was not up to it, so that functionally the idea of the multifold circulation of books was revived.

Both of these aspects highlight the haptic aspect of samizdat books and texts, the uniqueness of the goods, which bear material

discovered a way of transforming animal skins into wafer-thin sheets for use in era's finest books', *Independent*, 23rd November 2015: http://www.independent. co.uk/news/science/archaeology/medieval-europes-first-large-scale-publishing-industry-revealed-a6745981.html (11th January 2016).

and corporeal traces of their unique production, just like the traces of individual readings and thus of individual readers, i.e. their personal 'imprints'. Although this applies to all books, in the case of samizdat manuscripts and typescripts at least, the situation is different because a specific physical activity and uniqueness is behind every copy, every page and every letter. The body behind the text or other record stands out in its vivid presence, which is succinctly conveyed by X-ray photographs used instead of gramophone records or tape recorder tapes. Hence in a certain sense samizdat exercises a claim made by some heretics who reject books and promote records on 'tablets of memory', i.e. direct physical and corporeal communication from bearers of the spiritual tradition, who pass it down from one generation to the next. That is how, for example, the Russian '*duchoborci*' used to operate.[9] Of course, those engaged in samizdat had various motivations, but what they had in common was intensified communication, in which an important role was played by the specific immediacy, corporeality and individual. Machine production of books is anonymous, and in contrast to manuscripts, uniform copies have no direct association with the author; they are only connected to him intellectually, through his authorship. In the case of samizdat, the author, or more frequently the transcriber, takes part in person in mediating the meaning, and her typewriter and its individual keystrokes can be retrospectively identified, which was routinely done by the state police, whose experts were able to associate each copy with a specific typewriter and thus identify the origin of the transcription and the individuals taking part in its production and distribution. The meaning of each text came to include the traces left behind on it by the 'workshop' in which it was produced and the readers, who were taken into account as an integral part of the meaning of the work. Hence a samizdat work is itself involved in the

---

9 GLANC, Tomáš. 'Ein Buch gegen die Schrift. Zhivotnia kniga' [One Book against the Letters], in *Mystifikation - Autorschaft - Original*, S. FRANK et al. (eds.). Tübingen: Gunter Narr Verlag, 2001, pp. 49–65.

creation of the community (of 'friends') that forms around it as it is produced and circulated.

A typical example of the interconnection between the body and a 'copy' of a samizdat work was known as 'music on the ribs' or 'music on bones'. This was a musical samizdat that started to thrive in Eastern Europe after the Second World War and ended some fifteen years later as a result of mass production of reel-to-reel tape recorders in the early 1960s. It was primarily thanks to this unofficial publishing activity that dance music, which was not brought out by the official Soviet publishers, became widespread, with used X-ray photographs utilized as media instead of gramophone records.[10] Recordings not only acquired the uniqueness of individually produced copies. That is also the case with samizdat. The transcribers' finger marks can be found or imagined on each copy, or ash marks from their cigarettes, underlinings, notes, bent corners, blots and other traces of individual readings.

X-ray photographs as a recording medium are even more radical in this respect: here the information is 'printed' directly onto the (image of) the patient's body. Supplies of photographs of people's innards acquired from hospitals and doctors' surgeries, or from hospital waste containers,[11] serve as a medium for recording dance and jazz music or the chansons of singers whose performances could not be attended by Soviet citizens, since the performers had emigrated abroad.

Emigration and repatriation after the end of the Second World War led to the presence of a considerable number of gramophone records of popular music in the Soviet Union, where the demand for them was infinitely larger than the supply, as they were unique

---

10   KRAVCHINSKI, Maksim. *Istoriya russkogo shansona* [History of Russian Chanson]. Moskva: Astrel', 2012, p. 254.

11   The clinics were allegedly glad to be rid of the onerous task of disposing of the X-ray photos that were gathering dust. See KRAVCHINSKI, *Istoriya russkogo shansona,* op. cit., p. 255.

copies brought home as very distinctive war trophies. At the same time Telefunken machines were being brought from Western Europe, which could be used in a relatively simple way to play gramophone records or to copy those records. As eyewitness Maksim Kravchinski described in his monograph, the unofficial production of gramophone records imitated or 'duplicated' official production – as in the case of text samizdat typologically in many respects it parasited on state publishers.[12] In 1946 the Zvukozapis' [Sound Record] company started operating on Nevsky Prospekt Boulevard, enabling Soviet citizens to record poems, songs, birthday greetings and the like for their nearest and dearest for a fee. The company's slogan was 'Letters in Sound'. Similar services also appeared in Moscow and several other Soviet cities. The recording was made on a special soft stencil from an existing recording or directly from the microphone.

At first, the recording machine itself was successfully copied – and then it started to be used to duplicate copies of recordings, most frequently of an entertaining nature (i.e. dance music), as well as chansons sung by authors who had emigrated, which were banned from public circulation, or jazz music, which was ideologically criticized in various forms in the Soviet Union. Production shifted from the public studio to the basement, where it started to serve alternative circles of customers.

Relations between the technologies and the message broadcast appear to differ between 'music on ribs' and typescript samizdat. In 'classic' samizdat the whole process is initiated by a work which the samizdat communicator cannot or will not publish or distribute through the only available state-guaranteed and controlled procedures and mechanisms. As a result of this unsatisfactory state, technologies are mobilized to achieve this result by alternative means, including, for example, the typewriter. In the case of 'music on ribs', the motivation is almost the opposite. The process is based on the acquisition of a copying machine, which has a capacity to motivate

---

12   Ibid, 8th Chapter, p. 253 ff.

publishing activity. In this case the machine and the media (X-ray photos) come to be crucial pivots of the entire operation, while the issue of what is actually duplicated becomes secondary, because anything can be recorded or reproduced. This subtle shift of emphasis throws important light upon samizdat output with production and distribution themselves at the centre of activities. Reports of some text or record being distributed in samizdat primarily impart specific information on this text and its inadmissibility from the standpoint of state reprographic networks and relevant editorial boards and other authorities responsible for deciding what is and is not to be published. However, as the case of recordings on X-ray photos highlights, the fact is that anything could be published and distributed in samizdat. This samizdat belongs to the history of media rather than to the history of literature or music.

Copies of recordings on X-ray photos highlight the economic or commercial aspect, which also existed in the case of paper samizdat, but remained in the shadow of the texts themselves and their distribution. In the case of 'music on ribs', sales and profit played a significant role from the outset, both for those who initiated the duplication, and later in court proceedings, at which some activists were sentenced to imprisonment, suspended or otherwise.[13] Whereas the typical image of a samizdat worker includes nights spent working at the typewriter and conspiratorial distribution in shopping bags, 'music on ribs' presents other associations: fabulous riches earned by producing illegal recordings. For example, two brothers of Greek parentage from the south Russian town of Gelendzhik in the North Caucasus on the shores of the Black Sea bought themselves a Mercedes in Leningrad from the proceeds of duplicating gramophone records.[14]

'Music on ribs' was not recorded for samizdat culture itself, but in the majority of cases it involved recordings made and brought out in the usual way either in Russia or (more frequently) elsewhere.

---

13   Up to three to five years in some cases, see ibid, p. 259.
14   This and similar cases are described by Kravchinski in his memoirs.

However, are books and recordings that were brought out sometime in the past at state-recognized publishers to be classified as samizdat, when they became analogous to samizdat in the way they were distributed and in their absence from public communications? Is there such a thing as 'secondary samizdat', i.e. books or other publications that might well have been brought out by state publishers, e.g. in the pre-Communist period or under the Communist regime at a stage when they were allowed to be published, but they were subsequently banned from public circulation, libraries and even catalogues, so in spite of the original publication, the work circulates 'as if' it were a samizdat? Opponents of the term 'secondary samizdat' will argue over the typological uniformity with all the other 'officially' published titles. The only difference in this case is the excommunication of the work from public circulation for a certain period of time. It is truly only the exclusion of the work from circulation that changes its status, in contrast to samizdat, which is book production sui generis in its very origins. However, if transcriptions of books published long ago or abroad are considered to be samizdat then why not also accord this status to those books, if their usage is the same as in the case of original samizdats? The dispute over such possibilities is a conflict between functional or realistic approaches and a nominalist standpoint.

Publication of 'secondary samizdat' correlates with some samizdat in terms of its timescale, i.e. first it was published and only then was it barred from circulation. Another example of this is books that were published for the first time as samizdats. A similar parallel with samizdat can be found in '*tamizdat*' [literally 'thereizdat'],[15] i.e. publications brought out legally in your own language but in another country where such publications can legally be produced. In addition

---

15   For details see KIND-KOVÁCS, Friederike – LABOV, Jessie. *Samizdat, Tamizdat, and Beyond: Transnational Media During and After Socialism*. New York – Oxford: Berghahn Books, 2013 – the value of this study lies inter alia in the fact that the issue of samizdat is not restricted to Eastern Europe, but offers a broader comparative perspective, including e.g. Asia.

to local usage, at least some of the print run as a rule is transported (smuggled) into the country where it could not be brought out. Tamizdat is a practice that has existed in various contexts (as a rule due to political, religious or moral restrictions) for centuries. In technical terms, this is unmarked book production that is functionally analogous to samizdat.

A subset of secondary samizdat publications is that of photocopies or other copies of books (previously) published, which also play the role of samizdat publications and are direct counterparts of music brought out on X-ray photos, the only difference being that photographic or other copying paper is not as specific as an X-ray record of a particular person's body parts.

It is the element of prohibition, whichever way it is applied, i.e. the illicitness, which provides the thin borderline separating any copy of any text from secondary samizdat.

Justification for the term 'secondary samizdat' finds support in the set of books which were actually published by state publishers and physically printed by state printers, but which never got onto the book market, ending up instead at the pulp mill, i.e. their distribution was halted and prohibited, and the print run (usually the majority of copies, but not all of them) was destroyed, pulped in the same way as wheat was once ground into groats at the pulp mill, or poppy seed, although in all cases where the publication processes were 'halted' in this way, some of the print run was successfully preserved either thanks to subversive activities or by chance. Several Czech titles can be named at random in this broad category: Vladimír Chrastina: *Strůjci neklidu* [Authors of Disquiet] (1968), Bohumil Hrabal: *Domácí úkoly* [Home Work] (1969), Jiří Stránský: *Štěstí* [Happiness] (1969), Jan Patočka: *O smysl dneška* [On the Meaning of Today] (1971), Zdeněk Kalista: *Karel IV. Jeho duchovní tvář* [Charles IV and His Spiritual Aspect] (1971), and many other books of translated literature were sent off to be pulped, the reason often being a preface written by an offending author, an undesirable translator or just some irksome detail or allusion in the text. Books from the pulp mill also find their way into secondary samizdat circulation, although their genealogy does make them different. These are books that do not exist from the legal standpoint, even though they have in fact been rescued from the waste and scrapyard for their original purpose, which has shifted into the realms of samizdat communication.

If we consider samizdat primarily as a medium, the question arises as to which aspects of mediality should be taken into account. To obtain a physical idea of the term medium, its performativity is of primary importance, i.e. the mediating role of the medium or apparatus. Just as sound is disseminated through the air, samizdat represents a substance that disseminates certain works. For the sake of clarity we usually base ourselves on an idea of a text written on a typewriter, even though clearly samizdat-circulated albums with pictures or drawings, music recordings, photographs, film recordings and the like are typologically similar or identical cases. An important and previously little explored aspect of samizdat is the oral and performative level.[16]

The most widespread conception of the medium, which does latently reflect its material nature, but which is primarily based on the fact that the medium is a mediating mechanism, is as a means of communication between the broadcaster and the receiver, something in between (medius), while mediality is not just an empty common denominator, but it also takes an active part in the sense of a mediated medium. Hence samizdat means a particular platform and a particular mode of intercourse. The tangibility of the text is highlighted by its unique and individually confirmed genesis. In contrast to ordinary books we are confronted by singular features that lend this medium

---

16 Samizdat production, consumption and distribution were e.g. on the one hand oral, and on the other hand performative. See 'Innovative Forms of Hungarian Samizdat. An Analysis of Oral Practices', *Zeitschrift für Osteuropaforschung*, in print. Cit. based on manuscript, pp. 1, 9. As an example the author refers to the Hungarian magazine *Lélegzet*, which only 'came out' in an oral version. Ibid., pp. 11–15. See also CSEH-VARGA, Katalin. 'Innovative Forms of the Hungarian Samizdat. An Analysis of Oral Practices', *Zeitschrift für Ostmitteleuropa-Forschung*, No. 1, 2016, Vol. 65, pp. 90–107.

its singular validity: the strength of the typist's keystrokes, the colour and quality of the typewriter ribbon, the type of typewriter and the individual letters, the margins, the way typos were corrected, the pagination, the notes and binding, the title, the imprint, the illustrations if any, the line spacing, sometimes the manually performed corrections, the errata... all these signs are unique. And all of them reduce the distance between the producer and the product. Moreover, this does not just involve those cases where the author himself is the samizdat publisher. In those cases we can speak of a text as a physical extension of the author's body: his hands and the performance that his writing represents.[17]

Even if the transcriber is not the author, his or her proximity and presence remain obvious. In the samizdat environment the author as a rule personally knows the person reproducing the work and making it a reality in physical form. And in theory he can follow the trajectories along which his work moves and physically meet up with all his readers. This does not come into consideration at a book market. As goods distributed by a state book market or wholesalers, the book leaves the boundaries of the traceable communications chain behind it. Samizdat retains the private dimension and the intimity of the potentially traceable circulation of individual copies. This may indeed be disrupted or halted by confiscation, loss, mistaken distribution or a trick played by the state police and the like – but these are merely unfortunate deviations in a system that is primarily based on traceable distribution 'amongst ourselves'.

The uniqueness of samizdat lies in its attributes, which are usually conceived politically as literature resisting suppression, prohibitions and the like. However, this fact can also be understood from a different perspective offered by the concept of 'tactical media' (the pioneers of this term are considered to be David Garcia and Geert

---

17 B. SABEL - A. BUCHER (eds.). *Der unfeste Text : Perspektiven auf einen literatur- und kulturwissenschaftlichen Leitbegriff* [The Infirm Text. Perspectives on a Literature and Culture Studies Term]. Würzburg: Königshausen - Neumann, 2001.

Lovink in the late 1990s), i.e. alternative information media expressing the positions of minorities that feel themselves to be underrepresented in the mass media, the press, the news and in public. Tactical media are described by communication theorists as media of crisis, criticism and opposition. Their trigger mechanism is activism, participation and solidarity.

Samizdat creates a community, but one that cannot be reduced to 'opponents of the regime', because its interests and standpoints, as mentioned above, cannot be brought down to a single common denominator. Participants in the samizdat medium project a broad range of content, and the connection between these standpoints is undefinable, even if we remain on the general level of tactical media, because the methods, motivations and intentions of individual types of participation and solidarity, activism and resistance cannot be brought down to a single factor, so samizdat remains a mere medium between the broadcasters and the receivers.

However, samizdat in its individual manifestations undoubtedly forms a community, a unique constellation of confidentiality, kinship and shared values (however much these may be unarticulated and imaginary), while it is also clear that this community only existed as an aura or a disposition that could never materialize, because the participants and their preferences were too varied, or formed a network of communities, only some of which were interconnected. Samizdat anticipates a phenomenon whereby people who need not know or physically meet one another (mainly because samizdat involves conspiracy) nevertheless belong to the same media circle, within which they take part in shared platforms. In the digital revolution era that followed immediately after the natural end of the classic samizdat era, the name virtual community (as in the title of a book brought out in 1993 by Howard Rheingold) became established for this phenomenon.

Samizdat involved an 'impossible community' whose popularity was fostered to some extent by Jean-Luc Nancy, Maurice Blanchot, Giorgio Agamben and Alain Badiou, while Russian authors primarily include Elena Petrovskaya and Oleg Aronson with *Bogema: opyt soobščestva* [Bohemia, The Experience of a Community] (2002),[18] which is set in the 19th century, but whose theoretical bases and scope also relate to later periods. Briefly, the idea of an 'inconceivable' or 'impossible' community is based on the notion that communities can exist without having any firm basis, core or consolidating meaning – this is certainly the case for samizdat communities, which biographically, historically and in some (few) cases even aesthetically carry on from avant-garde concepts of groups and typographical radicalism, even though they change these basic ideas beyond recognition.

Actually, the connection between samizdat and the avant-garde is not so much historical or aesthetic, because only a tiny proportion of those involved in samizdat were representatives and upholders of avant-garde art (primarily the Surrealist group in Czechoslovakia) as typologically media-oriented.

Just as in some manifestations of avant-garde aesthetics, when books were printed on wallpaper or were produced by hand, because established book production seemed inadequate to the needs of the 'new book', so samizdat also involves a quest for a medium that is suitable for publishing purposes and reflects contemporary circumstances. At first glance it seems inappropriate to make comparisons for a simple reason: whereas in the avant-garde, innovative energy forms in circumstances of plenty and opportunity, samizdat is a reaction to deprivation. However, in both cases the outcome is a quest for a suitable medium. The connection between these two exceptional book publishing methods is personified in a pioneer in postwar samizdat and indeed the author of the word itself: Nikolai Glazkov, who as a poet upheld Russian avant-garde aesthetics. In 1939 Glazkov together with Julian Dolgin, who later advocated Pythagorean philosophy and esoteric mathematics, founded the neo-futurist Nyebyvalizm

---

18 PETROVSKAYA, Elena. *Nameless Communities*. Moscow: Falanster, 2012; ARONSON, Oleg. *Bogema: opyt soobshchestva*. Moscow: Fond 'Pragmatika kul'tury', 2002.

['Wasntism'] group, with references to the poetics of emptiness and the void in the avant-garde.[19] It was mainly the nichevoky ['Nothingies'] group, established in the early 1920s by the legendary poet Rurik Rok, whose original surname was probably Gering, which notoriously placed a Dadaist stress on nihilism, though this still had to be articulated in some way. As was often the case here, the intention was to formulate his own standpoint and doctrine:

Ot ikh ucheby i vozni
Uyti,
Nayti svoe uchen'e...
Vot tak nebyvalizm voznik –
Literaturnoe techen'e.[20]

[Escaping their education and toil,
To find one's own teaching,
That is how 'Wasntism' came about,
That literary stream.]

After the Second World War Glazkov moves away from declaring his own distinct way of writing poetry towards a rejection of all values and the creation of his own samizdat social network, while never understanding his task in some bombastic way. He might even have come up with the idea of a samizdat magazine on the toilet at a friend's, where they used sheets of paper full of rejected poetry by some of the apartment occupants when there was a lack of toilet paper. It occurred to Glazkov that this 'waste paper' could be collected and published on a do-it-yourself basis. Samizdat harmoniously brought together marginal technical elements with content that also

---

19 See A. HANSEN-LÖVE – B. GROYS (eds.). *Am Nullpunkt. Positionen der russischen Avantgarde* [At Level Zero. Positions of the Russian Avant-garde]. Frankfurt am Main: Suhrkamp, 2005.
20 VINOKUROVA, Irina. *'Vsego lish' geniy...': sud'ba Nikolaya Glazkova.* Moscow: Vremya, 2006, p. 91.

played a peripheral cultural role, even though on the contrary many people saw it as an archive of literary classics that would one day be canonized (which later turned out to be true in many cases).

The view of samizdat as a specific material medium also raises a question that has hitherto attracted little attention, even though it is directly associated with a basic characteristic of this publishing activity, i.e. with the specific material implementation of the publishing objective, which goes beyond all normal procedures and technologies. The question is: how can samizdat be understood as a production process and what can be learnt about the economic mechanisms on which samizdat operations are based?

Although samizdat was an alternative to the commercial book market, and the enthusiasm of its participants ensured they worked from conviction rather than for profit, still it cannot be take out of its economic context. Although samizdat comes into being as a pirate activity in relation to state institutions, its activities themselves become institutionalized. Between 1967 and 1982 a samizdat library operated in Odessa, which in individual cases covered the entire Soviet Union in its range, while in Hungary a samizdat 'boutique' was set up by László Rajk in the early 1980s. Samizdat output was production in which its participants invested material, machines and time. Hence it was production that could never have zero costs.

In his poetry entitled *Samizdat* in 1980, poet Alexandr Yeremenko implies some kind of miraculous, fairy-tale origin for samizdat texts, although samizdats are also (specific) goods, i.e. products, which have value that can be expressed (albeit with difficulty) in terms of money, and which are liable to be the subject of various types of transactions including commercial ones.

Za okoshkom svetu malo,
belyy sneg valit-valit.
Vozle Kurskogo vokzala
domik malen'kiy stoit.

Za okoshkom svetu netu.
Iz-za shtorok ne idet.
Tam pechatayut poeta –
shest' kopeek razvorot.[21]

[There is little light behind the window,
White snow lies all around,
At Kursk station,
There is a little house.
There's no longer any light behind the window,
It does not get through the curtains,
They are printing the poet's books there,
Six kopecks a double-page.]

Six kopecks refers to the capitalization of goods, i.e. of samizdat as a set of products available to a particular community of consumers, which (even though many people have worked on it selflessly for free, and the incoming cash flow often only served to cover costs, without any material profit ensuing) nevertheless had to implement its material production somehow. And it is the very hidden nature of these economic mechanisms that is on the one hand the reason behind the lack of research into this aspect of samizdat cultural practice and on the other hand a great challenge for the study of the medial nature of samizdat. In order to create samizdat, there was a need for at least paper, carbon paper, typewriter ribbons, often bindings, illustrations and above all labour expended over time. Transcription was normally paid for, and at least some of the output was not only loaned out and distributed, but also sold, but then activities which were not usually associated with remuneration were performed over time, in many cases during 'working hours', and hence they had not only symbolic but also material value. Analyses appeared in Russia of unofficial art as an activity indirectly sponsored by the state, which enabled people

---

21 Ibid, p. 91.

to make a living without spending their ordinary working hours in employment at work.[22]

The question mark over how samizdat was produced and distributed is also unavoidably a question mark over the material amongst other things, so it is this kind of research that is able to depict the highly varied breadth of samizdat output in a way that offers a common basis. This is a method that was highlighted in late 1980s humanities by Robert Darnton,[23] who actually dealt with the situation in pre-revolutionary France, but he based his observations methodologically on the way ideas spread through society and the communication channels that were used. In his monograph *The Forbidden Best-Sellers of Prerevolutionary France* (1995), summarizing his research and publications over the over the many previous years, Darnton uses simple equations concerning the market circulation of such goods as books in order to attempt to depict communications even in those cases where the readers 'used' books that were circulated clandestinely.[24]

As we seek a way to thematize samizdat while reflecting its breadth and variety, we come up against not only the material aspect, but also the unique form of authorship, which differs from that of 'unmarked' book production. In samizdat, not only is the text more closely physically connected to its author, as mentioned above, who has the potential opportunity to follow the trajectory of individual copies of the work circulating in the community of users. Samizdat authorship, i.e. the relationship of the author to his work, can generally be

---

22   E.g. DEGOT, Ekaterina. 'Zwischen Massenproduktion und Einzigartigkeit: offizielle und inoffizielle Kunst in der UdSSR - Berlin - Moskau. 1950-2000', in *Exhibition Catalogue to Martin-Gropius-Bau*, Vol. 2: *Chronik. Berliner Festspiele*. Berlin: Nicolaische Verlagsbuchhandlung, 2003, pp. 133–137.

23   I am grateful to Petr Steiner for introducing this research by Darnton, with whom I began to plan the previously unattempted project of studying the economic aspects of samizdat culture.

24   E.g. 'livres philosophiques', DARNTON, Robert. *The Literary Underground of the Old Regime*. Cambridge: Harvard University Press, 1982, p. 207.

considered to be an 'exceptional state'[25]. The author either voluntarily enters or is placed (even posthumously, or without it being his intention) in a sphere that differs from the overall situation on the book market. This is a risk-prone area (reading or production 'for one's own needs' is acceptable, but distributing samizdat is a criminal act, most frequently described in Czechoslovakia as *subversion of the state*, *disorderly conduct* or *damaging the interests of the state abroad* and may be punished by imprisonment, as in the case of numerous samizdat activists in many Soviet bloc countries), an area in which authorship is not only a creative gesture (the creation of the work) and subsequently a commercial and communicational gesture (publication of the work), but also a performative work. The author enters an area, or is drawn into it by the production of his work as a samizdat, in which each copy of the work has a special record available, which includes the set and order of readers of a particular 'copy', the method of production and the conspiratorial circumstances which led to its existence – and all the other 'acts' associated with these processes.

The 'eventful' physical urgency of the samizdat work, as well as the highlighted presence of the authorship additionally turn attention to the particular material design of each publication, which is normally ascribed secondary importance in ordinary book production. The quality of the typewriting, the paper, the type and the detailed features of the cover and similar features of the book are not usually considered to be an immediate part of the 'contents', and in the case of samizdat, two seemingly opposing phenomena occur: on the one hand the text is emancipated from the medium, which is a priori makeshift, while on the other hand this makeshift state becomes part of the actual meaning, so even after decades many readers identify the reading experience with the physical attributes of the copy they had available, which is surely the case for every text, but in the case

---

25   This metaphor formed the basis for my comparative study 'Autoren im Ausnahmezustand' [Authors in an Exceptional State] on Russian and Czech alternative culture. Publication of the study is forthcoming.

of samizdat it seems to be a more frequent, prominent and motivated phenomenon.

Because there has been an almost complete lack of a comparative standpoint in research to date, we know little yet about the local differences in publication conventions that illustrate the specific media and material used by individual samizdat circles. As an example of such surveys I shall mention several differences between Czech and Russian samizdat, while the phenomenon of the Polish 'drugi obieg' is a separate category that is only partially applicable to samizdat, as mentioned above. The difference between the situation in Czechoslovakia and the Soviet Union lies in their overall conception of samizdat. In Czechoslovakia, structures were formed that copied publishing institutions: Texty přátel (Peter Mikeš and Eduard Zacha), Expedice [Dispatch], Půlnoc [Midnight], Petlice [Padlock], Popelnice [Dustbin], Prostor [Space], Hermetická edice [Hermetic series] and so forth. In this way book culture was revived as an institutional mechanism, whereby part of the meaning of individual texts came to be the circumstances of their publication: the publisher (editor), the context of the particular publication within the publishing plan and in some cases the graphic lay-out.

In Russia samizdat was distributed primarily as an enormous set of individual texts, periodicals or possibly anthologies, while there were hardly any series and prestige publications like Šiktanc's Český orloj [Czech Astrological Clock] (1973), Blatný's Poblíž katedrál [Near the Cathedral] (1981) and dozens of similar works. The reasons behind this difference are hard to identify. In spite of the post-1948 nationalizations in Czechoslovakia, there was no brutal parallel in the traditional crafts of book production, whether illustration, typesetting, typography or book binding, with the Soviet Union, where we might speak of a complete absence of pre-revolutionary book culture,[26] after

---

26 FROLOVA, Irina. *Kniga v Rossii* [Book in Russia] *1861–1881; Kniga v Rossii 1881–1895; Kniga v Rossii 1895–1917.* Moskva: Kniga, 1988–1991;

the average typographical standard moved to a completely different level than the pre-revolutionary one following the total proletarianization of society, the civil war and the 'cultural revolution' of Stalinism. In Czechoslovakia the prewar standard was preserved to a far greater degree, though of course only to some extent at state publishers (e.g. export companies Artia, Odeon, Klub čtenářů and Albatros).

The samizdat medium, which came to be of such fundamental importance to the Soviet bloc states in the latter half of the 20th century with regard to the continuation of cultural communication in spite of the particularly straitened circumstances, is by no means a mere stopgap solution that makes up for the unavailability of certain other texts. It also fulfils other ancillary roles in various ways within different contexts. In Czechoslovakia the institutional micro-environment was revived thanks to samizdat, as it was at the end of the 18th century or following the establishment of Czechoslovakia in 1918. In some cases these activities even bear explicit hallmarks of National Revival objectives – one of the foremost publishers, for example, went under the name of Krameriova Expedice [Kramerius Dispatch] after Václav Matěj Kramerius, the publisher of the first Czech newspaper and organizer of 'alternative' Czech culture in the Austro-Hungarian context at the turn of the 18th and 19th centuries.

The samizdat publisher set up an original company, with which he identified, but which also represented an act of faith in the authority of civic society and in the coexistence of those within a particular field (in this case publishing). The coexistence of those sharing a particular profile makes sense because of their quantity and variety, implying both differences and competition. At the same time it suppressed the imposed reality that the books were 'prohibited' or 'secret', or this makeshift state turned into an advantage – this specific feature of production was implicitly highlighted as its bibliophilic quality. In spite of the poor conditions, publications in small

Sankt-Peterburg: Rossiyskaya natsional'naya biblioteka, 1997; Sankt-Peterburg: Rossiyskaya natsional'naya biblioteka, 2008.

Examples of magnetizdat

print-runs came to be a rarity even in the media and material sense, offering not only the value of the distributed text itself, but also the aesthetic value to the collector.

The situation was different in Russia, where the paralysis of social confidence[27] led to the circulation of texts whose physical design was only of importance when the form made up part of the publication plan. Hence, for example, the *Transponans* magazine, which was published in Yeysk from the mid-1970s by Sergei Sigei and Ry Nikonova, is outstanding for its prominent graphic design. However, this is in no way a general characteristic of publishing culture, but a symptom of the interest in visual poetry and another way of experimenting with paper, typeface and the connection between the typeface and the work of art as a whole. Otherwise it was primarily the partisan

---

27   J. KORNAI – B. ROTHSTEIN – S. ROSE-ACKERMAN (eds.). *Creating Social Trust in Post-socialist Transition*. New York: Palgrave Macmillan, 2004.

method of text circulation that was fostered, i.e. outside any institutional framework, even of a 'shadow' nature.

Circles of samizdat readers did indeed come together, but these were distinguished either by the shared aesthetic which they on principle identified with (e.g. within the community of so-called Conceptualists, Chertkov's group and the like) or through personal friendship, i.e. private connections. The lack of social coordination, which was apparent in the absence or limited occurrence of ties between political dissent and the unofficial culture, increased pressure to 'dematerialize' the samizdat medium. Russian samizdat was utilitarian, it did not form any superstructural values involving aesthetic objects and the 'unnecessary' creation of impressions, which were not economically incentivized. As a rule texts were distributed without hard bindings or illustrations, and without any association with other texts (e.g. from the same publisher). Such additional ornamental semantics would have been a 'burden'.

The natural consequence and continuation of this phenomenon was that the samizdat heritage was institutionalized in the post-Communist era. Whereas Czechoslovakia saw the establishment in the early 1990s of the extensive Libri prohibiti samizdat library, which in spite of its pitiful funding has been expanding its collections and sphere of operations for twenty years, including its exhibition and adult education activities, no institution of this kind exists in Russia to this day, even though several institutions deal systematically with samizdat with outstanding results, primarily the Memorial group and the Kollektsiya netraditsionnoy pechati [Non-traditional Printed Matter] collection at the Public Historical Library in Moscow. Moreover, Russian samizdat is prominently represented at such foreign institutions as the Open Society Archive in Budapest and Forschungsstelle Osteuropa in Bremen. The primary source for charting samizdat and its modern-day counterparts in Russia remains first and foremost the internet.

Commentary

Passages omitted from the original text due to editorial intervention are always indicated thus [...].

Czech titles of articles, books and publishers are translated into English in brackets, followed by the year of publication (if any). Bibliographical entries in footnotes are also translated into English.

Commentary to each essay included in this anthology is divided into separate parts listed alphabetically by the authors' names:

Miroslav Červenka

The translation of the first two essays included in this anthology is based on these versions of the texts: 'Dvě poznámky k samizdatu' [Two Notes on Samizdat], *Kritický sborník*, No. 4, 1985, Vol. V, pp. 1–12, reprinted in K. PALEK (ed.). *Kritický sborník 1981–1989. Výbor ze samizdatových ročníků* [Critical Review. Samizdat Anthology Selection]. Praha: Triáda, 2009, pp. 21–29 and 'K sémiotice samizdatu' [The Semiotics of Samizdat], *Slovenské pohľady* [Slovak Views], No. 6, 1990, pp. 57–62, reprinted in ČERVENKA, Miroslav. *Obléhání zevnitř* [Beleaguerment from the Inside]. Praha: Torst, 1999, pp. 366–373. The later essay is a restructured version of the first one, i.e. this restructured text is based on the 'first note on samizdat'. Thus we have inserted the complete text of 'K sémiotice samizdatu' into this anthology and from 'Dvě poznámky o samizdatu' we have only chosen the part which the texts do not have in common, i.e. 'the second note'. A detailed editorial note to both of the essays was also published here: ČERVENKA, Miroslav. *Textologické studie* [Textological

Studies]. M. Kosák – J. Flaišman (eds.). Praha: Ústav pro českou literaturu AV ČR, 2009.

Josef Jedlička

This text was published in the émigré journal *Zpravodaj: časopis Čechů a Slováků ve Švýcarsku* [Reporter: Journal for Czechs and Slovaks in Switzerland] No. 4, 1980, pp. 28–29. The journal was published by the Federation of Czechoslovak Associations in Switzerland and came out in Zurich between 1974 and 1995. We have omitted the accompanying fiction texts (poems) from the original.

František Kautman

The original article was published in the samizdat journal *Kritický sborník* [Critical Review] No. 4, 1982, where it is only signed with the initial -n-. The translation is based on the text version published in K. Palek (ed.). *Kritický sborník 1981–1989. Výbor ze samizdatových ročníků.* [Critical Review. Samizdat Anthology Selection]. Praha: Triáda, 2009, pp. 5–10. An edited version was also published in the journal *Acta* No. 1, 1987.

Petr Fidelius

This article was published in the samizdat journal *Kritický sborník* [Critical Review], No. 2, 1983 as a reaction to the previous text by František Kautman 'Question Marks over "Unpublished" Literature'. We include both texts in this anthology in consecutive order. This translation is based on the version of the text published in K. Palek (ed.). *Kritický sborník 1981–1989. Výbor ze samizdatových ročníků* [Critical Review. Samizdat Anthology Selection]. Prague: Triáda, 2009, pp. 11–13. The original article was only signed with the mark -pf-, an abbreviation of the author's pen-name Petr Fidelius [Karel Palek]. An edited version of the text was also published in the magazine *Acta* No. 1, 1987 and in the anthology Kritické eseje [Critical Essays]. Praha: Torst, 2000.

Jiří Gruša

Here we are only publishing an extract from the original article dated 1983 at the end of the text by the author. The selected basis for the translation was the text version published for the *V.Z.D.O.R. Výstava nezávislé literatury v samizdatu a exilu 1948–1989* [RESIST-ANCE: Exhibition of independent literature in samizdat and exile, *1948–1989*] exhibition arranged in January–June 1992 at the Museum of Czech Literature (PNP) in Strahov, Prague, by the Czechoslovak Documentary Centre, the CAS Institute of Contemporary History, the National Library in Prague, Libri prohibiti and the Museum of Czech Literature itself. The extract is a translation of this original text from pp. 14–24. The original text was written for a meeting in the German town of Franken where it was read aloud for the audience. A fragment of the whole essay was also published later in a journal *Soudobé dějiny* [Modern History] No. 4–5, 1993/1994, Vol. I, pp. 551–559. A critical edition of the complete article was published in GRUŠA, Jiří. *Eseje a studie o literatuře a kultuře I.* [Essays on Literature and Culture]. *Dílo Jiřího Gruši Vol. 2.* Brno: Barrister & Principal, 2015.

Tomáš Vrba

This text was published in an anthology of studies on postwar independent culture in Czechoslovakia: J. ALAN (ed.). *Alternativní kultura. Příběh české společnosti 1945–1989* [Alternative Culture. The Story of Czech Society, 1945–1989]. Praha: Nakladatelství lidové noviny, 2001, pp. 265–305. We have abridged this original text by omitting several chapters: *Co tedy je a co není samizdat, Svobodné informace, Ideová východiska, Lidové noviny* and *Svobodné myšlení* [What Samizdat Is and Is Not: Free Information, Ideological Starting Points, Lidové noviny and Independent Thinking].

Jiří Gruntorád

This text was published in the anthology entitled Josef ALAN. (ed.). *Alternativní kultura. Příběh české společnosti 1945–1989* [Alternative

Culture. The Story of Czech Society in 1945–1989]. Praha: NLN, 2001, pp. 493–507. Our translation is based on this version.

Martin Machovec

The first text was initially published here: *O slušnou odměnu bude pečováno: Ekonomické souvislosti spisovatelské profese v české kultuře 19. a 20. století.* [Economics of Writers' Career in 19th and 20th Century Czech Culture] T. Breň, P. Janáček (eds.). Praha: Ústav pro českou literaturu AV ČR, 2009 on which our translation is based.

The second text was originally published as a sub-chapter entitled *Skupina literátů kolem edice Půlnoc (1949–1955)* [The Circle of Writers around the Půlnoc Series (1949–1955)] as an example of particular underground activity within the chapter entitled *Od avantgardy přes podzemí do undergroundu* [From the avant-garde to the underground], in *Alternativní kultura. Příběh české společnosti 1945–1989* [Alternative Culture. The Story of Czech Society, 1945–1989]. Praha: NLN, 2001, pp. 156–167. Our translation is based on the reworked and supplemented edition of M. Machovec (ed.). *Pohledy zevnitř. Česká undergroundová kultura ve svědectvích, dokumentech a interpretacích* [Views from the Inside: Czech Underground Culture in Testimonies, Documents and Interpretations]. Prague: Pistorius & Olšanská, 2008, where the text came out with the same title as the sub-chapter on pp. 101–114 as part of the chapter entitled *Od avantgardy přes podzemí do undergroundu, skupina edice Půlnoc 1949–1955 a undergroundový okruh Plastic People 1969–1989* [From the Avant-garde to the Underground, the Půlnoc Series Group, 1949–1955, and the Underground Circle around the Plastic People, 1969–1989].

Alena Přibáňová and Michal Přibáň

This text was written for the Italian anthology *Il samizdat tra memoria e utopia. eSamizdat* 2010–2011, Vol. VIII, where it was published on pp. 233–238 under the title 'I rapporti di Sixty-Eight Publishers con il samizdat cecoslovacco e la concorrenza con le altre case editrici dell'emigrazione' Our translation is based on the Czech version presented to us by the author.

Petr Šámal

This text was originally published as part of a monograph on the history of censorship in the Czech lands: WÖGERBAUER, Michael – PÍŠA, Petr – ŠÁMAL, Petr – JANÁČEK, Pavel et al. *V obecném zájmu. Cenzura a sociální regulace literatury v moderní české kultuře 1749–2014* [In the General Interest: Censorship and Social Regulation of Literature in Modern Czech Culture, 1749–2014] Volume II. Praha: Academia – Ústav pro českou literaturu AV ČR, 2015. The present excerpt summarizes and characterizes the model of literary samizdat that was typical of Czechoslovakia in the 1970s and 1980s (during the period known as normalization). A section is left out of the original version of the text on *Legalismus disentu a perzekuce literárního samizdatu* [Legalism in Dissent and the Persecution of Literary Samizdat] describing the primary strategies of opposition activities and the elements of the repressive state apparatus that had an effect on literary activity.

Weronika Parfianowicz-Vertun

The Czech version of the text was first published in the *Podoby samizdatu* [Forms of Samizdat] thematic issue of *A2* cultural magazine No. 18, 2012 on p. 8. Its edited and longer version makes up a part of the anthology *Europa Środkowa w tekstach i działaniach. Polskie i czeskie dyskusje* [Middle Europe in Texts and Activities. Polish and Czech Discussions]. Warszawa: Wydawnictwa Uniwersytetu Warszawskiego, 2016.

Tomáš Glanc

His text was published in the Italian anthology *Il samizdat tra memoria e utopia. eSamizdat* 2010–2011, Vol. VIII, where it came out under the title 'Il samizdat come medium' on pp. 31–40. The text was published here in Czech: 'Samizdat jako médium', *Souvislosti*, No. 3, 2013, Vol. 24, pp. 183–193. The selected basis for the translation is the Czech version of the article with alterations made by the author.

Bibliography

J. ALAN (ed.). *Alternativní kultura. Příběh české společnosti 1945–1989.* Praha: NLN, 2001.

ARONSON, Oleg. *Bogema: opyt soobshchestva.* Moscow: Fond 'Pragmatika kul'tury', 2002.

BARTHES, Roland. *Writing Degree Zero.* London: Jonathan Cape, 1967.

BÍLEK, Petr. *175 autorů. Čeští prozaici, básníci a literární kritici publikující v 70. letech v nakladatelství Československý spisovatel.* Praha: Československý spisovatel, 1982.

BŁAŻEJOWSKA, Justyna. *Papierowa rewolucja. Z dziejów drugiego obiegu wydawiczego w Polsce 1976–1989/1990.* Warszawa: Instytut Pamięci Narodowej, 2010.

BLJUM, Arlen. *Zakat Glavlita.Kak razrushalas' sistema sov. tsenzury: dokument khronika 1985–1991.* Moskva: Terra, 1995.

BOLTON, Jonathan. *Worlds of Dissent. Charter 77, The Plastic People of the Universe and Czech Culture under Communism.* Cambridge (MA) – London: Harvard University Press, 2012.

BONDY, Egon. '2000', *Revolver Revue*, No. 45, 2001.

BONDY, Egon. 'Kořeny českého literárního undergroundu v letech 1949–1953', *Haňťa Press*, No. 8, 1990.

BONDY, Egon. *Básnické dílo I.–IX.*, M. MACHOVEC (ed.). Praha: Pražská imaginace, 1990–1993.

BONDY, Egon. *Básnické spisy I.–III.*, M. MACHOVEC (ed.). Praha: Argo, 2014–2016.

BONDY, Egon. *Prvních deset let.* Praha: Maťa, 2002.

BORN, Adolf – JELÍNEK, Oldřich. 'Urajt', *Haňťa Press*, No. 17, 1995.

BOUDNÍK, Vladimír. *Z korespondence I (1949–1956), II (1957–1968).* Praha: Pražská imaginace, 1994.

BOUDNÍK, Vladimír. *Z literární pozůstalosti*. Praha: Pražská imaginace – Pragma, 1993.

BRABEC, Jiří – GRUŠA, Jiří – HÁJEK, Igor – KABEŠ, Petr – LOPATKA, Jan. *Slovník českých spisovatelů. Pokus o rekonstrukci dějin české literatury 1948–1979*. Toronto: Sixty-Eight Publishers, 1982.

BRABEC, Jiří et al. *Slovník zakázaných autorů 1948–1980*. Praha: Státní pedagogické nakladatelství, 1991.

T. BREŇ – P. JANÁČEK (eds.). *O slušnou odměnu bude pečováno: Ekonomické souvislosti spisovatelské profese v české kultuře 19. a 20. století*. Praha: Ústav pro českou literaturu AV ČR, 2009.

A. CATALANO – S. GUAGNELLI (eds.). 'La luce dell'est: il samizdat come costruzione di una comunità parallela', *Il samizdat tra memoria e utopia. eSamizdat* 2010–2011, Vol. VIII.

CSEH-VARGA, Katalin. 'Innovative Forms of the Hungarian Samizdat. An Analysis of Oral Practices', *Zeitschrift für Ostmitteleuropa-Forschung*, No. 1, 2016, Vol. LXV.

CUHRA, Jaroslav. *Trestní represe odpůrců režimu v letech 1969–1972*. Praha: Ústav pro soudobé dějiny AV ČR, 1997.

ČERNÁ, Jana. *Adresát Milena Jesenská*. Praha: Klub mladé poezie, 1969 (1st edition); Praha: Concordia, 1991 (2nd edition); Praha: Torst, 2014 (3rd edition).

ČERVENKA, Miroslav. 'Dvě poznámky k samizdatu', *Kritický sborník*, No. 4, 1985. Vol. V.

ČERVENKA, Miroslav. 'K sémiotice samizdatu', *Slovenské pohľady*, No. 6, 1990.

ČERVENKA, Miroslav. *Obléhání zevnitř*. Praha: Torst, 1996.

ČERVENKA, Miroslav. *Textologické studie*, M. KOSÁK – J. FLAIŠMAN (eds.). Praha: Ústav pro českou literaturu AV ČR, 2009.

DARNTON, Robert. *The Literary Underground of the Old Regime*. Cambridge: Harvard University Press, 1982.

DAY, Barbara. *Sametoví filozofové*. Brno: Doplněk, 1999.

DEGOT, Ekaterina. 'Zwischen Massenproduktion und Einzigartigkeit: offizielle und inoffizielle Kunst in der UdSSR – Berlin – Moskau. 1950–2000', in *Exhibition Catalogue to Martin-Gropius-Bau*, Vol. 2: *Chronik. Berliner Festspiele*. Berlin: Nicolaische Verlagsbuchhandlung, 2003.

DEMSZKY, Gábor – RAJK, László – SASVÁRI, Edit. *Földalatti vonalak*. Pécs: Jelenkor, 2000.

Dočekal, Jaroslav. *Dopisy Jaroslava Dočekala Vladimíru Boudníkovi I.–II.* Praha: Jan Placák – Ztichlá klika, 2017.

Dočekal, Jaroslav. 'Smršťovače – hořké dávky', *Revolver Revue*, No. 29, 1995.

Duchastel, Philippe. 'Textual Display Techniques', in *The Technology of Text: Principles for Structuring, Designing, and Displaying Text*, D. Jonassen (ed.). Englewood Cliffs (NJ): Educational Technology Publications, 1982.

W. Eichwede (ed.). *Samizdat. Alternative Kultur in Zentral- und Osteuropa. Die 60er bis 80er Jahre.* Bremen: Edition Temmen, 2000.

Feindt, Gregor. 'Opposition und Samizdat in Ostmitteleuropa. Strukturen und Mechanismen unabhängiger Periodika in vergleichender Perspektive', *Zeitschrift für Ostmitteleuropa-Forschung*, No. 1, 2016, Vol. LXV.

Fidelius, Petr. 'Kultura 'oficiální' a 'neoficiální' ', *Kritický sborník*, No. 3, 1981, Vol. I.

Formanová, Lucie – Gruntorád, Jiří – Přibáň, Michal. *Exilová periodika.* Praha: Libri prohibiti – Ježek, 1999.

S. Frank – R. Lachman – S. Sasse et al. (eds.). *Mystifikation – Autorschaft – Original.* Tübingen: Gunter Narr Verlag, 2001.

Frolova, Irina. *Kniga v Rossii 1861–1881.* Moskva: Kniga, 1988–1991.

Frolova, Irina. *Kniga v Rossii 1881–1895.* Sankt-Peterburg: Rossiyskaya natsional'naya biblioteka, 1997.

Frolova, Irina. *Kniga v Rossii 1895–1917.* Sankt-Peterburg: Rossiyskaya natsional'naya biblioteka, 2008.

Glanc, Tomáš. 'Ein Buch gegen die Schrift. Zhivotnia kniga', in *Mystifikation – Autorschaft – Original*, S. Frank et al. (eds.). Tübingen: Gunter Narr Verlag, 2001.

Glanc, Tomáš. 'Samizdat jako médium', *Souvislosti*, No. 3, 2013, Vol. XXIV.

M. Goetz-Stankiewicz (ed.). *Good-bye, Samizdat: Twenty Years of Czechoslovak Underground Writing.* Evanston: Northwestern University Press, 1992.

Gottwald, Klement. *Spisy XIV. and XV.* Praha: Státní nakladatelství politické literatury, 1958 and 1961.

Gruntorád, Jiří. 'Z bibliografie samizdatu: Edice Expedice', *Kritický sborník*, No. 3 and 4, 1994, Vol. XIV.

Gruntorád, Jiří. 'Z bibliografie samizdatu: Edice Popelnice', *Kritický sborník*, No. 2, 1992, Vol. XII.

GRUNTORÁD, Jiří. 'Samizdatová literatura v Československu sedmdesátých a osmdesátých let', in *Alternativní kultura. Příběh české společnosti 1945–1989*, J. ALAN (ed.). Praha: NLN, 2001.

GRUŠA, Jiří. *Cenzura a literární život mimo masmédia.* Praha – Scheinfeld-Schwarzenberg: Ústav pro soudobé dějiny ČSAV – Československé dokumentační středisko nez. literatury, 1992.

GRUŠA, Jiří. 'Cenzura a literární život mimo masmédia', *Soudobé dějiny*, No. 4–5, 1993/1994, Vol. I.

GRUŠA, Jiří. *Eseje a studie o literatuře a kultuře I. Dílo Jiřího Gruši Vol. 2.* Brno: Barrister & Principal, 2015.

GRUŠA, Jiří. *Umění stárnout. Rozhovor s Daliborem Dobiášem.* Praha – Litomyšl: Paseka, 2004.

HAGEN, Trever. *Musicking in the Merry Ghetto. The Czech Underground from the 1960s to the 2000s.* Exeter: University of Exeter, 2012.

HANÁKOVÁ, Jitka. *Edice českého samizdatu 1972–1991.* Praha: Národní knihovna ČR, 1997.

Haňťa Press, No. 10–17. Praha: Pražská imaginace, 1991–1995.

A. HANSEN-LÖVE – B. GROYS (eds.). *Am Nullpunkt. Positionen der russischen Avantgarde.* Frankfurt am Main: Suhrkamp, 2005.

A. HARTMANN – B. MRÁZ (eds.). 'Boudník a Medek, korespondence', *Umění / Art*, No. 3/4, 1997, Vol. XVL.

A. HARTMANN – B. MRÁZ (eds.). 'Boudník a Medek, dodatek ke korespondenci a další 'texty pro Mikuláše Medka'', *Umění / Art*, No. 5, 1997, Vol. XVL.

HAVEL, Václav – JANOUCH, František. *Korespondence 1978–2001.* Praha: Akropolis, 2007.

HAVLÍČEK, Zbyněk – PRUSÍKOVÁ, Eva. *Dopisy Evě / Dopisy Zbyňkovi.* Praha: Torst – Levret, 2003.

HIRŠAL, Josef – GRÖGEROVÁ, Bohumila. *Let let.* Praha: Rozmluvy, 1993.

G. HIRT – S. WONDERS (eds.). *Präprintium. Moskauer Bücher aus dem Samizdat (Ausstellungskatalog). Dokumentationen zur Kultur und Gesellschaft im östlichen Europa, Forschungsstelle Osteuropa an der Universität Bremen.* Bremen: Edition Temmen, 1998.

HODOSÁN, Róza. *Szamizdat történetek.* Budapest: Noran, 2004.

L. HOPTMAN – T. POSPISZYL (eds.). *Primary Documents: A Sourcebook for Eastern and Central European Art Since the 1950s.* Cambridge (MA): The MIT Press, 2002.

HRABAL, Bohumil. *Bambino di Praga – Barvotisky – Krásná Poldi*. Praha: Československý spisovatel, 1990.

HRABAL, Bohumil. *Jarmilka*. Praha: Pražská imaginace, 1992.

HRABAL, Bohumil. *Poupata*. Praha: Mladá fronta, 1970.

HRABAL, Bohumil. *Vita nuova*. Toronto: Sixty-Eight Publishers, 1987.

HRABAL, Bohumil. *Židovský svícen*. Praha: Pražská imaginace, 1991.

HVÍŽĎALA, Karel. *České rozhovory ve světě*. Köln: Index, 1981.

HYNEK, Karel. *S vyloučením veřejnosti*. Praha: Torst, 1998.

JANOUCH, František. 'Stockholmská Nadace Charty 77 a podpora nezávislé literatury a jejích tvůrců', in *Česká nezávislá literatura po pěti letech v referátech*, F. KAUTMAN (ed.). Praha: Primus, 1995.

JEDLIČKA, Josef. 'Samizdat', *Zpravodaj: časopis Čechů a Slováků ve Švýcarsku*, No. 4, 1980, Vol. XIII.

JELÍNEK, Oldřich. 'Jak to všechno začalo...', *Haňťa Press*, No. 14, 1993.

JEŽEK, Vlastimil. 'Revolver Revue (Jednou nohou)', *Kritický sborník*, No. 3 and 4, 1991, Vol. XI.

JIROUS, Ivan Martin. 'Autodafé', *Revolver Revue*, No. 41, 1999, Vol. XV.

JIROUS, Ivan Martin. *Magorův zápisník*, M. ŠPIRIT (ed.). Praha: Torst, 1997.

JUNGMANNOVÁ, Lenka. 'Neoficiální, nezávislá, paralelní, alternativní, nelegální, druhá, jiná, nelicencovaná, samizdatová, ineditní, undergroundová, podzemní..., ale naše. Pokus o vymezení problematiky neoficiální dramatiky v letech 1948 až 1989', *Divadelní revue*, No. 3, 2003, Vol. XIV.

KANDZIORA, Jerzy – SZYMAŃSKA, Zyta. *Bez cenzury 1976–1989: literatura, ruch wydawniczy, teatr: bibliografia*. Warszawa: Instytut Badań Literackich, 1999.

F. KAUTMAN (ed.). *Česká nezávislá literatura po pěti letech v referátech*. Praha: Primus, 1995.

KEYS, David. 'Secrets of medieval Europe's large-scale publishing industry revealed', *Independent*, 23rd November 2015: http://www.independent.co.uk/news/science/archaeology/medieval-europes-first-large-scale-publishing-industry-revealed-a6745981.html [accessed: 11th January 2016].

KIND-KOVÁCS, Friederike – LABOV, Jessie. *Samizdat, Tamizdat, and Beyond: Transnational Media During and After Socialism*. New York–Oxford: Berghahn Books, 2013.

KLEE, Paul. *Paul Klee in Jena 1924, der Vortrag*, T. Kain et al. (ed.). Jena: Kunsthistorisches Seminar, 1999.

KLÍMA, Ivan. *Der Gnadenrichter.* Luzern – Hamburg: Hoffmann und Campe, 1979.

KLÍMA, Ivan. *Machtspiele: Roman.* Luzern: Reich, 1977.

KLÍMA, Ivan. *Moje šílené století.* Praha: Academia, 2009.

KLÍMA, Ivan. *Moje šílené století II.* Praha: Academia, 2010.

KLÍMA, Ivan – ČERMÁK, Miloš. *Lásky a řemesla Ivana Klímy.* Praha: Academia, 1995.

KOMAROMI, Ann. *Uncensored: Samizdat Novels and the Quest for Autonomy in Soviet Dissidence.* Evanston (IL): Northwestern University Press, 2015.

KOMAROMI, Ann. 'Samizdat as Extra-Gutenberg Phenomenon', *Poetics Today,* No. 29, 2008.

Jarmark umění (Bulletin Společnosti Karla Teiga), No. 11/12, 1996.

J. KORNAI – B. ROTHSTEIN – S. ROSE-ACKERMAN (eds.). *Creating Social Trust in Post-socialist Transition.* New York: Palgrave Macmillan, 2004.

J. KOSTECKI – A. BRODZKA (eds.). *Pismiennictwo, systemy kontroli, obiegi alternatywne (Z dziejów kultury czytelniczej w Polsce).* Warszawa: Biblioteka Narodowa, 1992.

KOWALCZUK, Ilko-Sascha. *Freiheit und Öffentlichkeit. Politischer Samisdat in der DDR 1985–1989.* Berlin: Robert Havemann Gesellschaft, 2002.

KRAVCHINSKI, Maksim. *Istoriya russkogo shansona.* Moskva: Astrel', 2012.

KREJCAROVÁ, Jana. *Clarissa a jiné texty.* Praha: Concordia, 1990.

KREJCAROVÁ-ČERNÁ, Jana. *Tohle je skutečnost (Básně, prózy, dopisy).* Praha: Torst, 2016.

KUNDERA, Milan. 'The Joke', *Times Literary Supplement,* No. 3531, 30th October 1969.

KUNDERA, Milan. *The Joke.* London: Macdonald, 1969.

LAZORČÁKOVÁ, Tatjana. 'Divadelní disent. K historii neoficiálních divadelních aktivit v sedmdesátých letech 20. století', in *Kontexty III. Acta Universitatis Palackianae Olomucensis,* M. SÝKORA (ed.). Olomouc: Univerzita Palackého, 2002.

LEDERER, Jiří. *České rozhovory.* Köln: Index, 1979.

LOPATKA, Jan. 'O původu, vzniku a dosavadní historii Edice Expedice', magazine of the *Nové knihy* weekly, Winter 1990 and Spring 1991.

LUKEŠ, Jan. *Hry doopravdy.* Praha – Litomyšl: Paseka, 1998.

MACHOVEC, Martin. 'Jak si undergroundoví autoři financovali svůj samizdat', in *O slušnou odměnu bude pečováno: Ekonomické souvislosti spisovatelské profese v české kultuře 19. a 20. století,* T. BREŇ, P. JANÁČEK (eds.). Praha: Ústav pro českou literaturu AV ČR, 2009.

MACHOVEC, Martin. 'Literární dílo Karla Maryska', *Revolver Revue,* No. 34, 1997.

MACHOVEC, Martin. 'Náčrt života a díla Egona Bondyho', in *Bouda Bondy. Projekt Bouda IV.* Praha: Národní divadlo, 2007.

MACHOVEC, Martin. 'Několik poznámek k podzemní ediční řadě Půlnoc', *Kritický sborník*, No. 3, 1993, Vol. XIII.

MACHOVEC, Martin. 'Od avantgardy přes podzemí do undergroundu', in *Alternativní kultura. Příběh české společnosti 1945–1989.* Praha: NLN, 2001.

MACHOVEC, Martin. 'Pokus o náčrt geneze a vývoje básnického díla Egona Bondyho', *Vokno*, No. 21, 1990.

MACHOVEC, Martin. 'Šestnáct autorů českého literárního podzemí (1948–1989)', *Nezávislá literatura, libri prohibiti a samizdat: Literární archiv*, 1991, Vol. XXV.

MACHOVEC, Martin. 'The Types and Functions of Samizdat Publications in Czechoslovakia, 1948–1989', *Poetics Today*, No. 1, Spring 2009, Vol. XXX.

MACHOVEC, Martin. 'Vídeňská bohemistika o Půlnoci (Česká podzemní literatura 1948–1953)', *Kritický sborník*, No. 2–3, 1999, Vol. XVIII.

M. MACHOVEC (ed.). *Pohledy zevnitř. Česká undergroundová literatura ve svědectvích, dokumentech a interpretacích.* Příbram: Pistorius & Olšanská, 2008.

M. MACHOVEC (ed.). *Views from the Inside. Czech Underground Literature and Culture (1948–1989).* Prague: Karolinum Press, 2018.

M. MACHOVEC (ed.). *Židovská jména.* Praha: NLN, 1995.

MAINX, Oskar. *Poezie jako mýtus, svědectví a hra. Kapitoly z básnické poetiky Egona Bondyho.* Ostrava: Protimluv, 2007.

MARTIN, A. D. *Atomový věk.* Stockholm: Česká kulturní rada v zahraničí, 1956.

L. MATĚJKA – B. STOLZ (eds.). *Cross Currents. A Yearbook of Central European Culture.* Ann Arbor: Michigan Slavic Publications, 1982.

MEDEK, Mikuláš. *Texty.* Praha: Torst, 1995.

MERHAUT, Vladislav. *Zápisky o Vladimíru Boudníkovi.* Praha: Revolver Revue, 1997.

MORGENSTERN, Christian – BONDY, Egon. *Galgenlieder / Šibeniční písně.* Praha: Labyrint, 2000.

MORGENSTERN, Christian. *Bim bam bum.* Praha: Československý spisovatel, 1971.

MORGENSTERN, Christian. *Morgenstern v Čechách. 21 proslulých básní ve 179 českých překladech 36 autorů.* Praha: Vida vida, 1996.

MÜLLER, Adolf – UTITZ, Bedřich (Prepared by K. NEŠVERA). 'Hovoří Index', *Telegram*, No. 2, 1973.

-n [KAUTMAN, František]. 'Otazníky kolem ineditní literatury', *Kritický sborník*, No. 4, 1982, Vol II.

-n [KAUTMAN, František]. 'Otazníky kolem ineditní literatury', *Acta*, No. 1, 1987, Vol. I.

NĚMEC, Jiří. 'K Zapomenutému světlu Jakuba Demla', *Kritický sborník*, No. 2, 1986, Vol. VI.

ONG, Walter J. *Orality and Literacy. The Technologizing of the Word*. London: Methuen, 1982.

ONG, Walter J. *Technologizace slova*. Praha: Karolinum, 2006.

ORSÁG, Petr. *Média československého exilu v letech 1948–1989 jako součást alternativní veřejné sféry*, dissertation. Olomouc: Univerzita Palackého, 2011.

OSTRÝ, Antonín. *Československý problém*. Köln: Index, 1972.

K. PALEK (ed.). *Kritický sborník 1981–1989. Výbor ze samizdatových ročníků*. Praha: Triáda, 2009.

PARFIANOWICZ-VERTUN, Weronika. 'Postgutenbergovská revoluce', *A2*, No.18, 2012.

PARFIANOWICZ-VERTUN, Weronika. *Europa Środkowa w tekstach i działaniach. Polskie i czeskie dyskusje*. Warszawa: Wydawnictwa Uniwersytetu Warszawskiego, 2016.

PARISI, Valentina. *Il lettore eccedente. Edizioni periodiche del «Samizdat» sovietico (1956–1990)*. Bologna: Il Mulino, 2013.

V. PARISI, (ed.). *Samizdat. Between Practices and Representations. Lecture Series at Open Society Archives. Budapest, February–June 2013*. Budapest: Central European University, Institute for Advanced Study, 2015.

PASTERNAK, Boris. *Doktor Živago*. Praha: Lidové nakladatelství, 1990.

T. PAVLÍČEK – P. PÍŠA – M. WÖGERBAUER (eds.). *Nebezpečná literatura? Antologie z myšlení o literární cenzuře*. Brno: Host, 2013.

PECKA, Karel. *Štěpení*. Toronto: Sixty-Eight Publishers, 1974.

PEKÁRKOVÁ, Iva. *Péra a perutě*. Praha: Maťa, 1998.

PELC, Jaromír – SÝS, Karel. 'Rozhovor s Bohumilem Hrabalem', *Tvorba*, No. 2, 1975, *Literatura – umění – kritika* supplement, No. 1.

PETROVSKAYA, Elena. *Nameless Communities*. Moscow: Falanster, 2012.

-pf [FIDELIUS, Petr]. 'Zapomenutý otazník nad 'ineditní' literaturou', *Kritický sborník*, No. 2, 1983, Vol. III.

-pf [FIDELIUS, Petr]. 'Zapomenutý otazník nad ineditní literaturou', *Acta*, No. 1, 1987, Vol. I.

Pilař, Martin. *Underground*. Brno: Host, 1999.

Placák, Petr. 'StB a 'protizákonné písemnosti' v osmdesátých letech', *Securitas imperii*, No. 1, 1994.

Poetics Today, Publish & Perish: Samizdat & Underground. Cultural Practices in the Soviet Bloc II, No. 1, Spring 2009, Vol. XXX.

Posset, Johanna. *Česká samizdatová periodika 1968–1989*. Brno: Továrna na sítotisk, 1991.

Povolný, Daniel. *Operativní technika v rukou StB*. Praha: Úřad dokumentace a vyšetřování zločinů komunismu, PČR, 2001.

Prečan, Vilém. 'Čs. dokumentační středisko nezávislé literatury', *Svědectví*, No. 78, 1986, Vol. XX.

Prečan, Vilém. 'Independent Literature and Samizdat in Czechoslovakia in the 1970s and 1980s', in *Literature and Politics in Central Europe: Studies in Honour of Markéta Goetz-Stankiewicz*. Columbia (SC): Camden House, 1993.

Prečan, Vilém. 'Unabhängige Literatur und Samizdat in der Tschechoslowakei der 70er und 80er Jahre', in *Der Zensur zum Trotz: Das gefesselte Wort und die Freiheit in Europa*, P. Raabe (ed.). Weinheim: Wiley-VCH Verlagsgesellschaft, 1991.

V. Prečan (ed.). 'Ke spolupráci dvou posrpnových exilových nakladatelství. Korespondence z let 1971–1987 s dodatky z roku 1996', in *Ročenka Československého dokumentačního střediska 2003*. Praha: Československé dokumentační středisko, 2004.

V. Prečan – M. Uhde (eds.). *Ve službách společné věci / Im Dienst der gemeinsamen Sache. Wolfgang Scheur und Prag 1981–1989*. Brno: Atlantis, 2001.

Procházka, Vladimír. *Příruční slovník naučný. Vol. 2*. Praha: Ústav pro českou literaturu, 1963.

Přibáň, Jiří. 'Meze politiky. Jak a proč číst George Orwella po samizdatu', *Právo* 12th February 2015, *Salon* supplement.

Přibáňová, Alena – Přibáň, Michal. 'I rapporti di Sixty-Eight Publishers con il samizdat cecoslovacco e la concorrenza con le altre case editrici dell'emigrazione', in *Il samizdat tra memoria e utopia*, A. Catalano – S. Guagnelli (eds.). *eSamizdat* 2010–2011, Vol. VIII.

Romanová, Gabriela. *Příběh Edice Expedice*. Praha: Knihovna Václava Havla, 2014.

'Rozhovor s Bohumilem Hrabalem', *Tvorba*, No. 2, 1975, *Literatura – umění – kritika* supplement, No. I.

RŮŽKOVÁ, Jana – GRUNTORÁD, Jiří. 'Samizdatový časopis Vokno', *Kritický sborník*, 1999/2000, Vol. XIX.

B. SABEL – A. BUCHER (eds.). *Der unfeste Text : Perspektiven auf einen literatur- und kulturwissenschaftlichen Leitbegriff.* Würzburg: Königshausen – Neumann, 2001.

SALIVAROVÁ, Zdena – ŠKVORECKÝ, Josef. 'Milí čtenáři…', in *Jak to bylo*, L. PACHMAN (ed.). Toronto: Sixty-Eight Publishers, 1974.

Z. SALIVAROVÁ – J. ŠKVORECKÝ (eds.). *Nakladatelství 68 Toronto.* Toronto: Sixty-Eight Publishers, 1971.

SIEKIERSKI, Stanisław. 'Drugi obieg. Uwagi o przyczynach powstania i społecznych funkcjach', in *Pismiennictwo, systemy kontroli, obiegi alternatywne (Z dziejow kultury czytelniczej w Polsce)*, J. KOSTECKI – A. BRODZKA (eds.). Warszawa: Biblioteka Narodowa, 1992.

SCHMIDT, Henrike. *Russische Literatur im Internet. Zwischen digitaler Folklore und politischer Propaganda.* Bielefeld: Transcript, 2011.

R. SCHOVÁNEK (ed.). *Svazek Dialog. StB versus Pavel Kohout. Dokumenty StB z operativních svazků Dialog a Kopa.* Praha – Litomyšl: Paseka, 2006.

SEELICH, Nadja – NEUBURGER, Berndt. *Sie sass im Glashaus und warf mit Steinen* – film, Austria, 1993.

SEIFERT, Jaroslav. *Morový sloup.* Praha: Československý spisovatel, 1981.

SKILLING, H. Gordon. 'Samizdat: a Return to the Pre-Gutenberg Era?', *Cross Currents*, No. 1, 1982.

SUK, Jiří. 'Podrobná zpráva o paralelní polis. Nad korespondencí Václava Havla a Františka Janoucha', in HAVEL, Václav – JANOUCH, František. Korespondence 1978–2001. Praha: Akropolis, 2007.

Svědectví, No. 47, 1974, Vol. XII.

SVOBODA, Pavel. 'Próza, poezie, korespondence', *Haňťa Press,* No. 17, 1995.

ŠÁMAL, PETR. 'Paralelní oběh jako důsledek cenzury', in WÖGERBAUER, Michael – PÍŠA, Petr – ŠÁMAL, Petr – JANÁČEK, Pavel et al. *V obecném zájmu. Cenzura a sociální regulace literatury v moderní české kultuře 1749–2014, Vol. II.* Praha: Academia – Ústav pro českou literaturu AV ČR, 2015.

ŠKVORECKÝ, Josef – DORŮŽKA, Lubomír. *Na shledanou v lepších časech. Dopisy Josefa Škvoreckého a Lubomíra Dorůžky z doby marnosti 1968–1989.* Praha: Books and Cards, 2011.

ŠKVORECKÝ, Josef – ZÁBRANA, Jan. *Jak je ve větě člověk. Dopisy Josefa Škvoreckého a Jana Zábrany.* Praha: Books and Cards, 2010.

ŠMORANC, Jiří. *Děti periferie.* Praha: Pražská imaginace, 1996.

ŠNEPPOVÁ, Daniela. 'Staging Samizdat: The Czech Art of Resistance, 1968–1989', *Zeitschrift für Ostmitteleuropa-Forschung,* No. 1, 2016, Vol. LXV.

ŠOTOLA, Jiří. *Kuře na rožni,* Praha: Československý spisovatel, 1976.

ŠVESTKA, Jaroslav. *Orwellův rok,* K. VOLKOVÁ – J. GRUNTORÁD – D. HAVRÁNEK (eds.). Praha: Libri prohibiti, 2013.

V. TODOROV (ed.). *Publish & Perish: Samizdat & Underground Cultural Practices in the Soviet Bloc (I) and (II): Poetics Today,* 2008–2009, Vol. XXIX and XXX.

TROUP, Zdeněk. 'Poezie totality', *Rozeta,* No. 1, 1991.

TUREČEK, Roman. *Neoficiální informační kanály mezi Československem a Západem v období 1969–1989 se zaměřením na tzv. kurýrní cestu,* thesis. Brno: Masarykova Univerzita, 2010.

TYPLT, Jaromír F. 'Absolutní realismus a Totální hrobař', *Host,* No. 1, 2006.

TYPLT, Jaromír F. 'Dvě svědectví o Židovských jménech', *Host,* No. 3, 1997.

TYPLT, Jaromír F. 'Fascinantně divý muž Zdeněk Wagner', *Host,* No. 5, 2000.

VANICEK, Anna. *Passion Play: Underground Rock Music in Czechoslovakia, 1968–1989,* thesis. Toronto, North York: York University, Faculty of Graduate Studies, 1997.

VAŠINKA, Radim. 'Bondy a Orfeus', in *Bouda Bondy. Projekt Bouda IV.* Praha: Národní divadlo, 2007.

VAŠINKA, Radim. 'Vydolováno z nepaměti I.–V.', *Divadelní noviny,* No. 5–9, 2001, Vol. X.

VÁVRA, Stanislav – TYPLT, Jaromír F. 'Ukázat pramen a podat pohár', *Iniciály,* No. 17/18, 1991, Vol. II.

VÁVRA, Stanislav. 'Záběhlická skupina surrealistů – Libenští psychici', *Jarmark umění,* No. 2, April 1991.

VÁVRA, Stanislav. *Libeňští psychici. Sborník básnických a prozaických textů z let 1945–1959.* Praha: Concordia, 2009.

VÁVRA, Stanislav. *Muž v jiných končinách světa.* Praha: Pražská imaginace, 1992.

VÁVRA, Stanislav. *Snovidění.* Praha: Pražská imaginace, 1992.

VÁVRA, Stanislav. *Zvířený prach.* Praha: MČ Praha 8, 2004.

VINOKUROVA, Irina. *'Vsego lish' geniy…': sud'ba Nikolaya Glazkova.* Moscow: Vremya, 2006.

J. VLADISLAV (ed.). 'Dialog přes hranice 1985–1990. Z korespondence Jindřicha Chalupeckého s Janem Vladislavem', in *Ročenka Československého dokumentačního střediska 2003*. Praha: Československé dokumentační středisko, 2004.

VODSEĎÁLEK, Ivo – MAZAL, Tomáš. 'S Ivo Vodseďálkem o letech radostného budování 49–53', *Vokno*, No. 18, 1990.

VODSEĎÁLEK, Ivo. 'Hra prstečků mých neklidných', *Haňťa Press*, No. 9, 1991.

VODSEĎÁLEK, Ivo. *Bloudění*. Praha: Pražská imaginace, 1992.

VODSEĎÁLEK, Ivo. *Nalézání*. Praha: Pražská imaginace, 1992.

VODSEĎÁLEK, Ivo. *Probouzení*. Praha: Pražská imaginace, 1992.

VODSEĎÁLEK, Ivo. *Snění*. Praha: Pražská imaginace, 1992.

VODSEĎÁLEK, Ivo. *Zuření*. Praha: Pražská imaginace, 1992.

VODSEĎÁLEK, Ivo. *Felixír života*. Brno: Host, 2000.

K. VOLKOVÁ (ed.). *Přadénko z drátů*. Praha: Libri prohibiti – Gallery, 2010.

VRBA, Tomáš. 'Nezávislé písemnictví a svobodné myšlení v letech 1970–1989', in *Alternativní kultura. Příběh české společnosti 1945–1989*, J. ALAN (ed.). Praha: NLN, 2001.

WAGNER, Zdeněk. *Virgule*. Praha: Cherm, 2007.

WILSON, Paul. 'Living Intellects: An Introduction', in *Good-bye, Samizdat: Twenty Years of Czechoslovak Underground Writing*, M. GOETZ-STANKIEWICZ (ed.). Evanston: Northwestern University Press, 1992.

WÖGERBAUER, Michael – PÍŠA, Petr – ŠÁMAL, Petr – JANÁČEK, Pavel et al. *V obecném zájmu. Cenzura a sociální regulace literatury v moderní české kultuře. 1749–2014*. Praha: Academia – Ústav pro českou literaturu AV ČR, 2015.

ZÁBRANA, Jan. *Celý život, I*. Praha: Torst, 1992.

ZACH, Aleš. *Kniha a český exil 1949–1990*. Praha: Torst, 1995.

ZANDOVÁ, Gertraude. 'Básník – svědek – aktivista: Poetický program a vydavatelský projekt Egona Bondyho v čase stalinismu', *Česká literatura*, No. 6, 1998, Vol. XLVI.

ZANDOVÁ, Gertraude. *Totální realismus a trapná poezie. Česká neoficiální literatura 1948–1953*. Brno: Host, 2002.

ZAND, Gertraude. *Totaler Realismus und Peinliche Poesie. Tschechische Untergrund-Literatur 1948–1953*. Frankfurt am Main: Peter Lang, 1998.

Profiles

Petr Fidelius [Karel Palek]

A Czech essayist, philologist and linguist, during the normalization period he studied the semantics of the language of Communist propaganda and edited the samizdat journal *Kritický sborník* (Critical Review). In 1983 his book *Jazyk a moc* (Language and Power) was brought out by the Arkýř publishers in exile in Germany. At present he teaches at the Faculty of Humanities at Charles University and writes articles on Czech orthography as a freelance editor. In 2000 a volume of *Kritické eseje* (Critical Essays) was brought out, containing a selection of his texts from 1981 to 2000. He focused on the semantics of ideological language in *Řeč komunistické moci* (Language of communist power) anthology.

Tomáš Glanc

A Czech Russist, literary theorist and translator (of K. Malevich and the Tartu School), documentarist (collaborating with Czech Television) and Slavisches Seminar professor at University of Zurich. He is primarily involved in contemporary Russian literature (J. Mamleyev, E. Limonov, V. Sorokin and I. Kholin) and visual art (the aesthetics of the interwar avant-garde). He translated *Memoria fantastika*, a monograph by Renate Lachmann. He was awarded grants from the Fulbright Commission in the USA and Alexander von Humboldt Stiftung in Germany. 2000–2003 he was Director of the Institute of Slavonic and Eastern European Studies, and 2005–2007 Director of the Czech

Centre in Moscow. He is a member of the editorial boards at the *Česká literatura* (Czech Literature) and *Novoye literaturnoye obozreniye* (New Literary Review in Moscow) journals and a member of the Scientific Council at the Slavonic Library. A regular contributor to the cultural review *Revolver revue*. In 2017 he brought out a monograph *Autoren im Ausnahmenzustand*.

Jiří Gruša

A Czech poet, prose writer, translator (of Franz Kafka, Rainer Maria Rilke and P. Celan) and diplomat. His debut came in the early 1960s with poems in the Czechoslovak *Literární noviny* (Literary Journal), and he contributed to such cultural journals and magazines as *Plamen, Kulturní tvorba, Listy* and *Sešity pro mladou literaturu*. Together with Ludvík Vaculík he established the samizdat series Petlice, where he published a number of his prose works: *Dámský gambit* (1972), *Mimner aneb Hra o smrďocha* (1974) and *Dotazník* (1975). A Charter 77 signatory and co-compiler of *Slovník českých spisovatelů* (Encyclopedia of Czech Writers, samizdat 1978; published 1991 with the title of *Slovník zakázaných autorů* (Encyclopedia of Prohibited Authors), portraying the literature suppressed by the Communist regime from 1948 to the late 1970s. From 1981 he lived involuntarily in emigration and after the Velvet Revolution he held various diplomatic positions (member of the Czech government and ambassador to Germany, later to Austria), 2004–2009 President of the International PEN Club, multiple award winner (Inter-Nationes).

Josef Jedlička

Czech prose writer, philosopher and editor (*Sešity pro mladou literaturu, Host do domu, Tvář*) author of numerous radio programmes and plays for young people, in exile from 1968 (Munich), where he worked as an editor at Radio Free Europe and a number of journals in exile (*Obrys, Svědectví*). He made his debut in 1966 with his autobiographical novel *Kde život náš je v půli se svou poutí* (*Midway upon the Journey of our Life*), and he summarized his radio essays in his book *České typy* (Czech Types, 1992, extended edition 2009). In his study *Dodatek k nenapsaným Dějinám české literatury* (Appendix to an Unwritten History of Czech Literature, 1987) he focused on literature not tolerated by the regime in postwar Czechoslovakia.

František Kautman

A Czech literary theorist and historian, writer and philosopher. Between 1949 and 1952 he was Editor-in-Chief at the Československý spisovatel publishing house, during the 1950s his scholarly career focused on Marxist literary theory (studying at the Maxim Gorki Literary Institute in Moscow), 1961–1971 he was a researcher at the Czechoslovak Academy of Sciences, Institute of Czech Literature, and a Charter 77 signatory. He also worked on a number of samizdat series and journals in exile (*Listy, Svědectví, Proměny, Obrys*). Together with J. Vladislav he established the samizdat literary journal *Kritický sborník*. His specialist papers focused on Fyodor Dostoyevsky's and Franz Kafka's work, as well as Jan Patočka's philosophical legacy.

Jiří Gruntorád

Czech archivist, founder and director of the Libri prohibiti Library of Samizdat Literature in Prague, editor and publisher. During the Communist regime in Czechoslovakia he took various menial jobs (boilerman or labourer), a Charter 77 signatory and political prisoner. In 1978 he established the Popelnice samizdat series. In 1994 he became a member of the Committee for the Defence of the Unjustly Persecuted, in 2002 he received the Order of Merit First Class, and in 2010 he was appointed a member of the Advisory Committee to the Director of the Institute for the Study of Totalitarian Regimes.

Martin Machovec

Czech editor and literary critic focusing on underground literary scene in Czechoslovakia from the 1950s to the 1990s. He compiled a number of prose and poetry works for publication (e.g. the works by E. Bondy, I. Vodseďálek, I. M. Jirous, P. Zajíček, M. Koch). Before 1989 he contributed to samizdat periodicals *Vokno* and *Revolver Revue*, after 1989, to a number of Czech and foreign journals and anthologies, e.g. *Tvorba, Lidové noviny, Revolver Revue, Babylon, Host, Tvar, A2, Česká literatura, Slovo a smysl, Poetics Today, Voice Text Hypertext, Czeski underground* etc. He teaches at Comenius University and at Charles University, Faculty of Arts. He also translates from English, e.g. works by A. Ginsberg, J. Fowles, A. Waldman, R. O. Paxton, P. Wilson, G. Scholem, W. Reich.

Weronika Parfianowicz-Vertun

Polish Central-European and Czech Studies expert. She works at the Institute for Polish Culture (University of Warsaw), a member of the Workshop for Urban Studies. She's the author of a book entitled *Teksty i działania. Europa Środkowa w polskich i czeskich dyskusjach* (Warszawa 2016) and of articles on contemporary Czech culture and Central European literature (published in *Teksty Drugie, Kultura Współczesna* and the Czech journal *A2*). Her research interests involve Central European urban culture, the Czech avant-garde and the underground. In 2012 she was a Visegrad Fund scholar at the Faculty of Arts (Charles University, Prague) and in 2017 she obtained Zdeněk Pešat's scholarship at the CAS Institute of Czech Literature.

Michal Přibáň

Czech literary historian, editor and prose writer, specializing in Czech literature from the latter half of the 20th century, particularly the work of Josef Škvorecký (Bibliography of the work of Josef Škvorecký, and edited Škvorecký's correspondence inter alia). In book form he published chapters from the history of his pre-1968 exile, *Prvních dvacet let* (The First Twenty Years, 2008), and he headed the team of authors working on the encyclopedia of Czech literary publishers *Česká literární nakladatelství 1949–1989* and the Encyclopedia of Czech Literary Samizdat *Encyklopedie českého literárního samizdatu*. Between 2002 and 2004 and then 2010 and 2012 he was a member of the Czech Ministry of Culture Literary Commission, 2004–2005 he was a member of the Czech Academy of Sciences, Institute of Czech Literature Literature Council. In 2017 he was nominated for a Magnesia Litera award for his debut novel *Všechno je jenom dvakrát* (Everything Only Happens Twice).

Alena Přibáňová

Czech literary historian, English specialist, editor and translator (of Paul Wilson and Norbert Frye). Since 2005 a research assistant at the Department for Research into the History of 20th Century Literature at the Czech Academy of Sciences, Institute of Czech Literature. She has taken part as a lexicographer inter alia in such projects as the Encyclopedia of Post-1945 Czech Literature Online (*Slovník české literatury po roce 1945 online*) and the Encyclopedia of Czech Literary Samizdat (*Encyklopedie českého literárního samizdatu*). She deals with modern Czech prose, and above all the theory of prose. Together with Michal Přibáň she has edited a number of publications on the work of Josef Škvorecký, on whose work inter alia she has written such studies as *Nalezeno v překladu: Anglické verze Škvoreckého románů Příběh inženýra lidských duší a Scherzo capriccioso* (Found in Translation: The English versions of Škvorecký's novels The Engineer of Human Souls and Dvořák in Love, 2009), and *Opus magnum z Nového světa* (Opus magnum from the New World, 2013).

Petr Šámal

Czech literary historian, since 2003 he has been the editor-in-chief of the specialist journal *Česká literatura*. At the Czech Academy of Sciences, Institute of Czech Literature he is a member of the team researching literary culture, he deals with the sociology of literature and the literary culture of the 1950s. A member of the Czech Academy of Sciences, Institute of Czech Literature Council (2012–present; since 2017 Chairman), and a member of the Council of the Institute for Contemporary History at the Czech Academy of Sciences; a member of the editorial boards of *Slovenská literatúra* and *Literární archiv* journals. He has co-authored a collective monograph on literature censorship *V obecném zájmu: Cenzura a sociální regulace literatury v moderní české kultuře 1749–2014* (In the common interest: Censorship and the social regulation of literature in modern Czech culture 1749–2014, 2015) and the multi-volume *Dějiny české literatury 1945–1989* (History of Czech Literature 1945–1989, 2007–2008).

Tomáš Vrba

Czech editor, translator (of Madeleine Albright, Yehuda Bauer, Flannery O'Connor, and others) and editor. He worked as an editor of samizdat publications (Expedice series, *Spektrum* journal). He was a member of Civic Forum and a signatory of Charter 77. Founder and former President of the Czech Section of the Association of European Journalists. During the 1990s Editor-in-Chief of the monthly magazine *Nová Přítomnost* (1997–2000) and of the Czech and Slovak edition of *Lettre Internationale* quarterly (1990–1995). Between 2002–2004 International Vice President of the Association of European Journalists and Chair of the Czech News Agency (ČTK) Council (2004–2007). He teaches the Central European literature at the New York University of Prague. Since 2007 he has been Chairman of the Board of Directors of Forum 2000 Foundation.

Encyclopedia of Czech Literary Samizdat

Czech samizdat or independent literature from the period between February 1948 and November 1989 has long ceased to be an unknown quantity, but to some extent it remains a mysterious phenomenon to this day. Research into it started immediately after the fall of the old regime. A specialist library called Libri prohibiti was established, a collection of samizdat literature created in exile was moved to Prague and collections of samizdat literature are being put together at various archives, museums and academic institutions. Several bibliographical catalogues have been compiled, and numerous articles, studies and books have been published describing and analysing individual series, magazines and works from different circles engaged in publication and distribution.

However, we have previously lacked a publication providing the specialist and lay public with a comprehensive summary of key information on this topic. As we have frequently come up against this lack in our specialist work, we decided to endeavour to lay the foundations for a work of this kind.

The Encyclopedia of Czech Literary Samizdat, which is due to come out in book form at the end of 2018, is taking shape at the Czech Academy of Sciences, Institute of Czech Literature, with the participation of external co-workers from other research institutes. Its working index so far includes over 120 series entries, 120 periodical entries and 40 entries on selected anthologies of a non-periodical nature, while the number of entries continues to rise, covering regional activities, many of which have not previously been researched by specialists. Entries include all the information that has been gathered on publishers, editors, technical collaborators and the distributors behind a particular title, duplication methods and basic bibliographical descriptions including print-run details, and if the need arises we also include information on the funding methods and the circle of readers involved. An essential part of each entry also comprises an information-rich description and the content of the series or magazine, an exposition of the publishers' objective and information on any development in the title in question in the liberal post-1989 conditions. The set of entries will be preceded by an extensive introductory study attempting to comprehensively deal with the development of the samizdat phenomenon in Czech culture from 1948 (taking into account similar methods of publishing literary works in previous historical periods), characterizing its economic conditions, production procedures and distribution methods, and unfortunately we cannot avoid a chapter on the police suppression that the publishers of independent literature were often exposed to.

The fact that the scope of the entries in the forthcoming Encyclopedia is restricted to literary samizdat, i.e. fiction, literary studies and essays, art studies and associated disciplines, stems from the specialized nature of our establishment, the CAS Institute of Czech Literature. However, this need not be a final and binding restriction: as our work approaches its goal, we can attempt to take another step in collaboration with politologists, historians, sociologists, art historians and other researchers to expand the scope of the Encyclopedia to include the other artistic and social fields that have hitherto seen samizdat publishing activity.

Contact: www.ucl.cas.cz/cs/projekty/encyklopedie-ceskeho-samizdatu
samizdat@ucl.cas.cz

Czech Literary Bibliography

The Czech Literary Bibliography has been compiled over almost 70 years at the Czech Academy of Sciences Institute of Czech Literature, a public research institute. It comprises a set of bibliographical databases that are updated on an ongoing basis, systematically covering cultural journalism and specialist texts on Czech literature and literary life in the Czech lands.

The parameters of the ICL bibliographical databases (chronologically covering the period from 1770 to the present, with approximately 1,500 titles and over two million records) make them the most extensive specialist bibliography in the Czech Republic. The interconnected Czech Literary Figures database of individuals includes key biographical details for some 37,000 figures in literary life. During 2014 the complete set successfully underwent an assessment by the Czech Ministry of Education and under the title Czech Literary Bibliography (CLB) it was included with effect from 2016 in the Roadmap of Large Czech Infrastructures for Research, Experimental Development and Innovation. CLB activities centre around the compilation, systematic utilization and further ongoing development of bibliographical, biographical and auxiliary ICL databases.

In 2016, the Czech Literary Samizdat article bibliography inter alia also started to be processed within the framework of the Czech Literary Bibliography research infrastructure project. The plan over the next few years is to create and make accessible online an analytical bibliography of Czech samizdat periodicals dealing with Czech literature, other national literatures and literary studies. Particular use is made for excerption purposes of the Libri prohibiti and Czechoslo-vak Documentation Centre libraries, as well as material from other libraries and private collectors. One important digital resource is the Scriptum.cz website, where scans of selected literary samizdat titles can be viewed. Source material is selected in collaboration with the *Encyklopedie českého literárního samizdatu* [Encyclope-dia of Czech Literary Samizdat] project, the core of the excerption base being made up in particular of literary and cultural magazines, although regional, social, specialist and various community titles are also represented along with the periodicals of particular subcultures.

Contact: clb.ucl.cas.cz (website)
biblio.ucl.cas.cz (online catalogue)
clb@ucl.cas.cz